MOUNDS FOR THE DEAD: AN ANALYSIS OF THE ADENA CULTURE

By Don W. Dragoo

Curator, Section of Man
Carnegie Museum

ANNALS OF CARNEGIE MUSEUM

PITTSBURGH, PA.

Vol. 37

Published by The Carnegie Museum of Natural History, Pittsburgh, PA 15213
Copyright © 1963, The Board of Trustees, Carnegie Institute
Manufactured in the United States of America

Third printing 1989

ISBN 0-911239-09-X

MOUNDS FOR THE DEAD: AN ANALYSIS OF THE ADENA CULTURE

By DON W. DRAGOO

Curator, Section of Man

Carnegie Museum

CONTENTS

INTRODUCTION

No remains of prehistoric man in the eastern United States have excited the imagination and interest of laymen and scientists alike more than the great burial mounds and earthworks now known to belong to the Adena and the Hopewell cultures in the Ohio Valley. Speculations as to the origin of the people who constructed these imposing earthworks to hold the remains of their dead was a favorite mental exercise of many from the first discovery of the mounds by Europeans.

Because the Indian with whom the white people first came into contact in the Ohio Valley knew nothing of the origin of the mounds, it was believed that the Indian could not have built these structures. It was suggested by some that one of the lost tribes of Israel was responsible, by others the Egyptians, the Norsemen, or some other fabled people of western history and mythology. Improved methods of excavation and dating and the evidence of physical anthropology have demonstrated the Indian ancestry of the "Mound Builders."

Of the early "Mound Builders" the Adena peoples dominated the Ohio Valley from about 1000 B.C. until their contact and absorption by Hopewellian peoples in the central Ohio Valley starting about 200 B.C. The spectacular results of this merger, known as Hopewell culture, received so much attention by early archeologists that the presence and separate identity of Adena was masked for many years. The eventual discovery and study of Adena came as an outgrowth of the investigations of Hopewell. The realization that the Adena culture was perhaps the foundation upon which the spectacular Ohio Hopewell culture rose has led to increasing interest in the Adena peoples who in the Ohio Valley developed the first extensive burial cult, built the first substantial homes, made some of the earliest ceramics, and practiced agriculture.

The path leading to the understanding of the important part of Adena in American prehistory has not been easily or quickly traveled. It has been nearly sixty years since the great earth mound on the estate of Governor Worthington in Ross County, Ohio, was excavated and reported by W. C. Mills (1902, p. 452-479). Governor Worthington had named the mound and his mansion Adena. Mills extended the use of the name Adena to include the cultural manifestation found within the mound. Since that time, excavations and researches by many workers have demonstrated the extent and importance of Adena culture in the prehistory of the eastern United States.

The first extensive study of Adena was made by Emerson F. Greenman (1932, p. 369-523). In this study he presented and described 59 cultural traits found in common in two or more of 70 mounds he assigned to Adena. Greenman was beset with difficulties in giving a detailed report. Many of the mounds had been only partially and carelessly excavated and in many instances field notes of the excavators were missing. In spite of these impediments, Greenman produced a work that brought previously scattered and obscure data into the most complete summary of Adena culture to that time.

In the years following Greenman's report in 1932, a large mass of new data was collected with funds made available by the federal government through the Works Progress Administration. Many large mounds, especially in Kentucky, were investigated with the use of relief labor. Many new traits and traits previously unknown to belong to Adena were discovered and placed in relationship with old and well known traits of the culture. Several sites, long ago partially excavated, were reinvestigated in the light of new evidence and many sites unknown to Greenman at the time of his report were excavated and reported upon.

In 1945 William S. Webb and Charles E. Snow published their book, "The Adena People" in which they summarized the new evidence. A complete revaluation of all old traits was achieved and many new traits were added to the Adena trait list. Webb and Snow retained Greenman's original 59 traits, with some changes in description, and added 159 new traits to make a total of 218 traits characteristic of Adena. To the Greenman list of 70 Adena sites, they added 99 new sites. At last the full impact and importance of Adena culture in the sequence of cultural development in the East was well documented. The Webb and Snow report was a firm foundation and framework for future research.

Since 1945 several Adena mounds in Ohio were excavated by Raymond Baby of the Ohio State Museum. From this work came additional information and good charcoal samples for radiocarbon dating. During this same period the Natrium Mound in Marshall County, W. Va., was excavated by Ralph Solecki of the Smithsonian Institution in 1948. Additional evidence of Adena occupation and influence was discovered by T. Latimer Ford as far distant from the Ohio Valley as the Chesapeake Bay region of eastern Maryland.

In order to make this newly discovered information available, Webb and Baby compiled and published "The Adena People No. 2" in 1957 as a supplement to the original Webb and Snow report. To the trait list were added 23 new traits, and the descriptions of several old traits were expanded. The list of known Adena mounds was increased from 173 to 222. More important than the addition of new traits and sites was the attempt of Webb and Baby in this report to delve more intimately into certain functions and basic orientations of Adena culture. Upon the skeleton of Adena traits and sites the flesh of a once vibrant culture was now being reconstructed.

The finds within recent years and the reports of Webb and his associates have enabled others to interpret more clearly the Adena remains in far-flung areas of the eastern United States. A recent study by Ritchie and Dragoo (1959, p. 43-50) has shown the movement of Adena culture out of the Ohio Valley into the Northeast and the East Coast. Of major interest in this study were the causes for movement of Adena from its Ohio Valley homeland and the influence these movements had upon the area it invaded.

Interest in the origins of Adena culture has been intensified within recent years. Among the most important contributions to this subject are the works of Webb and Snow (1945), Dragoo (1949), Griffin (1952), and Spaulding (1952, 1955). The diversity of opinions held by these workers still makes the origins of Adena a fascinating and critical problem in Adena research.

In the present study there was no intention of duplicating the excellent materials presented in the two volumes of "The Adena People" by Webb and associates. My main objectives in this project were as follows:

1. To present the recent findings in the excavation of the stratified Cresap Mound in Marshall County, W. Va.

2. To synthesize the information now available on the Adena culture in the Upper Ohio Valley.

3. To compare and contrast the Adena manifestations of the Upper Ohio Valley with Adena in the central Ohio Valley and in other areas where Adena remains have been found.

4. To reinvestigate the chronological development and spread of Adena culture in the light of the evidence found at the Cresap Mound and to re-examine all major Adena collections and records at various institutions in the Ohio Valley.

5. To present additional insights into the organization, customs, and beliefs that made Adena culture so important in the cultural development of the eastern United States.

6. To look again at the evidence concerning the origins of Adena culture.

Although much of the information contained in this report has been compiled since 1957, the project had its original inception at Indiana University in 1948. It began with my interest in the origins of Adena and the subsequent writing of a Master's dissertation entitled "Origins of the Adena Culture," in 1949. During the succeeding years additional information on Adena was gathered in the field, from collections, and from libraries. In 1957 and early 1958 William A. Ritchie and I conducted extensive research into the problems concerning the extensions of Adena from the Upper Ohio Valley to the East Coast and into the Northeast. With my excavation of the stratified Cresap Mound in West Virginia, I was at last presented with the previously missing key to Adena chronology. Much of the information that I had gathered over the years had done little to shed new light upon the overall picture of Adena culture. Now, the key to the ordering of this material was available. Scraps of information that meant little before now took on new meaning. Collections of Adena items scattered in various institutions could be studied from a new perspective.

Upon completion of the initial study of the Cresap Mound materials early in 1959, I made arrangements to visit William S. Webb and Charles Snow at the University of Kentucky, Raymond Baby at the Ohio State Museum, Glenn A. Black of the Indiana Historical Society, George K. Neumann at Indiana University, Ellis Crawford at the Behringer Museum of Covington, Kentucky, Ralph Drury at the Cincinnati Natural History Museum, and Delf Narona at the Mound Museum in Moundsville, W. Va. From all of these individuals I received invaluable aid and counsel. All the major collections of Adena materials at their respective institutions were made available for my study. Without their help the success of this project would have been impossible.

In addition to the above individuals, information, counsel, and access to collections were made available to me by the following—James B. Griffin of the University of Michigan, William A. Ritchie of the New York State Museum, Alfred K. Guthe of the Rochester Museum of Arts and Sciences, T. Latimer Ford of the Maryland Archeological Society, Oscar Mairs and C. L. Paxton of the West Virginia Archeological Society. To these individuals and many others too numerous to list here, I extend my sincere thanks for their aid.

I also wish to express my gratitude to Joseph Quill for his aid in typing the manuscript, to Richard W. Lang for his preparation of many of the drawings, and to Dorothy E. Dragoo and James L. Swauger for their many comments and editorial duties pertaining to the manuscript.

ANATOMY OF A MOUND. THE CRESAP MOUND

INTRODUCTION

The exploration of the Cresap Mound was directed by the author for Carnegie Museum during the summer of 1958. The project was jointly sponsored by Carnegie Museum, Hanna Coal Company, and the West Virginia Archeological Society. The greatest burden of expense in the mound's removal was borne by Hanna Coal Company, which has plans for the erection of a new industrial plant on the area where the mound was located.

The Cresap Mound, located approximately 6½ miles down the Ohio River from Moundsville, W. Va., was located on land once claimed by George Washington and later owned by the Cresap family in whose hands the land remained until its recent sale to the Hanna Coal Company. During the many years the mound was owned by the Cresap family, great care had been taken to guard it from vandalism and total destruction. Several years ago the mound and a small parcel of land surrounding it were turned over to the West Virginia State Highway Department for a small rest park along Route 2 with the understanding that the mound was not to be disturbed in any fashion. In the meantime, the surrounding Cresap lands passed into the ownership of the Hanna Coal Company. During 1958 the State Highway Department relocated Route 2, abandoning their old right of way to Route 2 and the rest park to the Hanna Coal Company who then owned the lands on both sides of the right of way.

Mr. Delf Narona of Moundsville, W. Va., upon learning of the proposed change in the highway and the plans of the Hanna Coal Company to construct an industrial plant on the area, took active steps in 1957 to assure the scientific salvage of the mound. Mr. Narona with the aid of Mr. Sigfus Olafson, President of the West Virginia Archeological Society, and Reverend Clifford Lewis, then Secretary of the Society, contacted officials of the Hanna Coal Company, the West Virginia Highway Department, and Carnegie Museum to establish a plan of operation. All of these organizations willingly pledged their support and preliminary technicalities were cleared away. On April 21, 1958, the author; Dr. James L. Swauger, Assistant Director of Carnegie Museum; and Reverend Lewis held separate meetings with Mr. George McCaa of the Hanna Coal Company and Mr. Oren Trout of the West Virginia Highway Department. Mr. McCaa pledged his full support and offered to put at the disposal of Carnegie Museum a crew of able men and power machinery sufficient to do the excavation. Mr. Trout extended the services of his department and made arrangements for fencing needed to protect the mound during the excavation.

The excavation of the mound was started on June 2, 1958, and was completed on August 26, 1958. Before beginning the work, we had estimated that it would take about six weeks for the excavation if we could use power equipment to remove much of the top layers of earth on the mound. After completion of the first tests to determine the structure of the mound, it was evident that power equipment could be used only in removal of dirt to the spoil pile after it had been carefully dug from the mound by hand. So many features were found throughout the mound that it took 13 weeks to do the job. The use of power machinery to carry the earth away from the piles at the base of the mound saved many additional days of hard labor.

The Hanna Coal Company did all in its power to make the project a success. Four, young, college-trained men were assigned to the work full time, and additional men were available on occasions for part-time service. The four permanent men, Louis Gmeindl, Jerry L. Lyseski, Julius H. Olzer, and Tom Sarff showed a keen interest in the work and became quite proficient in their tasks after a short training period. They were an excellent crew. Always ready to lend a helping hand were George McCaa, Ralph Snyder, James Reilley, Anthony Zitko, and many other officials of the Hanna Coal Company. Their support of this project can not be praised too highly.

During the course of the excavation, assistance was rendered by various members of the West Virginia Archeological Society and of the Society for Pennsylvania Archaeology. Among the most frequent helpers at the site were Delf Narona, Reverend Clifford Lewis, Charles Lally, Sigfus Olafson, George Sutton, and Arthur Hayes. To these people and to many others, too numerous to list here, I extend my thanks and appreciation for their efforts.

Mr. William C. Reeves of the Carnegie Museum staff gave invaluable aid in the photography connected with the excavation. To him fell the task of doing all the developing of films and printing of test prints as the films arrived from the field.

THE MOUND

The Cresap Mound, designated 46Mr7 in the trinominal system of site designation used by the West Virginia Archeological Society and Carnegie Museum, was located on Cresap Bottom at 80° 49′ W., 39° 50′ N. in Marshall County, W. Va. The Mound was situated 6½ airline miles southwest of Moundsville directly adjacent to Route 2. (Map 1).

Cresap Bottom is a wide, sloping terrace on the east side of the Ohio River which at this point flows north to south. The mound was 1090 feet east of the bank of the river and 10 feet west of Route 2, at an elevation of 675 feet above mean sea-level. At a distance of 610 feet east of the mound the hills bordering the Ohio Valley rise abruptly from an elevation of 700 feet to approximately 850 feet. The base of the mound was approximately 50 feet higher than the edge of the terrace at the river's edge where the elevation is 625 feet. The present normal pool level of the river is 610 feet.

Cultural materials of various periods can be found scattered over much of Cresap Bottom. Except near the river's edge where flooding has occurred, most of this material is on or near the surface of the ground. The terrace, which is composed of a gravel of Pleistocene origin, immediately surrounding the mound appears not to have been flooded since glacial times. Items typical of Adena have been picked from the surface of this area. Since Cresap Bottom has been cultivated for more than 150 years it has long been a favorable spot for collectors.

South of the Cresap Mound 2375 feet on a small spur jutting from the hills bordering Cresap Bottom to the east are twin conical mounds of just slightly smaller dimensions. Both of these mounds have disturbances in their tops. Although the contents of these mounds are unknown, they, too, are probably of Adena origin.

EXCAVATION OF THE MOUND

The first step in the excavation of the Cresap Mound was the clearing of all vegetation from its surface. At the base of the mound a ring of shrubs had been planted when the area had been turned into a rest park.

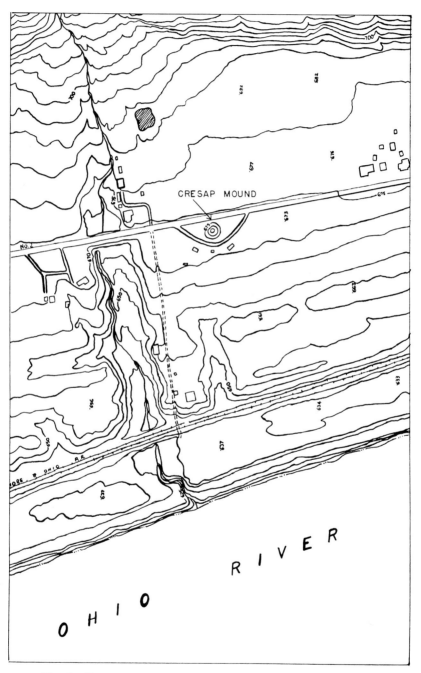

Map 1.   Topography of the area surrounding the Cresap Mound

These shrubs had grown to a height of more than 10 feet, nearly hiding the mound. It was possible to pull them without damage to the mound by the use of a high-lift machine. (Plate 1).

Plate 1.   General view of the Cresap Mound at the beginning of excavation in June 1958

Just slightly northwest of the top center of the mound was the only tree, a locust about 22 inches in diameter at the base. Its removal presented more of a problem. The first step was to cut this tree near the base. After the excavations in that area had removed the dirt from around the stump and the large roots were undercut, a cable and power winch was used to pull it from the mound. The small feeder roots of this tree, however, plagued our operations from top to bottom of the mound. The roots of this tree and others that had grown on the mound in the past had done much to break up and destroy the burials in the mound. All bones, except those in the subfloor tombs, were covered and permeated by tiny rootlets.

The second step in our operation was the survey and establishing of a grid of squares 10 x 10 feet, over the entire mound and the immediately surrounding area. This grid had its central point at a stake placed in the top center of the mound. From this point the mound was divided into four sectors with the main control lines running east to west and north to south. When all the stakes were set, it was possible to establish a series of profiles along each of these lines as the excavation progressed. In order to draw the contours, and in situations where additional profiles were needed at intervals of less than 10 feet, tape measures and temporary pins were used between the main stakes of the grid. As the earth of the mound was removed the stakes were progressively lowered and reset with accuracy being maintained by use of control stakes outside the limits of the mound. All measurements for location of burials, features, etc., found in the mound were made from the east-west and north-south base-lines that bisected the mound.

The property survey maps of the Hanna Coal Company established the elevation of the terrace at the base of the mound as 675 feet above mean sea-level. All vertical measurements were taken from a base point of this elevation established 40 feet south of the mound center on the north-south center-line. This same elevation coincided almost exactly with the floor of the mound as revealed in the excavation. All elevations of features, burials, etc., were taken from this base and, since the mound floor was of the same elevation, the elevations mentioned in the following sections are given in relation to the distance above or below the mound floor.

The mound was 15.0 feet in height and about 70 feet in maximum diameter. The vertical profiles of the mound indicated that the mound had been originally somewhat taller by perhaps 2 feet but that the diameter would have been as much as 10 feet less. This change could be attributed directly to erosion over the centuries. The general profile of the mound was that of a classic conical Adena mound. The outline of the mound at the base was nearly circular except for a slight projection on the southwest side where the prevailing winds and rain had caused more erosion. Except for general erosion, no other disturbances of importance had altered the surface of the mound. Damage to the interior of the mound was confined to the penetration of roots and the burrowing of ground hogs.

The excavation of the mound was begun by digging a trench 10 feet wide and 50 feet long N.-S. between 30 and 40 feet west of the center of the mound at the base level. This trench, cut into the subsoil, exposed a small profile at the western edge of the mound and indicated the general depth of the top-soil and underlying subsoil surrounding the mound. From this cut we were able to determine the base level of the mound and its relationship to the terrace soils below the mound.

Having established the mound base, we began digging at the outer margin of the mound on the blocks composing the SW.¼ of the mound. The approach from this side would give the best light for photography. As the work proceeded inwards, profile walls one foot thick were left standing between the blocks in order to reveal completely the mound's interior structure. All such walls were left standing as long as they did not interfere with the removal of the earth. Accurate sketches, black and white, and color photographs were made of these profile walls before their removal. These walls not only served as reference points during the excavation but also provided a complete series of profiles every 10 feet north-south and east-west. This system was used very successfully throughout the entire excavation of the mound.

The actual digging was done mostly with hoes by gradually cutting away thin layers of earth of about one inch thickness following the surface contour of the mound. As the earth was carefully removed by the hoe, it was then shoveled to the outer margins of the mound to be removed later by the high-lift machine. When any feature or burial was discovered, the trowel and smaller tools were used. An attempt was made to follow the actual structure of the mound throughout the digging rather than to excavate by arbitrary levels.

As the earth was gradually stripped from the blocks in the SW.¼ of the mound, an old humus zone ranging from 0.3 to 0.5 foot thick was discovered at a depth of 1.5 feet below the surface at the top of the mound. This dark zone terminated at the base of the mound approximately 26.0 feet from the center of the mound. At the outer margin this zone was about 5.5 feet below the surface. Once this zone was found, all the earth in the blocks of the SW.¼ was removed until the entire zone was exposed. It was obvious that this zone was the humus laden surface of a large inner mound (Plates 2 and 3).

Upon the surface of this inner mound were found the first burials and features encountered in the excavation. All the soil in the outermost

Plate 2.   Old humus layer separating the top zone from the lower zones
in the southwest quarter of the Cresap Mound

layer of the mound above this zone was devoid of cultural materials. The upper layer, composed mainly of gravel with a small amount of sandy clay, had been added as the last addition to cover the above burials and features. The thickness of the humus zone and the placement of the burials on the top of this zone indicated that these burials and the earth that covered them had been added after a lapse of considerable time after the completion of the inner mound.

The next step was to begin the cutting away of the inner mound in the SW.¼, still maintaining the profile walls between blocks (Plate 4). By exposing this quarter we would then have a key to the structure of the remaining three-quarters of the mound. As the digging proceeded downward, it became necessary to remove the earth completely from the blocks near the outer margins of the mound in order to facilitate

Plate 3.   View of the inner mound after the top zone had been removed from the southwest quarter of the Cresap Mound

the removal of the earth from the upper blocks. The profile walls were photographed, sketched, and then removed in these areas. In order to stabilize the large profile walls running N.-S. and E.-W. through the center of the mound, a block 10 feet square was left standing at the center of the mound at a height of 6.5 feet. Similar blocks were left in the other three-quarters of the mound when work reached those areas. These four blocks were removed as the final stage in the excavation (Plate 5).

The technique used in the removal of the SW.¼ proved so successful that it was extended to the remainder of the mound. The NW.¼ was removed next, followed by the SE.¼, and finally the NE.¼. The four blocks left standing as a key and support for the profiles were removed by first cutting away the two west blocks and finally the two east blocks. With the removal of subfloor features under these blocks, the excavation of the mound was completed.

Plate 4. Profile walls of the inner mound in the southwest quarter of the Cresap Mound

From beginning to end the excavation took nearly 13 weeks or 7 weeks more than we had anticipated at the start. The removal of the mound was slowed mainly by the complicated structure of the mound and the many features that required slow, painstaking care in uncovering them. Rain also hampered our operations throughout the period of work. During the month of July alone, rain fell at the mound on 20 days. Only 1½ days, however, were lost because of rain. The Hanna Coal Company supplied large sheets of heavy clear plastic 100 x 16 feet in size with which we completely covered the mound at the end of each day. On rainy days a framework was placed under the plastic to form a shelter and the work continued. We found this material extremely satisfactory for protecting the excavation and it was not subject to rot as is the case with canvas coverings. Its light weight made it easy to handle.

Plate 5.   View looking east at the central blocks that were left standing as support for the profile walls. These blocks were removed as the final stage in the excavation

MOUND STRUCTURE

In order better to understand the structure of the Cresap Mound, it is best to reconstruct the original steps taken in the building of the mound.

The area upon which the mound was built seems to have been originally the location of a house. Near the center of the mound was a large circular fire pit containing ashes and burned stones. Surrounding the fire pit was a prepared circular clay floor about 40 feet in diameter and ranging from 0.2 to 0.4 foot in thickness. In most areas under this layer of clay the old humus soil had been removed until the clay rested directly upon the loose gravel subsoil of the terrace. Around the clay floor was a circular ditch dug into the subsoil ranging from 1.8 to 2.75 feet in width and from 0.1 to 0.7 foot in depth. The soil filling this ditch was dark and contained pieces of charcoal, burned earth, and small fragments of midden refuse such as bones and shells. In the southwest sector of this ditch where it was most distinct, five dark round stains 0.6 to 0.8 foot in diameter were found within the ditch. They were spaced about 1.75 feet apart. These stains had the appearance of post molds, but it was impossible to trace them below the ditch into the loose gravel subsoil. Although no complete post mold pattern could be traced, it is my opinion that a structure was at one time present and that the early features of the mound had been placed within the structure (Fig. 1).

Features and burials to be described later, are referred to here as F.1, B.1, etc.

The first use of the area for burial purposes occurred when a shallow subfloor tomb (F.19) was dug through the clay floor just west of the fire pit. Before this tomb was covered with earth a large crematory basin (F.10) was dug into the clay floor just southwest of the tomb. Two extended adult burials (B.11 and 28) were placed on the clay floor just south of the above features. A dark humus-laden earth was then placed over these features to a depth sufficient to cover them. Additional features (F.2, 3, 4, 5, 12, and 18) containing human remains were gradually added and more earth over them until a small mound with a maximum height of 4.75 feet was formed. The earth of this small mound was a very dark, organic-laden, loamy soil. In contrast to other soil of the mound it was damp and heavy. Pieces of charcoal were mixed in the soil and were present on the surface.

About midway in the build up of this mound another tomb (F.20) was dug into the clay floor just north of tomb F.19. Dark earth was placed over it to form an annex to the small mound over F.19. At about this time another crematory basin (F.13) was dug into the dark earth with its base resting directly on the clay floor. This group of features and the dark earth that cover them composed the W. primary mound.

After the W. primary had reached its maximum height of 4.75 feet, activity shifted to the area south of the fire pit at the center of the clay floor. There at about 15 feet south of the fire pit, a large, clay, crematory basin (F.29) had been built directly on the mound floor. Over this basin was placed a dry, ashy, gray soil of fine texture forming a small mound with a maximum height of 3.1 feet. In addition to the large crematory basin containing the remains of six individuals, two other burials (B.21 and 32) had been placed on the mound floor and were covered by this small mound.

Upon the completion of this small mound the scene shifted to the area directly east of the central fire pit. There another subfloor tomb (F.28) containing Burial 54 had been cut through the clay floor. Over the tomb was another small mound of dark, humus-laden earth that reached a

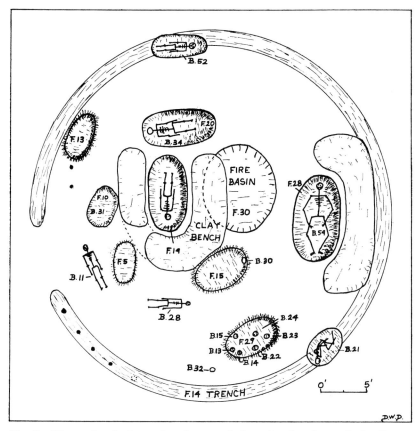

Fig. 1. The major features found on or below the clay floor of the Cresap Mound. All numbered features and burials discussed in the text

maximum elevation of 5.3 feet. The construction of this small mound had been in stages for inclosed within it were eight burials (B.40, 41, 43, 48, 49, 50, 51, and 53). Extended burial 53 had been placed 2.75 feet directly above the subfloor tomb. Under this burial was a compact layer of clay. Since this dense layer had restricted the passage of water through it, the tomb and its contents below had been kept relatively dry.

Small particles of charcoal found upon the surfaces and around the edges of these three small mounds indicated that the structure within which the small mounds had been built may have been destroyed by fire at this time. The absence of erosion gullies on the surfaces of these mounds lends additional support to the belief that they had been covered by a structure up until this time.

The next step in the construction was addition of a large crematory basin (F.15) in the saddle formed by the adjoining sides of the west and south primary mounds. Additional earth and features were then added to fill in the depressions between the small mounds and to form a single conical mound that had its peak elevation at 6.75 feet. The mound seems to have stood at this level for some time. A humus zone 0.1-0.2 foot thick developed and a few shallow erosional gullies were cut into the surface.

After the lapse of some time, additional features (F.9, 24, and 26) were placed upon the mound and a new layer of earth was added to the entire structure until it reached a height of 8.2 feet. Again a thin humus zone developed. Then a depression was dug into the top center of the mound until the floor of the depression rested at 6.5 feet. Within this depression was placed F. 8. In the profile above this feature were lines indicating that the earth that covered it had slumped into the depression. Such a situation clearly indicated that the feature had been covered by small logs.

Upon the surface of the mound at the 8.2-foot elevation was placed Feature 7. A cap of earth was then added until the summit of the mound was at 13.25 feet. At this point the mound appears to have been abandoned for a considerable length of time. A thick humus zone 0.3-0.5 foot in thickness developed upon the entire surface of the mound.

Eventually the mound again was used for the burial of the dead. This final act in the construction of the mound centered around a fire (F. 6) built at the top of the mound at the 13.25-foot elevation. On the surface of the mound around the fireplace had been placed burials 1, 2, 3, 5, 7, 8, 10, and 25. Over these burials and the fireplace a thick mantle of gravelly earth was placed until the mound was probably at least 17.0 feet in height. At the time of our excavation, erosion over the centuries had reduced the mound to 15.0 feet in height (Fig. 2).

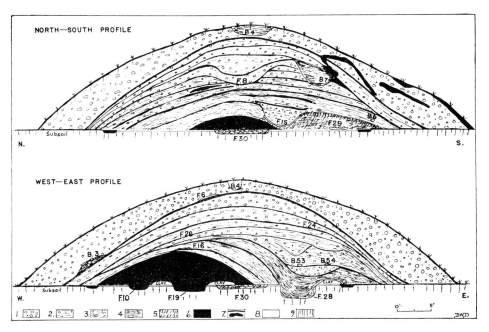

Fig. 2. North-South and East-West profiles through the center of the Cresap
      Mound. Feature and burial numbers discussed in the text
Explanation of numbered symbols: 1. Gravelly soil and large pebbles.
2. Earthy gravel. 3. Mixed gravelly loam. 4. Gray soil. 5. Mixed gray and
dark soil. 6. Concentrated zone of dark earth. 7. Lens or streak of dark earth.
8. Light-colored clay. 9. Sterile gravelly subsoil

With the addition of the above earth mantle, the building of the Cresap Mound by the Adena people drew to a close. The mound appears
not to have been disturbed again until the Late Prehistoric (A.D. 1200-
1600) when a man (B. 4) of that period was buried in a shallow pit dug
into the top of the mound. Neither this intrusion nor two shallow prob-
ings of the mound during the past century caused any disturbance or
damage to the mound's structure or contents. To us was presented the
rare opportunity of excavating a basically undisturbed mound in which
a clear chronological sequence of events could be traced.

In the succeeding sections of this report the individual features, burials, and objects are discussed in detail. Following these descriptions,
the significance of these findings is summarized.

FEATURES AND BURIALS

During the excavation of the Cresap Mound, 31 distinctive features and 54 burials were recorded. A feature was considered to be any specially prepared structural component in the mound such as a crematory basin, subfloor tomb, clay floor, fire pit, or an area prepared for a burial, etc. Many features contained one or more burials, but some burials were not associated with distinct features. In the sections that follow, each of the features and its associated items or burials is described in detail. Following the features each of the burials is discussed. When a burial was associated with a feature most of the details appear in the discussion of the feature. Cross-references are given in such cases.

All locations of features and burials are given as distances from the co-ordinate base-lines which ran through the center of the mound N.-S. and E.-W. All elevations are given in relation to the floor of the mound which also approximated the general ground level surrounding the mound.

An interpretative summary of the mound features and burials is given at the end of the descriptions.

Features

Feature 1. A cluster of stones ranging in size from 0.2 to 0.4 foot in diameter was found at 25.0 feet west and 18.2 feet south at an elevation of 0.2 foot above the mound floor. Some of these stones which appeared to be ordinary river pebbles were burned. The stones were heaped in a small pile about 1.2 feet in diameter and 0.8 foot in height. No cultural materials were found with or near the stones. It seems quite possible that this small pile of stones represented an individual load of materials added in the building of the mound. No similar cluster of stones was found elsewhere in the mound.

Feature 2. Elliptical basin found between 11.0 and 13.0 feet west and 2.0-6.0 feet south at an elevation of 3.6 feet above the mound floor. The basin was molded of fine yellow clay with well defined lips. The center of the basin was depressed 0.15 foot below the outer margin. Particles of red ocher were scattered throughout the clay used in the basin. Over the top of the basin was a layer of yellow and gray material which appeared to be a mixture of bark and yellow ocher. This layer covered the entire surface of the basin. Immediately below this covering were small patches of red ocher and particles of charcoal and burned bone. The clay of the basin had been reddened by intense heat. This reddening did not extend to the surrounding soil which was dark in color. Except for the few whitish flakes of burned bone and the charcoal the basin had the appearance of having been cleared of any contents it may have contained.

The basin was oriented almost directly N.-S. with a maximum length of 4.0 feet and a width of 2.25 feet. The elevation, 3.6 feet, of this basin was well above the mound floor and near the surface of the small W. primary mound. If this structure were used for crematory purposes, most of its contents were removed and redeposited elsewhere.

Feature 3. An ovate layer of reddish clay was uncovered between 1.2 feet north and 3.0 feet south and between 12.1 and 14.3 feet west at an elevation of 1.8 feet. This oval area was 4.2 feet long, 2.2 feet wide, and had a maximum thickness of 0.05 foot. The clay soil of which the layer was composed was burned a bright red.

The general appearance of this layer was similar to F.2 except that it lacked the depressed center and raised lips. The inclination of the layer was basically parallel with the floor of the mound except near the south end where it curved downward about 0.02 foot. Near the center of the layer at the north end was a slight depression. Over this depression was a circular area of bark 0.9 foot in diameter. Under this bark were the remains of a small child (B.16). Around the neck of this child a small string of 43 copper beads had been placed.

Red ocher had been sprinkled over the entire layer. Except for the above-mentioned burial and associated beads, no other objects were present. The layer had been cleared of all other evidence of its former use except for a few flakes of charcoal.

This feature was below and directly to the north of F.2 in the west primary mound. Features 4 and 5 were immediately south of this feature and below F.2.

Feature 4. An orange-red layer of clay was located between 10.5 and 13.9 feet west and between 2.9 and 8.1 feet south at an elevation of 0.2-0.6 foot above the mound floor. This oval-shaped layer was 5.2 feet long, 3.4 feet wide, and 0.06 foot in thickness. It was oriented with the long axis north-south. Fragments of organic material covered the entire upper surface of the layer. Most of this material appeared to be the remains of bark. The orange-red color of the clay resulted from the combination of heat and the presence of red ocher which had been sprinkled over the layer.

Near the center of the layer was a circular area of bark 0.9 foot in diameter. Under this layer was found the badly decayed skull of a small child (B.12). Around the neck and covering the face were 24 small rolled copper beads and four small disk shell beads. Fragments of shell and copper indicated that more beads were once present but had crumbled under the ravages of the acid soil.

When the top covering of organic material and red ocher was scraped from the clay layer, several objects were found. Near the south edge of the layer was a large round poll celt of igneous stone. Scattered along the western and northern margins of the clay layer were two stemmed blades, one long expanded-base drill, one small celt, and one crude sphere of hematite.

This reddened clay layer was directly below F.2 and immediately above F.5. Feature 3 was above it and to the north. All these features are similar and represent stages in the construction of the small west primary mound.

Feature 5. An orange-red basin-shaped layer of clay was found between 12.4-14.3 feet west and 3.1-7.5 feet south at an elevation of 0.0-0.3 foot above the mound floor. This oval-shaped basin was 4.4 feet long, 1.9 feet wide, and 0.06 foot in thickness. It was composed of fine clay and had the same fire-reddened appearance as nearby features 2, 3, and 4. The outer edges of the clay lining were raised 0.2 foot above the floor giving a definite basin-shape appearance as was noted for F.2.

Within this basin was a layer of ash and burned organic material which ranged from 0.05 to 0.075 foot in thickness. Patches of red ocher were present in the ash as well as scattered over the clay lining of the basin. No objects were present.

This basin was directly on the floor of the mound and almost precisely under F.4 in the west primary mound.

Feature 6. Burned area between 6.0 to 8.0 feet west and between 1.0 south to 2.2 feet north at an elevation of 13.5 feet above the mound floor. This oval, burned area was 1.5 feet below the surface of the outer mound and at the top of the large inner mound. There was no clay lining present in this burned area. The earth of the mound was merely reddened by intense heat over an area containing about six square feet (Plate 6).

Plate 6.   Burned area (Feature 6) and part of the associated items found
near the top of the inner mound at the 13.5-foot level

Within this burned area and on the same general level surrounding it were a number of interesting items. Found within the burned area were one stemmed blade, one copper strip which had been folded and beaten flat, one grooved tablet carved in the shape of a turtle, one "kidney-shaped" grooved tablet, one plain rectangular tablet, one grooved rectangular tablet, one large plain rectangular tablet found in two pieces, one irregular-shaped grooved tablet, two fragments of plain rectangular tablets, one rectangular piece of crude sandstone, one blank for a tubular pipe made of Berea grit sandstone, one piece of worked stone, and one stone with a faceted surface (Plate 7).

Plate 7.   Tablets, pipe blank, stemmed blade, and copper strip found directly in the burned area of Feature 6

Immediately east of the burned area on the same surface were two reel-shaped gorgets of banded slate, one hemisphere of calcium carbonate, two ellipsoidal-shaped two-hole objects of calcium carbonate, five stemmed blades, and one fragment of a stemmed blade (Plate 8).

All of the objects found directly in the burned area showed the effects of heat and were specked with organic stains. Some of the objects from the surrounding area also were burned and covered by dark organic stains.

The position of this burned area and the objects found in and near it are of great interest. We may conjecture that this feature represented the remains of a major fire-oriented ceremony which occurred just prior to the placement of the earth over several burials on the same surface along the sides of the mound. This earth constituted the last major addition to the mound. The objects found were used in the ceremony and then cast into the fire as an offering. The cultural and chronological sig-

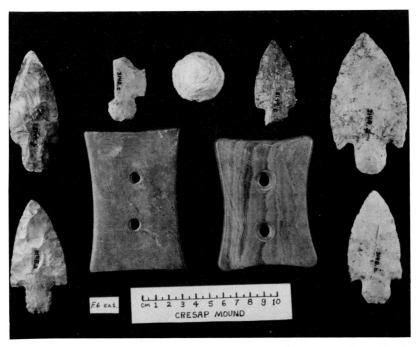

Plate 8. **Gorgets, blades, and hemisphere found in the area immediately surrounding Feature 6**

nificance of these objects in Adena will be discussed more thoroughly in a latter section of this report (Fig 3).

Feature 7. Burned area found between 2.0 and 7.6 feet W. and between 6.0 and 8.0 feet S. at an elevation of 8.82 feet above the mound floor. This rectangular area was 5.6 feet long and 2.0 feet wide. It was oriented in a SE.-NW. direction. The earth of the entire area had been reddened by heat and small particles of red ocher had been scattered over it.

The teeth and fragments of a skull (B.18) were found in the SE. end of this feature. No other bones were found. Near the skull fragments was a large piece of worked hematite and at the NW. end of the reddened area were two small celts.

The size and shape of this burned area coupled with the position of the skull fragments at the SE. end of the area indicated that, perhaps, an entire body had once been present. If the torso had been burned, all fragments of calcined bone had been removed from the area and redeposited elsewhere.

This feature was on an old mound surface at the 8.82-foot level.

Fig. 3. Artist's reconstruction of the probable ceremony centered around the fire (Feature 6) at the top of the Cresap Mound at the beginning of the final building phase when several burials were placed on the mound surface around the fire and then covered by a thick layer of earth

Feature 8. Reddened layer of clay located near the center of the mound between 1.6 N. and 1.4 feet S. and between 2.9 W. and 1.7 feet E. at an elevation of 6.5 feet above the mound floor. This oval-shaped layer was 4.6 feet long and 3.0 feet wide. It was oriented in an east-west direction. The entire area was burned intensely and the center was slightly depressed. It lacked, however, the definite turned-up margins noted for similar features F.2 and F.5.

Near the west end of this feature was a patch of yellow ocher 0.8 foot in diameter. Fragments of human bone were mixed with this yellow ocher. Red ocher had been scattered around the yellow ocher and throughout the reddened area. Under the yellow ocher were three stemmed blades, one small stone concretion, and one worked piece of hematite (Plate 7).

Plate 9.   Heat reddened layer of clay (Feature 8) upon which the remains of Burial 26 and associated objects were found

At the east end of the feature were found the badly broken fragments of a skull and the bundled long bones of a burial (B.26). Directly associated with this burial were three celts, one leaf-shaped blade, one section of a large blade, one stemmed blade, two large pieces of Flint Ridge flint with battered edges, one concretion paint cup stained with red ocher, 1 piece of worked hematite with grooves worn into it, one fragmentary deer scapula awl, one broken and burned blocked-end tubular pipe, and 15 small copper beads which had been strung on a string. Red ocher had been placed over and around these objects.

Fragments of bark and stains of other organic materials were present over the bones and objects. In the wall profiles directly over this feature the lenses of soil are depressed as if they had collapsed downward into the feature. It thus appears that this feature was dug into the mound when it was at the 8.82 foot level. Small logs probably held the earth above the burial for a considerable period of time before their collapse.

Feature 9. A small area of burned earth containing a deposit of red ocher was found at 7.5 feet S. and 8.0 feet E. at an elevation of 6.5 feet above the mound floor. This irregular area of burned earth was approximately 1.0 foot in diameter. With the small pile of red ocher at the center of the burned area were one piece of worked hematite, one concretion paint cup stained with red ocher, and two small flakes of flint. The fragmentary remains of Burial 39 were found directly east of this feature.

Feature 10. A clay-lined basin was found between 14.0 and 17.3 feet W. and between 3.0 N.-1.5 feet S. at an elevation of 0.0-0.6 foot below the mound floor. This well constructed oval-shaped basin was 4.5 feet long, 3.3 feet wide, and depressed in the center to a depth of 0.6 foot. It was oriented in a north-south direction. The clay lining of the basin averaged 0.05 foot in thickness and it had been burned to a brick-red color (Plate 10).

Within the basin a number of objects had been placed in definite positions. Along the west side there was a cache of five leaf-shaped blades and one stemmed blade. Scattered in the area near this cache were two stemmed blades, one stemmed blade base, one base of a leaf-shaped blade, one side scraper, and a small deposit of graphite near a few fragments of bone. Adjacent to the cache blades was a small pile of ash and calcined bones which probably represented the total remains of a cremation (B.31). At the north end of the basin were one stemmed blade, one leaf-shaped blade, one hematite hemisphere found with flat surface up, one stone sphere, and a pile of graphite so placed as to indicate that it had once been in a container of cloth or skin. Scattered along the east side of the basin were two stemmed blades, one drill, and one side scraper. At the south end of the basin were one stemmed blade, one blade tip, and one hematite hemisphere found lying on edge (Plate 11).

Plate 10. Feature 10, a clay-lined basin in the mound floor containing both artifacts and osseous materials

Most of the artifacts were found near the margins of the basin rather than on its floor. Except for a few flakes of charcoal scattered over the floor, all residue of fires had been removed. A few scraps of badly decomposed bone were scattered over the floor, but no definite form or placement could be determined from these scraps. Red ocher was present near all the artifacts and had been sprinkled over the entire surface of the basin.

This basin appeared to be a typical example of a crematory basin in the floor of a mound. Its location under the small west primary mound near subfloor tomb F.19 would make it one of the earliest features in the mound.

Feature 11. A basin-shaped layer of burned clay was found between 2.9 W. and 1.6 feet E. and between 7.8 and 10.2 feet S. at an elevation of 3.8 feet above the mound floor. This oval oriented in an east-west direction was 4.5 feet long and 2.4 feet wide, and the center was depressed

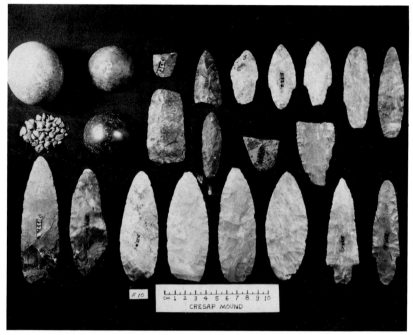

**Plate 11.   The blades, scrapers, hemispheres, stone ball, and particles of
graphite found in clay basin (Feature 10)**

about 0.15 foot below the outer margins. The clay lining of this feature
was not as intensely burned as was noted for similar features in the
mound.

At the west end of this shallow basin were the burned skull fragments
of Burial 27. No other bones or artifacts were present, and the basin had
been cleared of any ash of charcoal accumulations. Red ocher had been
sprinkled over the entire surface of the basin.

Feature 12. A basin-shaped layer of burned clay 0.04 foot in thickness
was uncovered between 11.5 and 14.2 feet W. and between 6.0 and 9.5
feet N. at an elevation of 0.9 foot above the mound floor. This basin was
oval in outline and depressed only 0.12 foot at the center. It had been
reddened by intense heat and red ocher had been scattered over its
entire surface. Tiny specks of calcined bone were found on the floor of
the basin.

Near the north end of the basin was a small area of bark about 0.5 foot in diameter. Under this bark was a circular string of 22 rolled copper beads and a small piece of cloth preserved by the copper salts. Near the beads were several fragments of enamel from the teeth of a small child (B.9). No other bones or objects were found.

Feature 13. Another clay-lined basin was found between 16.0 and 18.6 feet W. and between 5.0 and 10.5 feet N. at an elevation of 0.0-0.7 foot above the mound floor. This oval basin, oriented in a north-south direction, appeared to have been dug into the dark soil of the small west primary mound. The bottom of the basin rested directly on the mound floor but the sides rose steeply to a well defined rim 0.7 foot above the floor. The basin was 5.5 feet long and 2.6 feet wide, and its depth of 0.7 foot was the greatest of any similar feature found in the mound.

In the north end of this basin were the partially burned fragments of an adult skull (B.38). Under the skull was a thin layer of red ocher and 0.5 foot west of the skull was a large clump of red ocher. Red ocher had also been scattered over the entire inner surface of the basin which had been burned a bright orange. No other objects were found.

Feature 14. As the work progressed toward the center of the mound at the floor level, a circular trench was found which surrounded all the major features on the mound floor. This trench was located between 16.0 E. and 22.2 feet W. and between 18.1 N. and 21.0 feet S. at an elevation of 0.0-0.5 foot below the floor level of the mound. The maximum diameters of this shallow trench were 38.2 feet N.-S. and 39.1 feet E.-W. The trench varied in width from 2.1 to 3.2 feet. Its maximum depth occurred on the southwest segment where it was 0.5 foot deep. Along the north side of the arc it appeared as merely a dark stain in the soil. The clay floor of the central area of the mound was completely confined to the interior of this circular trench. Outside of the trench the top-soil had been removed down to the gravel subsoil. The clay floor also rested directly on the gravel subsoil except for one small area on the southwest quarter of the mound where an area of about 36 square feet of thin top-soil lay between the clay floor and the subsoil.

Where the trench had any depth it was filled with dark soil and village debris. In the southwest sector of the trench fine darker stains 0.6-0.8 foot in diameter were seen in the dark earth. These stains had the appearance of post molds but it was impossible to trace them into the gravel subsoil. Several faint circular stains were seen in the trench but none could be traced for any depth. An intensive effort was made to locate post molds all along the trench, but the loose gravel subsoil would not have preserved the shape of such intrusions.

Although only suggestive stains of what appeared to be a pattern of post molds could be found, it seems highly probable that a structure was once present. As none of the suspected post-mold stains occurred in pairs, the house would have had single wall posts more common to early Adena circular houses rather than the paired posts found in late Adena.

Along the northwest sector of the trench, Burial 52 had been placed into the ground through the trench. Burial 21 was placed over the trench in the southeast sector. The clay embankment along the east side of the subfloor tomb F.28 partially overlapped the trench at the east side of the mound.

Feature 15. A log-covered clay-lined basin was found between 5.0 W. and 0.9 feet E. and between 3.0 and 8.0 feet S. at an elevation of 0.2-0.6 foot above the mound floor. This feature was located in the saddle formed by the junction of the margins of the W. and S. primary mounds. The basin was oval in outline and was oriented in SW.-NE. direction. It was 5.9 feet long, 3.8 feet wide and 0.4 foot deep. The clay lining of the basin was 0.04 foot in thickness. It was hard and reddened from the effects of heat. The lips of the basin were distinct and were 0.09 foot in thickness (Plate 12).

Over the basin 10 small logs had been placed as a cover. These logs averaged 4.2 feet in length and 0.5 foot in diameter. The ends of the logs were supported on the sides of the two primary mounds. Along the SE. side of the basin the logs had slipped downward into the basin. Directly under the logs were fragments of bark which appeared to have once covered the entire area of the basin.

At the NE. end of the basin were the fragments of an adult skull (B.30). Scattered throughout the basin were other fragments of human bone but no definite form could be determined for these scraps.

A number of interesting items were found in the basin. In the area 0.5 foot south of the skull fragments (B.30) were a crude celt and a large leaf-shaped blade. West of the skull near the center of the basin was a large reel-shaped gorget of copper covered with a fibrous organic material. Under the copper gorget was a slender strip of bone 16.9 cm. long, 4.1 cm. wide and 0.8 cm. thick. Fibrous organic material was present around the bone object which appeared to have been attached to the gorget (Plate 13).

Plate 12.   Feature 15, a large clay basin located in the saddle between the south and west primary mounds. Note the copper gorget near the center of the basin

Under the bark covering at the SW. end of the basin were the fragile remains and the distinct impression of a small simple twined basket 21.6 cm. in diameter and 5.1 cm. in depth. Although most of the fibers of this basket were gone, enough remained to indicate that the basket had been tightly woven from small strands of fiber. It was impossible to remove this object before the few remaining fibers crumbled under the exposure to air.

Along the NW. side of the basin was a deposit of yellow ocher and a deposit of red ocher. Near the ocher was a crude grooved tablet made from a thin slab of fine-grained sandstone. At the center of the basin was another crude grooved tablet under a small deposit of ash and calcined bone fragments which probably represented the residue of a cremation. Around this deposit were one stemmed blade, two worked and faceted pieces of hematite, one blade tip, one end scraper, and one pitted stone.

Plate 13.   Crude tablets, faceted lumps of hematite, blades, scraper, celt, and
copper gorget from Feature 15

The size and shape of this basin along with the intense burning it had
received would indicate that it had been used primarily for crematory
purposes and then as a burial chamber for the skeletal material found
in it.

Feature 16. An orange-red layer of clay was found between 5.0 and
10.5 feet W. and between 0.5 S. and 4.0 feet N. at an elevation of 5.2 feet
above the mound floor. This oval layer of burned clay was just above
the apex of the small W. primary mound. It was 5.5 feet long, 4.5 feet
wide, and 0.04 foot thick. The layer was level, with no depression at
the center. Over the burned clay had been sprinkled red ocher and a
whitish material which upon laboratory examination proved to be small
pieces of calcined bone. Over the layer of clay was a mantle of decomposed organic material and bark. Under this mantle were several objects
and the burned fragments of an adult skull (B.29).

Near the skull at the west end of the layer were two hematite hemispheres, one crude grooved tablet, one mussel shell, and a small clump of red ocher. Scattered at the east end of the clay layer were three celts, one piece of quartzite, one large piece of Flint Ridge flint, and one piece of worked hematite. Along the north side of the layer were two stemmed blades and three fragments of a crude grooved tablet (Plate 14).

Fragments of human bone were found near the center of the layer and near the celts at the east end. These bones were so decayed that no definite relationship between these fragments and the skull could be seen.

At 0.2 foot directly above this feature a celt was found in the earth fill of the mound. This object may have only been an accidental inclusion.

Feature 17. A layer of ash was found directly north of F.16 between 5.5 and 8.6 feet W., between 4.1 and 6.0 feet N. at an elevation of 5.2 feet above the mound floor. This oval layer was 3.3 feet long, 1.9 feet wide, and 0.09 foot thick. It was oriented with its long axis east-west.

This feature was unusual in that it lacked the characteristic redness seen in surrounding features. It consisted of two layers of whitish-gray ash separated by a brownish layer of ash and decayed organic material. Each of these layers was about 0.03 foot in thickness. Very small particles of bone were present in the two layers of whitish-gray ash. Clay was not used as a base.

When the brownish layer was scraped away the following objects were found: one flint blank or scraper with well worked edges, one large chunk of flint with worked edges, one small piece of flint, and one mussel shell which had been partially burned.

Except for the particles of bone in the two ash layers, no other osseous material was found in this feature.

Feature 18. A reddened layer of clay was found between 1.0 and 3.9 feet W. and between 4.4 and 8.2 feet N. at an elevation of 0.7 foot above the mound floor. This elliptical-shaped layer of burned clay rested on the clay platform that surrounded the subfloor tomb (F.19) under the W. primary mound. The layer was 4.0 feet long, 2.5 feet wide, and 0.08 foot thick.

Over the layer of burned clay was a heavy lens of ash and carbonized organic material. Fragments of calcined bone were present in this ash.

Plate 14. Artifacts found associated with Burial 29 in Feature 16

The only other inclusion in the feature was a small deposit of red ocher at the southeast end.

Feature 19. Under the center of the W. primary mound was a bark and log covered subfloor pit located between 6.5 N. and 1.8 feet S. and between 6.2 and 10.1 feet W. at an elevation of 0.0-0.8 foot below the mound floor. This rectanguloid subfloor pit was 8.3 feet long, 3.9 feet wide, and 0.8 foot in maximum depth. The long axis was oriented N-S. (Plates 15-16).

The pit had been covered by strips of bark held up by small logs laid across the opening. Directly above the tomb, the lenses of soil in the profile showed a collapse into the tomb after about 2.0 feet of earth had been added to the W. primary mound. Since the lenses of soil were unbroken, the collapse seems to have been gradual and to have taken place as the small logs and bark slowly rotted away.

Plate 15. Cross-section of west primary mound directly over the subfloor tomb (Feature 19). Clay benches on south and west sides of tomb can be seen on the mound floor

Surrounding the subfloor pit on the west, south, and east was a raised clay platform approximately 2.0 feet in width and 0.8-0.9 foot in height from the mound floor upon which it was constructed. The interior earth of this platform was a mixture of gravel subsoil and humus laden top-soil like that used in the construction of the W. primary mound, but the surface of the platform had been deliberately covered with a coating of yellow clay about 0.09 foot in thickness. This clay was similar to that used to line the crematory basins and to build the mound floor. Two circular discolorations, 0.5 foot in diameter, were present at the north end of the pit where the clay platform was absent. These stains appeared to be post molds but it was impossible to trace them below the mound floor into the gravel subsoil.

Plate 16.   Subfloor tomb (Feature 19) after removal of the west primary mound. Clay benches on south and east sides of tomb still in position but west bench had been removed

When the collapsed covering of the tomb was removed to expose the contents, the fragmentary remains of a female or young male were found. The burial (B.30) was extended on its back with the head to the south. Only the enamel of the teeth and a few decayed scraps of bone remained of the skull which appeared to rest on its right side facing east. Only the left tibia and left tarsal bones were moderately well preserved. All the remaining bones of the skeleton were fragmentary or completely missing. Light colored stains in the clay floor of the pit attested to the former presence and position of these missing bones. Why the left tibia and tarsal bones were preserved seems a mystery for there was no noticeable difference in the soil around these bones and that around the missing bones.

The only objects associated with this pit were a celt of igneous stone at the south end of the basin near the top of the skull, a clump of red ocher

to the left of the skull, and a small deposit of white ash at the middle of
the pit near the west side of the burial. Dark stains on the floor and sides
of the pit indicated the former presence of organic material. Fragments
of bark were found under the burial and along the sides of the pit. The
entire tomb thus appears to have been lined with this material. The
scarcity of funeral furniture with the burial in this pit was in contrast
to the number of items found in subfloor pits F.20 and F.28.

Feature 20. A bark and log covered subfloor tomb was found directly
north of pit F.19 between 3.2 and 11.0 feet W. and between 6.5 and 11.6
feet N. at an elevation of 0.9 foot below the mound floor. This rectanguloid shaped pit was 7.8 feet long, 5.1 feet wide, and 0.9 foot in maximum
depth. It was oriented east-west.

A layer of bark over small logs also covered this pit. Unbroken lenses
of soil in the profile above the pit indicated a gradual collapse of the
covering as the logs rotted. Stains of the logs could be seen on the floor
of the tomb.

No raised clay platform was present around this pit as was the case for
F.19. The earth fill in the mound covering this tomb contained more
gravel and clay than the fill earth over F.19 where the soil was very
black and humus laden. The small mound which covered this tomb
appeared to be an addition to or an extension of the W. primary mound
over F.19.

This tomb was 0.1 foot deeper than tomb F.19 and the layer of bark
which covered the tomb was much thicker (ranging in thickness from
0.09 to 0.15 foot). Near the east end of the pit were the remains of
organic material which had the appearance of woven mats.

In the west end of the pit were the crowns of the teeth of a burial
(B.34) in a darkly stained area 0.8 foot in diameter. No other bones,
except a few tiny pieces of calcined bone near the center of the pit, were
found. The size of the pit and the finding of the fragments of teeth at
the west end of the pit indicated that an extended burial had been placed
in the pit. Faint brownish stains on the floor of the pit also attested to
the former presence of bone. The clay lining of the pit prevented free
drainage of water, making the pit a catch-basin. This coupled with the
general acidity of the soil seems to account for the total destruction
of bone.

In contrast to F.19, this tomb contained a number of artifacts. At the
west end of the pit near the fragments of teeth were a stone sphere and a

small hematite celt. Extending through the center of the pit but with the greatest concentration about midway along the north side were four large celts of igneous stone, one small celt of igneous stone, one hematite hemisphere, one barite hemisphere, two grooved tablets, two pendants of banded slate with engraved lines on their surfaces, one scraper, one drill, and two mineral deposits (one of manganese dioxide and the other of red ocher). Just below the tooth fragments near the center of the pit floor was a large stemmed blade. At the east end of the pit were three celts, two drills, one fragment of a grooved tablet, one small deposit of red ocher, and a small pile of Flint Ridge flint flakes. The small flint flakes were in a pile with no definite geometrical pattern. The red ocher deposit covered the flint flakes and red ocher had been lightly sprinkled over the surrounding area. The entire pit had been lightly sprinkled with red ocher and faint traces of yellow ocher were evident in certain scattered areas of the pit (Fig. 4 and Plate 17).

This subfloor pit was dug into the floor of the mound after pit F.19. The soil covering this pit partially overlapped the earth covering F.19.

Fig. 4. Artist's reconstruction of the activities associated with the interment of Burial 34 in subfloor pit, Feature 20

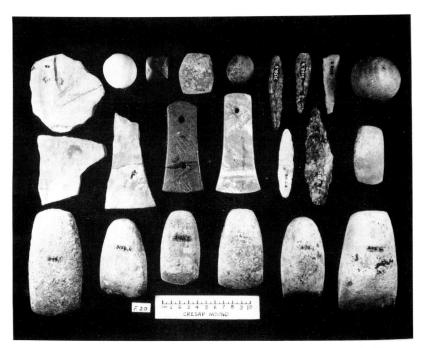

Plate 17. The artifacts associated with Burial 34 in subfloor tomb (Feature 20) under the northern extension of the west primary mound

Feature 21. A layer of heat-reddened soil was found between 8.1 and 10.2 feet W. and between 9.8 and 11.9 feet W. at an elevation of 5.1 feet above the mound floor. This circular, level area was 2.0 feet in diameter and 0.03 foot in thickness. It was not as reddened by heat as other areas seen in the mound.

At the west side of this layer was a mass of cremated bone (B.35). On the south section were unburned fragments of a skull and teeth (B.36). At the east side of the layer was another broken skull and some teeth (B.37). Near the center of the reddened area were several badly decayed fragments of long bones.

Near the pile of skull fragments and teeth (B.37) at the east side of the layer was a small pile of red ocher about 0.5 foot in diameter. In this red ocher and scattered nearby on the burned area were 1 drill, 1 base of a stemmed blade, 1 small stemmed blade, 1 section of a blade, 1 small hematite celt, 1 stone concretion, and 8 pieces of worked flint. All of these items appear to have been subjected to heat.

This layer of reddened soil and the associated skeletal material was on the apex of the earth which covered subfloor pit F.20 and formed an extension of the W. primary mound.

Feature 22. A burned area was located between 15.2-17.4 feet E. and between 2.9-5.1 feet S. at an elevation of 4.4 feet above the mound floor. There was no clay layer present in this burned area which was roughly circular in outline and 2.2 feet in diameter. Some fragments of burned bone were present in this feature and the skull of B. 40 was found immediately south of it. No other objects were present.

Feature 23. Another burned area was found between 9.5-11.2 feet N. and between 0.8 E.-2.5 feet W. at an elevation of 4.8 feet above mound floor. This oval area of burned soil was 3.3 feet long and 1.7 feet wide. It was oriented with its long axis E-W. Covering the burned area was a thin layer of bark. Under the bark at the west end of the feature were badly decayed bone fragments. No burial number was assigned to these fragments, but it seems quite possible that a burial may have been present before its nearly total destruction by the acid soil.

Feature 24. A burned area was found between 13.1-16.1 feet E. and between 0.0-3.2 feet N. at an elevation of 6.75 feet above the mound floor. This oval area was about 3.1 feet in diameter. It was covered by a heavy layer of charcoal ranging in thickness from 0.1 to 0.2 foot. The earth under and near the feature was stained black from the charcoal but was only slightly reddened by heat.

Along the southwest side of this feature was a pile of cremated human bone (B.44). Scattered throughout the charcoal were many small fragments of calcined bone. Except for several heat broken stones, no other cultural objects were associated with the feature.

In the charcoal layer were fragments of burned hickory nuts and the ends of twigs from the red spruce. The red spruce now grows only in the highlands of West Virginia many miles from the location of the Cresap Mound. There are three main possibilities of how the red spruce could have been included in the mound: 1. A spruce limb could have floated down the adjacent Ohio River from a much higher and distant elevation. 2. The Adena people could have traveled many miles to the spruce forests. 3. The climatic conditions could have been such that the red spruce was growing in the immediate area. In the latter event, a much cooler climate than at present would be indicated.

Feature 25. A layer of reddened clay was located between 4.9 and 10.3 feet W. and between 10.2 and 14.4 feet N. at an elevation of 0.2 feet above the mound floor. This rectanguloid layer of burned clay was 5.4 feet long, 4.2 feet wide, and 0.05 foot thick. The long axis was oriented in an east-west direction.

Upon this burned layer of clay was found the fragmentary remains of an extended adult burial (B.45). The head was to the east and had been crushed flat by the weight of the earth above it. Only traces of other bone were present except for the left radius and ulna which had been preserved by the copper salts of a string of 128 small copper beads which had been wrapped around the lower left arm. Although the body had been placed on its back, the head and thorax had been rotated to the right so that the burial faced north (Plate 18).

Surrounding Burial 45 on the burned clay were a number of interesting objects. To the left of the burial on the south side of the layer was a small deposit of calcined bone 0.4 foot in diameter. Near the calcined bone were one stemmed blade, one drill, one broken stemmed blade base, one broken blade tip, one piece of worked flint, one abrading stone of sandstone, one clump of black organic material, and three small clusters of red ocher (Plate 19).

Scattered from near the head to the feet along the right side of B.45 near the margin of the burned clay were five pieces of worked flint, four pieces of worked hematite, two large side scrapers, four stemmed blades, one stemmed blade base, one blade tip, one rectangular gorget or pendant, one piece of worked cannel coal, two abrading stones of sandstone, eight pieces of heat broken stones, and a small cluster of red ocher.

Red ocher had been sprinkled over the entire clay layer. Fragments of bark were also present, especially over the area surrounding the copper beads. It seems quite probable that the entire layer had been covered with bark at the time of burial.

This clay layer with B.45 and associated objects was on a thin layer of dark soil 0.2 foot above the mound floor directly north and partially overlapping subfloor pit F.20. This feature would have had to be added soon after F.20 was completed but before any great amount of earth covered F.20.

Feature 26. A set of elk antlers was found between 0.0 and 2.1 feet S. and between 9.2 and 10.8 feet W. at an elevation of 6.5 feet above the mound floor. These antlers rested on the dark soil layer at the level of

Plate 18. Prepared clay layer (Feature 25) on which Burial 45 and associated artifacts had been placed

F.8 and immediately west of that feature and almost directly above the apex of the small W. primary mound.

The antlers were still attached to the skullcap which had been carefully cut away from the remainder of the skull. The distal tips of the antlers had been shortened and modified. The fragmentary condition of these antlers made detailed inspection of this modification impossible. It seems quite likely that the antlers were shortened to reduce excessive bulk and weight. This modification coupled with the careful removal of the skullcap from the skull indicated that these antlers were part of a head-dress. The intentional placement of the antlers near F.8 would suggest that they were of importance in the burial ceremony that accompanied the internment of B.26 in that feature.

Feature 27. Another burned area was found between 1.6 and 2.7 feet E. and between 1.5 and 2.5 feet S. at an elevation of 1.8 feet above the mound floor. The area was nearly circular and was 1.1 foot in diameter.

The soil was reddened by heat and red ocher had been sprinkled over the entire area. There was no clay lining to this feature as was common at many of the other features in the mound. Over the burned area was a covering of bark. Under the bark was a thin layer of red ocher. Several fragments of calcined bone were scattered through the red ocher.

Plate 19.   Blades, scrapers, drill, abrading stone, faceted pieces of hematite, pendant, and copper beads associated with Burial 45 in Feature 25

Feature 28. On the east side of the mound the third log and bark covered subfloor pit was found between 5.1 and 10.5 feet E. and between 3.5 N. and 5.2 feet S. at an elevation of 0.0-3.3 feet below the mound floor. This oval-shaped pit was 8.2 feet long, 6.15 feet wide, and 3.3 feet deep. It was oriented with the long axis N.-S. The floor of the pit was level and slightly larger than the opening. The loose gravel subsoil accounted for the larger floor area of the pit as the gravel would have crumbled and collapsed as the digging progressed. Since the opening of the pit had been dug through the hard clay mound floor, the opening retained its shape and oval outline (Plate 20).

Over the pit small logs had been placed crossways. These were then covered by a layer of bark. The logs and the bark covering had collapsed in the pit after the pressure of the small earth mound that was constructed over it had become too great. The earth of the small primary mound was dark and humus laden. Within it were fragments of shell, bone, charcoal, burned stones, flint, and pottery. This earth seems to have come from the surrounding village area.

Along the east side of the tomb was a clay bench similar to the one that surrounded subfloor pit F.19 on three sides. This platform was confined to the east side and there was no evidence to suggest that it ever extended around the pit. The interior soil of the platform was mixed subsoil gravel and dark top-soil. The exterior was plastered with a coating of yellow clay about 0.07 foot in thickness. This platform was 10.2 feet in length, 3.2 feet in maximum width, and 0.9 foot in height. It was crescent shaped with the ends tapering to rounded points. This platform partially overlaid the shallow trench (F.14) which encircled the prepared clay floor of the mound.

At the southwest corner of the tomb some of the gravel subsoil tossed out of the pit overlaid the margin of the small S. primary mound which covered the crematory (F.29) containing six skulls. This situation seems to indicate clearly that this pit was later than the features on the south and west sides of the mound floor and was the last major intrusion into the mound floor.

Within the pit was the burial of a tall adult male. The skeleton lay on its back with the head to the north. The arms were at the sides with the elbows out slightly. The legs were partially flexed with the knees out in a "bow-legged" fashion. The skull was badly crushed and had been burned. The fire responsible for this burning may have been in the tomb soon after the burial. None of the bones below the head shows the effects of fire. Some pieces of charcoal were found in the soil around the skull (Plate 21).

Fragments of bark were found under the burial, around it, and at the sides of the pit, indicating that the tomb had been lined with this material. The bark and the bones of the burial were well preserved in contrast to the very fragmentary nature in all the other burials. This good preservation can be attributed to the well drained gravel subsoil, the

Plate 20.   Subfloor tomb (Feature 28) under the east primary mound. A clay
bench was located on only the east side of this tomb

absence of clay lining in the pit, and the presence of a layer of clay 2.75
feet directly above the pit, in the E. primary mound which covered
this feature.

Associated with Burial 54 in this tomb were many objects. To the left
of the skull at the northeast corner of the pit were two turtle carapace
cups. Inside one of these cups were a mussel shell and a piece of worked
flint. Near the left shoulder were a small pile of graphite, two bone awls,
two pieces of worked hematite, and a large piece of flint. At the left
knee was a piece of worked flint and a stemmed blade.. Lying between
the legs were a large stemmed blade, a deer scapula awl, a piece of
worked bone, a small ball of burned clay, a mussel shell, and six pieces
of burned shale. At the right hip were a turtle shell, an antler punch or
awl, a small celt, a piece of worked hematite, and a thin layer of dark
organic material 0.5 foot in diameter. Between the right arm and the
vertebral column were three stemmed blades, two mussel shells, a bone

Plate 21.   Burial 54 and associated artifacts in subfloor tomb (Feature 28).
The skull and upper portion of body had been partially destroyed by fire

awl, a piece of worked bone, and a piece of burned shale. At the right
elbow was a small deposit of ash 0.4 foot in diameter and a lump of
burned clay. Just above the right elbow was a crude rectangular tablet
made from mudstone. Near this tablet was a smooth river stone covered
by a layer of waxy organic material. At the right shoulder were a deposit of red ocher, three flint scrapers, and a piece of worked hematite.
On the floor of the pit at the head of the burial were two blades, one
stemmed blade, a section of broken blade, and two worked pieces of
hematite.

Around the neck of the burial was a string of 43 disks and tubular
conch shell beads and four tubular bone beads. In the same area were
31 marginella shell beads. Around the right wrist were 12 marginella
shell beads. In a line running across the pelvis from the left to right
hand were 10 large conch shell heads (Plate 22).

Near the beads at the neck of the burial was a mass of brown-colored organic material. Several similar areas were seen around and under the burial.

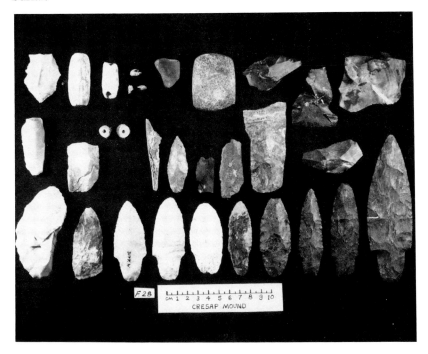

Plate 22.   The blades, scrapers, celt, faceted piece of hematite, bone awl, and shell beads associated with Burial 54 in Feature 28

Feature 29. Under the small S. primary mound a clay-lined basin was found between 2.6 W. and 2.4 feet E. and between 11.3 and 15.2 feet S. at an elevation of 0.3-0.8 foot above the mound floor. This oval-shaped basin was 5.2 feet long, 3.0 feet wide, and 0.5 foot deep. The long axis was oriented in NE.-SW. direction. The interior of the basin had been burned a brick-red color. Red ocher sprinkled over the basin surface further intensified the red color. The clay lining averaged 0.04 foot in thickness. This basin was the central feature under the S. primary mound.

The skulls of six adult males were found in the basin. Three skulls (B.13, 14, and 15) were clustered at the SW. end of the basin, two skulls (B.23 and 24) were at the NE. end, and one skull (B.22) was along the SE. side of the basin. Four of the skulls faced outward while the other two faced towards the center of the basin. All the skulls were crushed flat and very poorly preserved (Plate 23).

Plate 23.   The badly crushed skull of Burial 15 and associated artifacts found in the western portion of Feature 29

In the center of the basin were the long bones and the vertebrae of a dismembered body. The leg and arm bones were in proper anatomical order but they had been removed from the torso. The vertebrae were in proper anatomical order but they were not connected to either the skull or pelvic girdle. The position in which these bones were found indicated that a body had been decapitated, dismembered, and then buried with the six skulls (Plate 24). Since none of the skulls was attached to these bones, it was impossible to associate a particular skull definitely with the long bones. It seems reasonable to believe that one of the skulls probably belonged with the dismembered body.

A few other tiny scraps of bone were also present in the basin, but they were insufficient in number to account for another body. We can only surmise that the bodies of at least five, and perhaps of all six, skulls were disposed of by cremation or were buried elsewhere.

Plate 24. The crushed remains of skulls (Burials 22, 23 and 24) and the dismembered segments of a torso found in the eastern portion of Feature 29

Associated with these skulls were two celts, one crude grooved tablet, eleven pieces of worked hematite, one cone-shaped natural stone, one paint cup made from a stone concretion, and one large end scraper. All these items were placed at the back of the skull of B.15 at the west end of the basin. Scattered among the long bones near the center of the basin were two celts and one stemmed blade (Plate 25).

The mandibles were present in proper anatomical order with all the skulls. This would indicate that the skulls were placed in the basin while sufficient flesh still held the mandibles in place. None of the bones found in the basin showed any effects of fire except for a few pieces of calcined bone embedded in the floor of the basin. The basin, after use for crematory purposes, was apparently cleaned of its contents before the skulls and long bones were placed in it. The presence of small fragments of bark over the skulls and associated objects suggests that a bark covering once covered the basin.

Plate 25. Celts, scraper, crude tablet, paint cup made of a stone concretion, and faceted lumps of hematite associated with Burial 15 in Feature 29

Feature 30. Near the center of the mound between 3.5 E. and 4.0 feet W. and between 2.4 S. and 6.1 feet N. at an elevation of 0.0 foot a large burned area was found. This circular area was about 8.0 feet in diameter. The clay floor of the mound was missing in this area. The ashes which covered this area rested directly on the gravel subsoil.

This burned area was the central feature on the mound floor. It was slightly off center to the northeast on the clay floor that was surrounded by the circular trench (F.14). The clay platform along the east side of the subfloor tomb, F.19, partially overlapped the western side of the burned area. This clearly indicated that the burned area was older than the tomb which was the first disturbance of the clay floor for burial purposes.

The presence of the large burned area at the center of the clay floor lends additional credence to the assumption that the circular trench and the clay floor were features of a circular house that became the locus for the burial mound.

Feature 31. A burned clay layer was found between 11.8 and 17.3 feet S. and between 5.9 and 10.4 feet E. at an elevation of 0.7 foot above the mound floor. This oval-shaped burned area was depressed in the center approximately 0.2 foot. The area was 5.2 feet long, 3.1 feet wide, and 0.06 foot thick. It was oriented with the long axis NE.-SW. The clay layer had been reddened by heat and from the red ocher that had been sprinkled over the entire area.

Within this burned area was a partially flexed adult male burial (B.21). The head of the burial was at the southwest end of the basin while the feet were at the northeast end. The burial had been placed on its right side facing southeast. The legs had been flexed enough to keep them within the limits of the burned area. All the bones were crushed and very poorly preserved.

Several objects were found near this burial. Near the top of the skull was a large bone spatula. Under the spatula was a stemmed blade in juxtaposition with a worked section of antler which appeared to be a handle for the blade. The edges of the blade were worn and nicked from use. Near the mandible was a leaf-shaped blade and the three small bone awls. Near the bone spatula at the top of the skull were two large mussel shells. In one of these shells was a deposit of red ocher. Near the shells was a small hematite celt. (Plate 26).

Near the back of the pelvic region were two mussel shells and the fragmentary remains of a bone tool, possibly a bone handle. Next to the femorae was a large clump of red ocher. Scattered fragments of bark indicated that this material once covered the burial.

BURIALS

Burial 1. An extended burial of an adult male was found between 14.5 and 20.0 feet W. and between 8.25 and 12.0 feet S. at an elevation of 5.5 feet above the mound floor. This burial lay on its back with the head towards the center of the mound and the feet towards the southwest margin. The body had been placed on the sloping surface of the large inner mound which had its peak at 13.25 feet above the mound floor. The torso of the burial followed the general contour of this old mound surface, but an extra wedge of earth had been placed under the legs to make the body more level and to prevent it from slipping down the mound. The earth of the last addition to the mound covered the burial.

Plate 26. The badly crushed skull of Burial 21 and some of the associated artifacts found in Feature 31

Resting directly upon the pelvic region of this burial was the poorly preserved skull of an adult male (B.2). This skull faced the center of the mound and the head of Burial 1. This isolated skull appears to be a good example of a trophy skull.

No other objects were found in association with this burial except for a clump of carbonized organic material 0.3 foot in diameter directly behind the skull.

Burial 1 and the associated trophy skull (B.2) were among the last burials added to the mound. They were on the same contour surface as the fire pit (F.6) and associated tablets at the top of the mound.

Burial 2. This skull was found with B.1 at 9.0 feet S., 17.5 feet W. at an elevation of 5.25 feet above the mound floor. The skull lay directly on the pelvic region of B.1. Under this skull was a lens of gray, ashy-like material 0.09 foot in thickness and 0.5 foot in diameter. Although this skull was poorly preserved, the surface of the bone showed a polish not present on the skull of extended Burial 1. The disposition of this skull and the polish on its surface indicated its use as a trophy skull.

Burial 3. An extended burial of an adult female was found between 22.0 and 27.0 feet W. and between 1.0 and 1.5 feet N. at an elevation of 4.0 feet above the mound floor. The head was towards the center of the mound with the feet towards the west margin. The skull was on its left side facing south towards B.1 A small wedge of earth had been placed under the legs of this burial to prevent it from slipping down the slope of the mound.

This burial was very fragmentary with only portions of the long bones and skull remaining. No objects were associated with the bones. Burial 1 and Burial 3 had been placed in the mound at approximately the same time.

Burial 4. A flexed burial was found in an intrusive pit that had been dug into the top center of the mound. The burial was at an elevation of 13.5 feet above the mound floor. The burial was flexed on its left side with the head towards the south and the face to the west. The arms and legs were flexed with the hands at the knees which were drawn tightly to the chest.

Just 0.25 foot south of the head was a small stone pipe in the shape of a bird talon. Two small, slender, triangular points were found near the bones. One was in contact with the proximal end of the left tibia and the other would have been within the chest cavity. There is little doubt that these two points were once imbedded in the flesh of the burial and were probably the direct cause of death.

This burial and the three objects found with it were typical of the Late Prehistoric Period in the Upper Ohio Valley. This burial had no relationship to the Adena culture responsible for the mound.

Burial 5. A cremation was found on the surface of the large inner mound at 6.0 feet W. and 8.0 feet S. and at an elevation of 9.5 feet above the mound floor. This burial consisted of a pile of cremated bone 1.15 feet in diameter and 0.5 foot in thickness. Particles of charcoal and burned earth were mixed with the fragments of burned bone. A small platform of earth had been placed on the sloping side of the old mound to form a level surface for this bone deposit. No objects were with or near the bones.

Burial 6. An extended burial of an adult was found at 20.0 feet S. and between 0.6 and 5.9 feet W. at an elevation of 1.8 feet above the mound floor. This fragmentary burial was at the southern margin of the large inner mound. Only small portions of the long bones and the enamel of the teeth remained of this burial. It was impossible to determine age or sex. The head was to the west with the feet towards the east. Directly below the burial was a layer of hard clay upon which the burial had been placed. No objects were present.

Burial 7. An extended burial of an adult was located 12.8 feet S. and between 1.6 and 3.7 feet E. at an elevation of 7.1 feet above the mound floor. Much of this burial had been destroyed by the burrowing of ground-hogs in the area. The burial appeared to be just above the old surface of the large inner mound which had been covered by a cap of additional soil in this area.

In the area near the burial were several pieces of burned human bones. Near these bones, which would have been close to the chest region of the burial, were found a small strip of copper, a keeled boatstone, and a reel-shaped gorget. In the profile of the area a small disturbed area was present in addition to the disturbances attributed to the more recent activities of the ground-hogs. The copper strip, boatstone, and gorget may have been placed in a small pit with the cremated bones rather than having been placed with the extended burial. Both the burial and the near-by objects would have been placed in the mound after the large inner mound was completed but before the addition of the late outer mound layer.

Burial 8. An extended burial was found 9.0 feet S. and between 5.0 and 9.6 feet W. at an elevation of 6.75 feet above the mound floor. The head was to the northwest with the feet to the southeast. The bones were so poorly preserved and crushed that it was impossible to determine sex or approximate age. There were no associated objects. This burial was on the surface of the large inner mound but under the cap of soil which covered many of the features near its top.

Burial 9. A child burial was found in F.12 at 12.5 feet W. and 8.0 feet N. at an elevation of 0.9 foot above the mound floor. Only fragments of tooth enamel were recovered at this burial. See F.12.

Burial 10. A bundle burial of an adult male (?) was found between 21.5 and 22.5 feet S., and between 3.0 and 5.5 feet W. at an elevation of 0.6 foot above the mound floor. The long bones had been gathered together into a compact bundle. The skull was 1.5 feet W. of the long bones. All the bones were badly crushed and poorly preserved. This burial was near the outer margin of the large inner mound. Directly below the burial was a layer of gravel that appeared to be the result of the larger stones in the mound soil rolling to the outer margin as it was heaped on the mound. No artifacts were associated with the burial.

Burial 11. An extended burial of an adult male was found lying between 14.8 and 17.0 feet W. and between 3.9 and 9.2 feet S. at an elevation of 0.0-0.4 foot above the mound floor. This burial was on its back in a NW.-SE. orientation with the head to the northwest. The entire area around the skull was burned and a brick red in color. The skull appeared to have been burned by a fire built directly above the skull after a thin layer of earth had been placed over the burial. The result was the unintentional partial cremation of the burial. The lower portions of the burial showed no evidence of fire.

Associated with this burial were several items. Extending from the waist to the knee on the left side of the burial was a string of 148 small copper beads that had been attached to a band of skin 30.3 cm. long and 10.4 cm. wide. Fragments of this band had been preserved by the copper salts. Some pieces of bark were found near the beads. This material probably covered the entire burial.

Just below the left hip at about the level of the left hand was a hematite hemisphere. This object may have been in the hand but the bones of the hand and lower arm were so decayed that it was impossible to verify this assumption. Between the legs was a small hematite celt. Near the celt was a small clump of purple-colored mineral. Near the left ankle was a small greenstone celt and near the right knee was the tip of a broken blade and a crude side scraper. Near the right tibia was a section of very poorly preserved bone about 10.2 cm. long and 2.1 cm. in width that had been cut and worked. At the right shoulder was a small deposit of graphite. Directly under the skull were two portions of a broken blade that showed the effects of intense heat. Near the back of the skull fragments was a small pile of red ocher. A fragment of a crude grooved tablet was found in the ocher. Red ocher also had been sprinkled over the burial.

Burial 12. A child burial was found in crematory basin F.4 at 11.4 feet W. and 6.9 feet S. at an elevation of 0.5 foot above the mound floor. All that remained of this burial were a few fragments of skull bones and the enamel of the teeth. See F.4.

Burials 13, 14 and 15. Burials 13, 14 and 15 were skulls of adult males buried in the west end of crematory basin F.29 between 12.9 and 15.2 feet S. and between 2.4 E. and 2.6 feet W. at an elevation of 0.3-0.8 foot above the mound floor. Burials 22, 23, and 24 were in the east end of this basin. The position and description of these three skulls are as follows: Burial 13, adult male skull lying on right side facing east. Skull was crushed nearly flat but artificial deformation appeared to be present. Burial 14, adult male skull lying on its left side facing east. Deformation was present. Skull badly crushed. Burial 15, adult male skull lying on its right side facing west. This skull was too badly crushed to note presence of deformation.

See Feature 20 and Burials 22, 23 and 24 for further details.

Burial 16. Another child burial was found on burned area F.3 at 13.1 feet W. and 0.4 feet N. at an elevation of 1.8 feet above the mound floor. This burial had been placed on the burned area and covered with bark. All that remained of the burial were the crowns of the teeth and a few fragments of skull. Around the neck of the burial was a string of 43 small copper beads. See F.3 for further details.

Burial 17. An extended burial of undeterminable sex was found between 15.0 and 20.0 feet W. and between 1.1 S. and 3.0 feet N. at an elevation of 1.1 feet above the mound floor. Only fragments of long bones and skull were found. These bones were too poorly preserved to permit any observations. No objects were associated with the burial.

Burial 18. A fragmentary burial of an adult was found in burned area F.7 at 1.8 feet W. and 7.0 feet S. at an elevation of 8.82 feet above the mound floor. See F.7 for details.

Burial 19. An extended burial of an adult of undeterminable sex was found between 7.5 and 8.5 feet W. and between 1.03 and 4.3 feet N. at an elevation of 8.5 feet above the mound floor. This burial had been partially cremated. The skull was badly burned and crushed. Except for the fragmentary leg bones, all other bones had completely decayed. The soil near the legs also appeared discolored by heat but the leg bones had not been burned. The head of the burial was towards the south and the feet to the north. A stemmed blade was found 0.75 foot east of the lumbar region of the burial.

The soil under the burial was dark and humus laden. This burial, as well as B.18, was placed on an old mound surface at the 8.5-foot level above the mound floor.

Burial 20. A cremation was found at 5.1 feet W. and 0.8 feet S. at an elevation of 7.5 feet above the mound floor. Mixed among the bones of this cremation was red ocher. The earth around the bones was reddened by heat and indicated that burning of the bones may have taken place on the spot. Near the bones was a piece of worked hematite.

Burial 21. A partially flexed adult male burial was discovered in burned area F.13 between 11.8 and 17.3 feet S. and between 5.9 and 10.4 feet E. at an elevation of 0.7 foot above the mound floor. This burial was loosely flexed on its right side with the head towards the southwest and the feet to the northeast. The skull and long bones were badly crushed and decayed. The amount of wear on the teeth indicated a relatively old adult. See F.31 for objects found with this burial.

Burials 22, 23 and 24. These three skulls were found in the east end of crematory basin F.29 in which Burials 13, 14 and 15 were unearthed in the west end. The positions of these skulls were as follows: Burial 22, adult male skull that lay on its right side facing south. The skull appeared deformed but the crushed condition of the bones made this observation uncertain. Burial 23, adult male skull lying on its right side facing east. Although this skull was crushed, it appeared to be deformed. Burial 24, adult male skull resting on its right side facing northeast. This skull was badly crushed.

These three skulls, plus the three (B.13, 14 and 15) in the west end of Feature 29, had the appearance of mature males. In spite of their crushed and decayed condition, it is possible to state that they were of a round-headed, robust physical type. The square, projecting chin common to Adena males was particularly noticeable. See Feature 29 for details of objects found with these skulls.

Burial 25. Fragments of a skull were found at 5.0 feet N. and 6.0 feet E. at an elevation of 9.60 feet above the mound floor. The bones were so fragmentary that it was impossible to make any sex or age determinations. No other bones were near the skull. This skull was near the surface of the large inner mound just east of F.6. Several interesting items were found in this area but none was in direct association with the skull. See F.6 for details.

Burial 26. A bundle burial of a young adult was found in F.8 at 1.0 foot W. and 1.1 feet N. at an elevation of 6.5 feet above the mound floor. This burial consisted of the skull and long bones gathered together into a bundle. All the bones were crushed and decayed. See F.8 for details of objects associated with this burial.

Burial 27. A cremated skull of an adult was found at 9.0 feet S. and 1.8 feet W. at an elevation of 3.8 feet above the mound floor. Only fragments of this burned skull were present. An area about 2.5 feet in diameter around the skull had been reddened by heat but no special preparation in the way of a clay lining seems to have been made.

Burial 28. The extended burial of an adult was located between 5.6 and 11.0 feet W. and between 8.5 and 10.5 feet S. at an elevation of 0.0 foot above the mound floor. The bones were so fragmentary that it was impossible to determine sex. The head was to the east and the feet to the west. The area around the bones was slightly reddened from heat and red ocher had been sprinkled over and around the burial. The ocher was most heavily concentrated near the feet and the head. No objects were found in direct association with the burial but a broken blade was found in the earth 0.6 foot above and 1.1 feet south of the burial.

Burial 29. A cremation was uncovered in burned area F.16 at 10.2 feet W. and 1.25 feet N. at an elevation of 5.2 feet above the mound floor. Among the bone fragments were portions of an adult skull and partially burned long bones. See F.16 for details of objects associated with this cremation.

Burial 30. A crushed and decayed skull was found in a log-covered crematory basin (F.15) at 0.2 foot E., 5.0 feet S., at an elevation of 0.2-0.6 foot above the mound floor. It was impossible to determine the sex of this adult skull which had been placed at the east end of the basin. Several fragments of burned long bones were also found in the basin, but no direct association of these bones and the skull could be demonstrated. See F.15 for details of objects found in the basin near this skull.

Burial 31. Another cremation was uncovered in the large basin (F.10) at 7.0 feet W., 1.2 feet N. at 0.2-0.6 foot below the mound floor. This deposit consisted of finely broken and intensely burned bone piled in a small heap at the west side of the basin. See F.10 for details and associated objects.

Burial 32. The skull of an adult was found 16.2 feet S., 3.9 feet W. at an elevation of 0.0-0.2 foot above the mound floor. This badly crushed and decayed skull had been partially burned. No other bones were present near the skull which may have been removed from a crematory and reburied in the mound. Near the skull was a piece of worked hematite.

Burial 33. The extended burial of a female or young male was found in subfloor pit F.19 between 6.5 feet N. and 1.8 feet S., and between 6.2 and 10.1 feet W. at an elevation of 0.6-0.8 foot below the mound floor. The burial lay on its back with the head to the south. Only the crowns of the teeth remained of the skull. With the exception of the left tibia, fibula, and foot bones, all the bones were completely decayed. The small size and configuration of the lower left leg bones indicated that the burial probably was female. The condition of the bone made definite sex identification impossible. See F.19 for additional details.

Burial 34. An extended burial of an adult was uncovered in subfloor pit F.20 between 3.2 and 11.0 feet W. and between 6.5 and 11.6 feet N. at an elevation of 0.7-0.9 foot below the mound floor. Only the crumbling crowns of the teeth remained of the skeleton. Faint stains where the bones once had been could be seen on the floor of the pit. See F.20.

Burial 35. A cremation was located in burned area F.21 at 11.8 feet N., 10.0 feet W. at an elevation of 5.1 feet above the mound floor. Red ocher had been sprinkled over this small pile of intensely burned bone which was 0.7 foot in diameter and 0.3 foot high. See F.21.

Burial 36. The skull of an adult was found in burned area F.21 at 10.4 feet N., 8.8 feet W. at an elevation of 5.1 feet above the mound floor. This skull was in extremely poor condition. See F.21.

Burial 37. Another skull of an adult was found in burned area F.21 at 11.0 feet N., 8.2 feet W. at an elevation of 5.1 feet above the mound floor. This burial consisted of the teeth and a few crushed fragments of skull. See F.21.

Burial 38. The skull of an adult was located in crematory basin F.13 at 9.5 feet N., 17.4 feet W. at an elevation of 0.0-0.2 foot above the mound floor. This fragmentary skull had been partially burned. Directly under the skull was a thin layer of red ocher and just west of the skull was a large clump of red ocher. See F.13.

Burial 39. The skull of an adult was found at 8.0 feet S., 10.5 feet E. at an elevation of 6.5 feet above the mound floor. This skull was very fragmentary. Directly west of this skull was a small burned area and a clump of red ocher. See F.9.

Burial 40. A skull of an adult male was found at 5.8 feet S., 16.4 feet E. at an elevation of 4.4 feet above the mound floor. The skull faced southwest with top of skull upwards. A few fragments of decayed bone were found near-by but they appeared to be in no order. This skull and the bone fragments may mave been the remains of a bundle burial.

Burial 41. An extended burial of an adult male was found between 0.5 foot N. and 5.3 feet S. and between 10.8 and 12.4 feet E. at an elevation of 3.2 feet above the mound floor. This burial lay on its back facing upwards. Only the fragile skull and long bones remained.

Near the left knee was a small pile of red ocher. With this red ocher were five ovate-base stemmed blades, two side scrapers, and a natural stone concretion which may have been used as a paint cup. Scattered along the right side of the burial was some yellow ocher. In the soil near this burial were four sherds of "Fayette Thick" pottery and a reel-shaped gorget.

In the wall profile directly above this burial was an area which had collapsed downwards on to the burial. It seems possible that small logs had once been placed above the burial as a covering. No remains of these logs were present.

Burial 42. The extended burial of an adult was located between 4.5 and 10.0 feet W. and between 14.2 and 16.0 feet N. at an elevation of 0.9 foot above the mound floor. This burial lay on its back with the legs to the west and twisted slightly to the right. The skull was missing from the skeleton. Near the left shoulder, however, was a small pile of cremated bone which contained fragments of skull and teeth. It is possible that these fragments belonged to the skull of this burial.

Near the right hip of the burial were three leaf-shaped blades. At the chest on the left side of the burial were one stemmed blade, one leaf-shaped blade, one celt, three fragments of grooved tablets, several pieces of graphite, and red ocher. Near the right foot was a small pile of charcoal about 0.5 foot in diameter and 0.2 foot thick (Plate 27).

Plate 27.   Blades, celt, and three crude tablet forms found in association
with Burial 42

This burial was of particular interest since it presented a case where the skull was apparently removed from the body and intentionally cremated. Except for the skull the body had been buried like many other extended burials in the mound.

Burial 43. An extended burial of an adult female was found between 11.2 and 15.5 feet E. and between 5.75 and 10.3 feet N. at an elevation of 2.55 feet above the mound floor. The burial was oriented SE.-NW. with the head to the southeast. There were no objects with this poorly preserved burial.

Burial 44. A cremation was found in burned area F.24 at 1.4 feet N., 13.7 feet E. at an elevation of 6.75 feet above the mound floor. This cremation consisted of a pile of burned bone 0.8 foot in diameter and 0.2 foot thick. Many tiny fragments of burned bone were scattered throughout the feature. See F.24.

Burial 45. The extended burial of an adult was found in burned area F.25 between 4.5 and 10.2 feet W., 12.0-13.0 feet N. at an elevation of 0.02 foot above the mound floor. The burial was oriented E.-W. with the head to the east facing north. See F.25 for details of the feature and associated objects.

Burial 46. The burial of a small child was found in burned area F.27 at 2.0 feet E., 2.0 feet S. at an elevation of 1.8 feet above the mound floor. This burial consisted of fragments of skull and teeth covered with red ocher and bark. See F.27.

Burial 47. The skull of an adult was found at 15.3 feet E., 6.25 feet N. at an elevation of 0.8 foot above the mound floor. This skull was badly crushed and decayed. No other bones were found in the area .

Burial 48. An extended burial of an adult male was found between 0.25 and 5.45 feet N., 10.2-11.5 feet E. at an elevation of 2.9 feet above the mound floor. This burial was extended on its back with the head to the north facing west. The feet lay directly under the head of extended Burial 41 just slightly above and to the south of this burial.

Between the legs of this burial near the knees were fragments of a burned and broken blocked-end tubular pipe. Directly above the pelvic area, approximately 0.4 foot, were several small burned stones and fragments of charcoal. None of the bones of the burial appeared burned.

Burial 49. Fragments of an adult skull were found 5.2 feet E., 13.0 feet N. at an elevation of 1.6 feet above the mound floor. No other bones were near these fragments.

Burial 50. The extended burial of an adult was located between 8.1 and 13.0 feet N., 5.0 feet E. at an elevation of 1.6 feet above the mound floor. The head of the burial was to the south. The bones were so fragmentary that no observations could be made on them. The skull of Burial 49 was near the legs of this burial.

Burial 51. The remains of a bundle burial were found at 16.2 feet N., 1.5 feet E. at an elevation of 1.5 feet above the mound floor. Portions of long bones and badly decayed fragments of other bones were present.

Burial 52. An extended adult burial was found 8.2-14.3 feet W., 17.0 feet N. at an elevation of 0.0-0.5 foot below the mound floor. This badly decayed burial was in a shallow pit dug into the trench which surrounded the clay mound floor. The head was to the west with the feet to the east.

Scattered among the fragmentary remains of this burial were two leaf-shaped blades, two ovate-base stemmed blades, one side scraper, two celts, and one hematite hemisphere. Some red ocher was near the skull and at the feet.

Burial 53. An extended adult male burial was located between 2.2 feet S. and 4.2 feet N., 6.6-7.8 feet E. at an elevation of 2.75 feet above the mound floor. The head was to the south facing upwards. This burial was directly above subfloor tomb F.28.

At the right side of the skull was a straight-base stemmed blade, two concretions, and a worked piece of hematite. Near the left shoulder was a large ovate-base stemmed blade. At the left ankle were a straight-base stemmed blade and a small side-notched blade. At the right knee was a small clump of red ocher.

Although the skull of this burial was crushed, it had the general appearance of the typical Adena male with heavy, protruding, square, mandibular eminence and large brachycephalic skull with deformation. The mastoid processes were large and the supra-orbital ridges prominent.

Burial 54. This was the extended burial of an adult male in subfloor tomb F.28 between 5.2 feet S. and 3.5 feet N. and between 5.1 and 10.5 feet E. at an elevation of 3.3 feet below the mound floor. The head was towards the north and the feet to the south. The legs were slightly flexed with the knees protruding outward in a "bow-legged" fashion. The arms were at the side.

The skull had been partially destroyed by a fire which seems to have been kindled directly over it after a thin layer of earth had been placed over the body. Only the skull was affected by this fire. None of the long bones was burned.

This individual was of large proportions. When measured in the tomb his length was approximately 7.04 feet. All the long bones were heavy and possessed marked eminences for the attachment of muscles. See F.28 for details of objects found.

SUMMARY OF FEATURES AND BURIALS

Features. The 31 features found in the Cresap Mound ranged in elevation from 13.5 feet above datum to 3.3 feet below datum, or within a total distributional depth of 16.8 feet. The bottommost feature was No. 28, a subfloor tomb, located 3.3 feet below the mound floor. The topmost feature was no. 6, a large burned area found 13.5 feet above the mound floor and 1.5 feet below the top surface of the mound.

The greatest concentration of features occurred on, near, or below the mound floor. Five features extended through the mound floor into the subsoil while ten features ranged in elevation from 0.0 to 1.0 foot above the floor. Two features were between 1.0 and 2.0 feet, but no features were present between 2.0 and 3.0 feet. All of these features were associated with the three small mounds which composed the primary core. With the exception of features 1, 14 and 30, all these features were connected with the burial practices occurring in the mound. Of the above three features, two, the circular trench (F.14) and the large fire pit (F.30)belonged to the house over which the mound had been constructed. The other feature (F.1) was an unusual deposit of stones with no definite associations.

The second major concentration of features began with two features between 3.0 and 4.0 feet, two between 4.0 and 5.0 feet, three between 5.0 and 6.0 feet, and four between 6.0 and 7.0 feet. These features began near the tops of the three small primary mounds and reached a climax at the level of 6.5 feet above the mound floor. At this level there was clear evidence for an old sod line which had accumulated over a considerable period of time before features 8, 9, 24 and 26 were added to the mound.

Between the 7.0-foot and 8.0-foot level there were no features, but at 8.82 feet another major feature (No.7) was found. The last feature (No. 6) added to the mound was the burned area near the top center of the mound at 13.5 feet. This last-mentioned feature and near-by burials were the last additions to the mound and were separated from all the lower features by a distinct sod line ranging from 0.3 to 0.5 foot in thickness.

The distribution of the features and their relationships to the various constructional components of the mound clearly indicated that the mound had been built by increments as the burials were added. Although three major levels or concentrations of features were found, all the features and their associations conform to Adena. Important chronological differences within Adena, however, were noted for the objects associated with these features. These differences will be discussed thoroughly later in this report.

The remains of former fires were in marked evidence in 27 of the features. Slight traces of fire were found in two other features. Thus, of 31 features, 29 contained lenses of burned earth, blackened earth, or charcoal. In the features lined with clay, the earth had been burned a red-orange color. There can be little doubt that fire was a significant part of the activity that surrounded the use of these features.

The most numerous feature in the mound was an oval or elliptical layer of burned earth. Of 20 features of this type, 11 were lined with clay. Some of these layers were level but most were depressed at the center forming a shallow basin. Ten of these clay lined layers contained burials or traces of bone as attested by the presence of phosphate. Burials or traces of bone were present in seven of the nine burned areas which did not have the clay lining. The fragile remains of bark and other organic materials were present in 11 of these layers. Often this material covered the skeletal material that had been placed on these specially prepared areas. When copper was present in any of these features the bark and bone near the copper were well preserved. It seems highly probable that many of these features once contained organic materials and burials which had disappeared under ravages of the acid soil. The burned appearance of these layers and the presence of small pieces of calcined bone suggest that these layers were used for the burning of human bone. In two of these features (F.16 and F.21) cremated remains were deposited in neat piles, but in most cases the cremated bone and ash appeared to have been cleared from the burned area and redeposited elsewhere. Unburned bone, either dry or with flesh, was then placed on these areas for burial.

Four large clay basins were found at the base of the mound. One of these (F.10) had been dug through the clay mound floor into the subsoil under the small W. primary mound. Basin F.13, also under the W. primary mound, had been constructed on the mound floor. Basin F.15 had been built in the depression formed by the sloping sides of the W. and S. primary mounds. Its floor rested on the floor of the mound. The fourth basin, F.29, was placed on the clay mound floor and was covered by the small S. primary. All four of these basins were oval in outline with deeply depressed bottoms and distinct rims. The clay lining of these basins was thick and had been carefully molded to form the structure. Intense heat from the fires in these basins had turned the clay an orange-red color. Human remains were present in each of these structures. A pile of cremated bone was in basin F.10 and unburned burials were present in the other three basins. Tiny scraps of calcined bone were found on the floors of all the basins. Objects were associated with three of the basins and red ocher was present in all four. Basin F.15 had been covered by logs forming a small tomb. Fragments of these logs were present in the basin. Because of the soil conditions it was impossible to determine if logs had been placed over the other three basins. No wood fragments were seen in these features. The very nature of these basins and their contents indicated their primary use as crematories and their secondary use as receptacles for unburned remains. Webb and Snow (1945, p. 62) have shown that such basins are a common Adena trait. The basins of the Cresap Mound and those of Adena bear no resemblance to the rectangular crematories reported from Hopewellian mounds (Mills 1916, p. 278).

Three of the most interesting features in the Cresap Mound were the burial pits or tombs that had been dug through the clay mound floor. Two of these pits (F.19 and F.20) were on the west side of the mound and covered by the small W. primary. The other pit (F.28) was on the east side of the mound and covered by the small E. primary mound. Stratigraphic evidence indicated that the two western pits were earlier than the one on the east side of the mound. Both of the western pits were rectanguloid in outline with maximum dimensions of 8.0 feet long, 5.0 feet wide, and 0.9 foot deep. In each of these pits was a single extended burial in very fragile condition. The presence of clay linings in these two pits, which prevented the rapid drainage of water from them, appears to have contributed to the decay of the osseous material. Pit F.19 directly under the center of the W. primary contained only one object, a celt, in direct association with the burial. The other pit, F.20, had been furnished with 22 different objects. The pit (F.28) on the east side of the mound was oval in outline and was 8.2 feet long, 6.15 feet wide, and 3.3 feet deep. There was no clay lining in this pit and the single extended male burial was in a fair state of preservation. Associated with this burial were 126 objects. All three pits had been lined with bark and covered with small logs. Tomb F.19 was surrounded by an embankment of earth on three sides and tomb F.28 had an embankment on one side. There was a complete absence of embankment around tomb F.20. The simple construction employed in building these tombs was in marked contrast to the elaborate log tombs found at certain mounds in Kentucky and Ohio considered as late Adena sites by Webb and Baby (1957, p. 112-113). The Cresap Mound tombs appear to be of the early Adena variety.

It is of interest to note that red ocher was found in 23 of the 31 features in the mound. This high incidence attests to the importance of this material in burial practices of the Adena people who constructed the Cresap Mound.

Artifacts were found in 18 of the 31 features. Since three of the features were structural in that they pertained to the house remains under the mound, the proportion would actually have been 18 of 28 (or 65%) features with associated artifacts. It is entirely possible that many features contained items of a perishable nature that had disappeared in the acid soil. The finding of organic substances in several features clearly suggested the former presence of such objects. Unfortunately, except for the discovery of a basket in F.15, only items of stone and other relatively non-perishable materials were recovered.

Burials. The skeletal remains of at least 54 individuals were found in the excavation. The presence of fragmentary unburned bones and pieces of calcined bones found scattered in various places in the mound indicated that perhaps more individuals may have been interred in the structure. None of these fragments, however, was of sufficient concentration or preservation to warrant a number.

Of the 54 burials, 25 were associated with features and 29 were placed in the mound without any special preparation of the area surrounding the burial. The burials ranged in elevation from 3.3 feet below the mound floor to 13.5 feet above the floor. Five burials were found in features below the mound floor, 18 burials between 0.0 and 1.0 foot above the floor, seven between 1.0 and 2.0 feet, three between 2.0 and 3.0 feet, two between 4.0 and 5.0 feet, six between 5.0 and 6.0 feet, four between 6.0 and 7.0 feet, two between 7.0 and 8.0 feet, two between 8.0 and 9.0 feet, two between 9.0 and 10.0 feet, and one at 13.5 feet. The single burial at 13.5 feet was intrusive into the mound and belonged to the Late Prehistoric Period and not to Adena.

The largest concentration of burials (29 burials, 53%) occurred in the zone near the mound base between 3.3 feet below the floor and 2.0 feet above it. All of these burials were covered by or included in the three small primary mounds. Another concentration of burials (10 burials, 18.5%) was found between 5.0 and 7.0 feet above the mound floor in the layers of earth that capped the three small primary mounds. The remaining burials were scattered in intervening elevations. Seven burials (12.9%) were on the old inner mound surface that had been capped by the last layer of earth added to the mound. Thus, these burials represented the third and last concentration in the mound.

The positions of the burials were varied. There were 20 extended burials, 18 skulls, seven total cremations, three bundle burials, one semi-flexed burial, four child burials, and one flexed burial of non-Adena origin. Four of the extended burials and three of the skulls showed evidence of partial burning. In at least two of these instances the burning seems to have been accidental.

The poor preservation of the physical remains made observations as to exact age and sex on many of the burials impossible. Of the 54 burials, there were 45 adults, four children, and five cremations which appeared to consist mainly of adult bone. On the basis of sex, there were 16 males, three females, and 35 unidentifiable.

Of the few remains which were sufficiently preserved to note the physical type, it was evident that the people were brachycephalic with artificial head deformation generally present. The face was large both in length and breadth and there was moderate alveolar prognathism. The chin was prominent and broad with bilateral eminences usually present. The cheek bones were large with pronounced lateral projections. The stature was medium to tall and the bones were heavy with prominent areas for muscle attachment. The large male found in subfloor tomb F.28 was exceptional in height. Measurements taken of the skeleton while still in the grave indicated an individual approximately 7.2 feet tall. He would have been a splendid figure in any society and the darling of a primitive basketball team. In all respects the Cresap Mound skeletal material conforms to the physical type of the Kentucky and Ohio Adena mounds as previously described by Snow (1957, p. 47-60).

Of the 54 burials, grave objects were found in association with 34 of them. Red ocher was present with 31 burials. This high incidence of grave offerings and the number of such objects present afforded an excellent opportunity to study certain facets of Adena material culture. These objects and their important chronological implication are discussed in the next section.

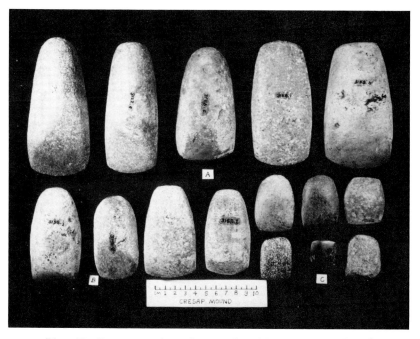

Plate 28.   Representative celt types found in the Cresap Mound
A. large celts 10-13 cm. long. B. medium celts 6-10 cm. long. C. small celts
3-6 cm. long

THE ARTIFACTS

A list of all the artifacts removed from the Cresap Mound is given
below. Following the list are detailed descriptions of all the items. The
list and the section on description have been divided into the following
major categories with the number of specimens assigned to each being
given: polished stone artifacts, 133; chipped stone artifacts, 141; copper
artifacts, 373; bone artifacts, 23; shell artifacts, 115; pottery sherds, 9;
and miscellaneous artifacts, 2. Each of these categories is divided into
various subdivisions. At the end of the artifact descriptions, a descrip-
tive list of the minerals found with the features and burials is given. The
total artifacts amount to 796 specimens. Since no intrusion of importance had disturbed the mound and great care was taken in the excavation to recover all specimens, the artifacts found are believed to be the
total of such items ever present in the mound.

ARTIFACT LIST

Polished stone artifacts:

Balls, round stone	2
Boatstone	1

Celts:

Nonferruginous stone:

Oblong poll	1
Rounded poll	21
Rectangular poll	10

Hematite:

Rectangular poll	3
Total celts	35

Gorgets and pendants:

Reel-shaped (quadriconcave)	5
Rectangular	1
Pendants	4
Total gorgets and pendants	10

Hemispheres:

Hematite	7
Barite	1
Calcium carbonate	1
Siltstone	3
Total hemispheres	12

Pipes:

Tubular, blocked-end	3
Claw-shaped (Non-Adena)	1
Total pipes	4

Tablets:

Effigy turtle	1
Rectangular	6
Kidney-shaped	1
Irregular	14
Total tablets	22

Miscellaneous stone artifacts:

Faceted hematite point stones 35
Cupstones 8
Hammerstones 2
Elliptical stone bars 2

    Total miscellaneous stone items 47

Chipped-stone artifacts:

Blades and projectile points:

Leaf-shaped 19
Stemmed, ovate base 37
Tapered stemmed, flat base, weak shouldered 5
Tapered stemmed, flat base 2
Straight stemmed, flat base 8
Straight stemmed, rounded base, wide 12
Straight stemmed, concave base 1
Side-notched 3
Expanded-stemmed 1
Triangular (Late Prehistoric) 2
Fragmentary specimens 3

    Total blades 93

Drills:

Expanded base 2
Straight base 4
Flat, stemmed base 1
Stemmed, rounded base 2

    Total drills 9

Scrapers:

End scrapers 4
Side scrapers 9
Utilized flakes 9
Crude scrapers 12
Crude blanks or scrapers 5

    Total scrapers 39

Copper artifacts:

Reel-shaped (quadriconcave) gorget 1

Beads, rolled 370

Strips 2

    Total copper artifacts 373

Bone artifacts:

Beads 4

Awls, scapula 2

Awls, splinter 5

Spatula 1

Punch or flaker, antler 1

Handles, antler 2

Cups, turtle carapaces 3

Head-dress, elk skull and antlers 1

Worked bone 1

Deer antlers (worked ?) 3

    Total bone artifacts 23

Shell artifacts:

Disk shell beads 51

Marginella beads 44

Large tubular, columnella beads 10

Small tubular, columnella beads 6

Spoons, mussel-shells 4

    Total shell artifacts 115

Pottery:

"Fayette Thick" 8

"Adena Plain" 1

    Total pottery 9

Miscellaneous artifacts:

Basket 1

Textile 1

    Miscellaneous artifacts 2

    Total artifacts 796

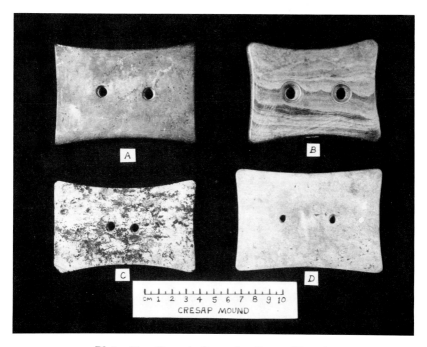

Plate 29.   Gorgets from the Cresap Mound
A. No. 3148. d. associated with Feature 6. B. No. 3106. associated with Feature
6. C. No. 3161. associated with Burial 41. D. 3108. near Burial 7

The artifacts in the above list are discussed in detail in the sections
below. Following these descriptions is a discussion of items such as
minerals and organic remains found in the Cresap Mound. Although
these latter items are not generally included on the artifact lists, they
are important Adena traits.

Round stone balls

Two round, polished stone balls were found associated with other
artifacts in two Cresap Mound features. One ball, 5.6 cm. in diameter,
was found in F. 10, and the other, 5.5 cm. in diameter, was in F.20. Both
were highly polished and on their surfaces were stains of a dark organic
material like that often present on many of the other artifacts found in
the mound. Stone balls were listed by Webb and Snow (1945, p. 88) as
a rare trait in Adena with only one occurrence in an Adena mound in

Plate 30.   Pendants and gorgets from the Cresap Mound
A. 3158. g. associated with Feature 20. B. 3158. f. associated with Feature 20.
C. 3168. c. associated with Burial 45. D. 3107. in mound fill. E. 3151. in earth
fill of west primary mound. F. 3093. a. and 3093. b. on surface of large inner
mound

Kentucky. Solecki (1953, p. 356) found two balls in the Natrium Mound
that were similar to the Cresap specimens (Plate 31, M and N).

Boatstone

Near Burial 7 an elongated boatstone of a yellow-tan colored siltstone
was found. The object is bar-like with an expanded center and with
pointed ends. On the top of the bar where the center expands there is
a raised keel. At each end of the keel is a hole which was drilled from the
underneath side. The lower surface of this specimen is flat. One end
of this boatstone was missing. On the basis of reconstruction made in
the laboratory this boatstone was 10.1 cm. long, 2.7 cm. wide at the
expanded center, and 2.3 cm. high from the bottom to the top of the
keel. The two holes averaged 0.6 cm. in diameter. This specimen is
similar in general outline to one illustrated by Moorehead (1917, p. 75,

Plate 31. Hemispheres and stone balls from various features of the
Cresap Mound
A. Hematite hemisphere in Feature 10. B. Hematite hemisphere in Feature 16.
C. Hematite hemisphere in Feature 10. D. Hematite hemisphere with Burial
11. E. Hematite hemisphere with Burial 52. F. Hematite hemisphere in Feature 20. G. Hematite hemisphere in Feature 4. H. Barite hemisphere in
Feature 20. I. Calcium carbonate hemisphere near Feature 6. J. Siltstone
hemisphere with Burial 7. L. Siltstone hemisphere in Feature 29. M. Stone
ball in Feature 10. N. Stone ball in Feature 20

fig. 49) except that there is no groove present on the keel on the Cresap
Mound specimen. Boat-shaped, barite and galena bars were reported
from Adena sites in Kentucky by Webb and Snow (1945, p. 89). These
objects appear to be similar in general design, and probable usage as
atlatl weights, to the specimen from the Cresap Mound and a boatstone
reported by Solecki (1953, p. 357) from the Natrium Mound (Plate
32. D).

Celts

A total of 35 celts was found in the Cresap Mound. All, except two
found in the earth fill of the mound, were associated with either features

Plate 32.   Pipes and boatstone from the Cresap Mound
A. Blocked-end tubular pipe of fireclay with Burial 48. B. Blocked-end tubular
pipe of fireclay with Burial 26. C. Blocked-end tubular pipe of sandstone found
near Feature 30 on mound floor. D. Boatstone of siltstone near Burial 7,
"claw-shaped" sandstone pipe with intrusive Burial 4

or burials. Thirty-two celts were of non-ferruginous stone and three were
of hematite. These celts tended to fall into three natural groupings
according to size—large 10-13 cm. long, medium 6-10 cm. long, and
small 3-6 cm. long. The descriptions of these celts according to size
group are as follows:

Large celts (10-13 cm. long). The six celts of this group ranged from
10.65 to 12.9 cm. in length, 5.1 to 6.5 cm. in width, and 3.15 to 4.5 cm.
in thickness. Four had been made of gabbro while the other two were
of diorite. On four of these celts the polls were round and the cross-
sections were oval. One celt had an oblong poll and a rectangular cross-
section, and one celt had a flat rectangular poll and a rectangular cross-
section. Only two of the six celts were polished over most of their
surface. Four specimens were polished only from one-third to one-half
at the bit end with the remainder of the surface left roughly pecked.

The polls on four of these celts have scars from being used as hammers (Plate 28, A).

Medium celts (6-10 cm. long). The 16 celts of this group ranged from 6.4 to 9.8 cm. in length, 3.4 to 5.3 cm. in width, and 1.4 to 3.1 cm. in thickness. Ten of these celts were made from gabbro and six were of diorite. Of the 10 celts with rounded polls, seven had oval cross-sections and three had rectangular cross-sections. Of six celts with flat rectangular polls, five were rectangular and one was oval in cross-section. Nine of these celts were polished only over about one-third to one-half of their surfaces near the bit end. Seven celts were polished over nearly their entire surfaces. Five of these celts have scars on the poll from having been used as hammers.

One celt of this group has the appearance of having been reworked from an adz. Since Archaic materials have been found on the surface in the area of the mound, it seems quite likely that an adz typical of this earlier period was picked up by the Adena peoples and refashioned into a celt (Plate 28, b).

Small celts (3-6 cm. long). The 13 celts of this group ranged from 3.05 to 5.95 cm. long, 2.4 to 4.1 cm. wide, and 0.7 to 1.7 cm. thick. Seven of these celts were of gabbro, three of diorite, and three of hematite. Of seven celts with rounded polls, six had rectangular cross-sections and one had an oval cross-section. Of six celts with flat rectangular polls, five had rectangular cross-sections and one had an oval cross-section. Nine of these small celts had been polished over most of their surfaces, while the remaining four had been only partially polished near the bit ends. Two of the larger celts of this group had polls scarred from use as hammers (Plate 28, c).

When taken as a group, rounded polls predominated with 21 (60%) of the 35 celts. Rectangular polls were present on 14 (37.14%), and one (2.86%) celt had a pointed oblong poll. Twenty-one (60%) of the celts had rectangular cross-sections and 14 (40%) were oval in cross-section. Igneous stones were used for 32 of the celts. Only three specimens were of hematite. Webb and Snow (1945, p. 88) have indicated that rounded-poll celts of igneous stone are most common on Adena sites. The presence of scars on many of the celt polls of the Cresap Mound specimens confirms Webb and Snow's belief that celts were often used as hammers. Celts of the types found in the Cresap Mound were listed by Webb and Snow (1945, p. 88) as Adena traits 123 and 124 respectively.

Gorgets and pendants, Stone

Five reel-shaped or quadriconcave gorgets, one rectangular gorget, and four pendants were found in the Cresap Mound. The descriptions of these items and their associations and provenience in the mound are as follows. (Numbers are field catalogue numbers in Carnegie Museum.)

3148. d. This quadriconcave gorget was found at 4.5 feet north 8.0 feet east at an elevation of 10.0 feet. It was on the surface of the large inner mound near the large burned area, Feature 6, which was the central feature of the last addition to the mound. It was made of dark-blue slate that had been carefully shaped and smoothed. The maximum dimensions are 10.1 cm. long, 7.2 cm. wide, and 0.95 cm. thick the minimum dimensions are 9.8 cm. long and 6.3 cm. wide at the constricted portions of the gorget. The two holes had been drilled from one side only and the diameter of the opening tapered from 0.85 cm. to 0.35 cm. (Plate 29, A).

3106. This quadriconcave gorget of gray-blue banded slate was found at 3.0 feet west 2.0 feet south at an elevation of 13.1 feet. It was near burned area Feature 6, on the surface of the inner mound. The maximum dimensions are 9.5 cm. long, 7.3 cm. wide, and 1.3 cm. thick and the minimum dimensions are 9.0 cm. long and 6.15 cm. wide at the constricted portions. The two holes were drilled from one side, but some widening of the holes from the opposite side seems to have occurred after the holes had been drilled completely through. The maximum diameter of the holes was 1.45 cm. tapering to 0.3 cm. at the actual opening. Only slight wear was indicated at the holes. This gorget was carefully made and finely finished. The edges are smooth and rounded. (Plate 29, B).

3108. 2. Another quadriconcave gorget was found at 13.1 feet S., 1.4 feet E., at an elevation of 7.0 feet near Burial 7. This gorget is of slate of a grayish-tan color. Since this gorget had been burned and scarred by heat, the grayish-tan color may not be that of the original slate. The maximum dimensions are 10.5 cm. long, 7.25 cm. wide, and 0.9 cm. thick, and the minimum dimensions are 10.05 cm. long and 6.6 cm. wide at the constrictions. The two holes had been drilled from both sides and had been smoothed by wear. The holes tapered from 0.65 cm. to 0.3 cm. at the opening. The entire gorget was carefuly made and finely finished. The edges had been slightly rounded (Plate 29, D).

3161. A quadriconcave gorget was found 10.2 feet south 1.2 feet east at an elevation of 3.1 feet above mound floor near, but not directly associated with, Burial 41. This gorget was of grayish-tan slate but it had also been burned and the original color changed by the heat. The maximum dimensions are 10.15 cm. long, 6.45 cm. wide, and 0.7 cm. thick, and the minimum dimensions are 9.95 cm. long and 5.4 cm. wide at the constrictions. The two holes had been drilled from one side only. The holes tapered from 0.6 cm. to 0.3 cm at the opening. This gorget had been carefully made and it was very thin. Stains of a dark organic material were present on both surfaces of this gorget (Plate 29, C).

3151. A portion of a broken bi-concave gorget was found at 4.0 feet north, 6.2 feet west at an elevation of 1.0 foot above mound floor in the earth fill of the small west primary mound. The reconstructed dimensions of this dark-gray slate gorget are 10.3 cm. long, 5.7 cm. wide, and 0.9 cm. thick. The ends of this gorget were slightly convex but the width was constricted at the center to a minimum width of 5.1 cm. The holes appear to have been drilled from one side and then slightly enlarged from the other side after the penetration of the drill. The breakage of this specimen was caused by heat (Plate 30, E).

3093.2. and 3093. b. Two pieces of a rectangular gorget were found. Piece 2 was found 18.0 feet west 1.1 feet south at an elevation of 5.9 feet. Piece b was found 4.0 feet south 0.4 foot west at an elevation of 13.2 feet above mound floor. Both pieces were on the surface of the large inner mound. The reconstructed dimensions of this gorget of blue-gray banded slate are 8.7 cm. long, 4.65 cm. wide, and 0.6 cm. thick. The two holes had been drilled from one side and they had been worn smooth. These holes tapered from 0.7 cm. to 3.5 cm. at the opening. Piece 2 had been discolored brown from the effects of heat (Plate 30, F).

3107. A rectangular pendant was found at 4.2 feet west 3.0 feet north at an elevation of 10.0 feet above mound floor in the earth fill of the mound. It was made of dark blue-gray slate and the dimensions are 8.7 cm. long, 4.7 cm. wide, and 1.1 cm. thick. The one hole tapered from 1.3 cm. to 1.0 cm. at the opening. The edges and interior surface of the holes are smooth and polished from wear. The hole appears to have been drilled from each side (Plate 30, D).

3168. e. A rectanguloid pendant was found in Feature 25 in association with Burial 45 at 6.2 feet west 14.0 feet north at an elevation of 0.2 foot above mound floor. This pendant of dark blue-gray slate is 11.6 cm. long, 4.55 cm. wide, and 0.75 cm. thick. The single hole, 0.5 cm. in diameter, had been drilled from both sides and showed smoothing from wear. Another hole had been started but never drilled completely through. The positions of the completed hole and the partial hole indicated that the maker may have intended to make a gorget. The edges of the pendant are smooth and polished from wear (Plate 30, C).

3158. f. An elongated bell-shaped pendant was found with Burial 34 in subfloor tomb F.20 at 7.2 feet west 7.2 feet north at an elevation of 0.9 foot below the mound floor. This pendant of blue-white slate is 11.15 cm. long, 5.1 cm. at lower end, 3.1 cm. wide at suspension end, and 0.9 cm. thick. The hole is 0.5 cm. in diameter and made smooth by wear. This hole probably was drilled through from one side and then enlarged from the other side. Across both faces of the pendant are oblique incised lines that form a cross-hatched design (Plate 30, B).

3158. g. Another elongated bell-shaped pendant was found with Burial 34 in Feature 20 as described above for pendant 3158. f. This pendant of dark blue-gray slate is 10.2 cm. long, 4.8 cm. wide at the bottom, 3.5 cm. wide at the suspension end, and 0.8 cm. thick. There are two holes, one near the upper or suspension end and one about two-thirds down the pendant. The upper hole is 0.5 cm. in diameter and made smooth by wear. The lower hole shows little wear. The holes were probably both drilled from one side, but only the lower hole that had not been used, clearly showed this type of drilling. The entire surface has been polished from use. On both surfaces are a series of incised geometrical designs. At the suspension end are six incised notches and along the edge of one side are 25 similar notches. This pendant appears to have been intentionally broken when it was placed with the burial (Plate 30, A).

It is of interest to note that four of the gorgets had been subjected to fire and that two of these had also been broken. It seems probable that these objects had been intentionally mutilated. This is a trait that has often been noted for Adena (Webb and Snow 1945, p. 69).

The reel-shaped or quadriconcave gorgets of the Cresap Mound are all of the types generally considered as early in Adena development by Webb (1941, p. 210-215).

Hemispheres

A total of 12 hemispheres was found, seven of which were of hematite, one of barite, one of secondary calcium carbonate, and three of siltstone. The bases of these hemispheres are flat and generally well polished. They are round or slightly ovate at the basal perimeters which range from 3.25 to 5.1 cm. in diameter. In height these specimens range between 2.2 and 3.3 cm. All of the hemispheres were associated with features or burials as follows:

Feature 4, Burial 12. A hematite hemisphere 3.4 cm. in diameter and 2.2 cm. in height was found in crematory basin, Feature 4. It was crudely formed and only partially polished. It was found with the flat base down. It had been discolored from the effects of heat (Plate 31, Q).

Feature 10. Two hematite hemispheres were found in this deep crematory basin in the floor of the mound. Specimen *A* was lying on its edge at the south end of the basin. It is 4.8 cm. in basal diameter and 2.95 cm. in height. It is symetrical and highly polished (Plate 31, D). Specimen *B* was at the north end of the basin with the flat basal surface facing upwards. It is 4.4 cm. in diameter and 2.35 cm. in height. This hemisphere was carefully shaped but had not been highly polished (Plate 31, C).

Feature 16. A hematite hemisphere was found at the west end of burial area Feature 16. It is 3.8 cm. in diameter and 3.1 cm. in height. The surface had been polished but the object had been subjected to intense heat that caused cracks and pits on its surfaces. Stains of a dark organic material were also present (Plate 31, B).

Burial 11. Another hematite hemisphere was found, base upwards, near the left hand of Burial 11. It is 3.8 cm. in diameter and 3.1 cm. in height. The surfaces are smooth but fractured from the effects of heat. Clinging to the basal surface are fragments of charred bark (Plate 31, A).

Feature 20. A hematite and a barite hemisphere were found in subfloor tomb, Feature 20, with Burial 34. The hematite hemisphere was found base downward near the head of the burial. It is 3.25 cm. in diameter and 2.65 cm. in height. The surface had been carelessly smoothed. It also had been burned and stained by a dark organic substance (Plate 31, F). The barite hemisphere was found along the north side of the tomb near the left hand of the burial with the base lying downward. It is symmetrical and the surface is highly polished. There are a few brown stains on the white surface. It is 3.8 cm. in diameter and 2.2 cm. in height (Plate 31, H).

Burial 52. A hematite hemisphere was found near the head of Burial 52. It is 4.2 cm. in diameter and 2.7 cm. in height. The surface is smooth but not too carefully finished (Plate 31, B).

Feature 6. Among the artifacts scattered around the fire pit near the top of the mound was a hemisphere of secondary calcium carbonate. It is 3.8 cm. in diameter and 2.0 cm. in height. The white surface of this object is extensively weathered and covered with dark-brown stains. It was found with the flat base down (Plate 31, I).

Burial 7. A hemisphere of dense siltstone was found with a gorget associated with Burial 7. It is 4.5 cm. in diameter and 3.3 cm. in height. This rough hemisphere appears to be of natural origin but its placement in the mound was such that its intentional use and deliberate interment were implied (Plate 31, K).

Feature 16. A roughly fashioned hemisphere of dense siltstone was found near a small deposit of cremated bone in Feature 16. It is 5.1 cm. in diameter and 3.15 cm. in height. It was found with the flat basal surface down (Plate 31, J).

Feature 29. Another hemisphere of dense siltstone was found with a cache of artifacts near the head of Burial 15 in Feature 29. It is 4.0 cm. in diameter and 2.4 cm. in height. This hemisphere, like the one mentioned above, is of natural origin, but there can be little doubt of its intentional placement within the mound (Plate 31, L).

Hemispheres of various materials are well known in Adena (Webb and Snow 1945, p. 89). Hematite appears, however, to have been used in their manufacture more extensively in the Upper Ohio Valley than in Kentucky and Ohio.

The probable use of hemispheres in Adena culture still remains somewhat of a mystery. Solecki (1953, p. 361) seriously doubted the use of the Natrium Mound hemispheres as rubbing, polishing, or abrading stones because of the polished surfaces and the careful shaping of these objects. He stated that "it does not seem probable that such well-trimmed objects were used as utilitarian pieces, especially in the presence of cruder objects which could have served the same supposed purpose". Solecki, however, did not suggest any alternate possibility for their use.

The evidence from the Cresap Mound adds little to the clarification of the problem. None of the hemisperes could be associated with any other object, or found in such a situation, as to suggest their use. They were definitely considered of sufficient worth to be given as burial offerings and in several instances they had been burned along with the body and other artifacts. The finding of these objects near the left hand of two individual burials in the Cresap Mound may indicate that they had a ceremonial significance. It seems possible that they were some type of symbol since no valid utilitarian purpose can be adduced for their use.

Pipes

Three tubular pipes of Adena origin and one intrusive Late Prehistoric pipe were found in the Cresap Mound. The descriptions of these pipes are as follows:

A tubular pipe of a fine-grained, compact, sandstone was found on the prepared clay floor of the mound just south of the large pit, F.30, near the center of the mound. This pipe is of the blocked-end variety with a slight flare at the blocked end. It is 5.1 cm. long, 2.6 cm. in outside diameter at the open end, 2.8 cm. at the flared blocked end. The bore at the open end is 1.5 cm. in diameter and the aperture at the blocked end is 0.7 cm. in diameter. The surface of the pipe is smoothly finished. Circular striae from the drilling are present in the bore. Areas of slight reddening on the surface of the pipe indicate that it had been subjected to heat.

A blocked-end tubular pipe of fireclay was found associated with Burial 26. This pipe had been intensely burned and was in many fragments when found. So many pieces were missing that it was impossible to determine its length. The block-end portion was sufficiently intact to permit some measurements. The outside diameter of the tube is 2.0 cm. while at the flare at the blocked end it is 2.65 cm. in diameter. The inside bore of the tube is 1.2 cm. in diameter and the aperture at the blocked end is 0.55 cm. in diameter. The interior of the tube is black and discolored from charred organic material (Plate 31, B).

Another blocked-end tubular pipe was found with Burial 48. This pipe also had been subjected to intense heat and was broken into several pieces, some of which were missing. Sufficient pieces were present to indicate that the pipe was at least 9.2 cm. in length and probably longer. The outside diameter of the tube near the open end is 2.2 cm., and at the flared blocked end it is 3.0 cm. The bore of the tube is 1.6 cm. and the aperture at the blocked end is 0.9 cm. in diameter. Incised notches are present around the circumference of the flared end. A sector of the flared end had been flattened. In the bore of the tube just inside the aperture of the blocked end was a cake of charred organic material (Plate 32, A).

The fourth pipe recovered from the Cresap Mound was not of Adena origin. It was found at the head of Burial 4 which was intrusive into the top of the mound. The intrusive nature of the burial, the two small triangular arrowpoints, and the form of the pipe indicated that these materials belonged to the Late Prehistoric period with specific affinities to the Monongahela complex of the Upper Ohio Valley and Fort Ancient of the central Ohio Valley.

This intrusive pipe of coarse sandstone was "claw-shaped" like the talon of a raptorial bird. The openings for the bowl and stem meet at an obtuse angle. The pipe is 6.6 cm. long, 4.7 cm. wide at top of bowl, and 2.1 cm. thick. The interior diameter of the bowl is 1.2 cm. and the diameter of the stem opening is 1.0 cm. (Plate 32, C).

The finding of charred organic material in the two tubular blocked-end pipes of Ohio fireclay and the presence of burned areas on the tubular pipe of stone afford additional evidence to support the use of these instruments as smoking devices. Bache and Satterthwaite (1930, p. 152-154) believed the tubular pipes found in the Beech Bottom Mound to have been used for smoking. Solecki's (1953, p. 363) observations on the pipes from the Natrium Mound led him to concur with Bache and Satterthwaite's conclusion. Webb and Snow (1945, p.86, 334) suggested that these tubes were used as shaman medicine tubes rather than as smoking devices. It is conceivable that both uses could have been made of these tubes but the evidence now clearly supports their use as smoking pipes.

Tablets

Twenty-two tablets were found associated with other featural materials in the mound. These tablets, often called whetstones, abrading stones, or grooved stones in the Adena literature, vary in form and degree of workmanship. Because of the significance of these items in Adena culture, their featural associations, and their stratigraphic position, the Cresap Mound tablets warrant full description.

Feature 6. Burned area near top of mound 13.5 feet above mound floor and 1.5 feet below the surface. The following tablets were clustered together within the burned area.

1. *Turtle effigy tablet* (Carnegie Museum 3091. c.). The outline of this tablet of fine-grain sandstone is that of a turtle. All major details of the dorsal and lateral surfaces of the turtle are shown. On the head, which is carved in the round, the eyes are depicted by two depressions and the mouth by an incised line. Around the neck are three incised lines which are cut into the dorsal and lateral surfaces but do not extend across the ventral surface. The legs project from the body and the digits of the feet are formed by three deep notches which give the effect of four toes. The outline of the carapace is marked in part by incised lines at the anterior and posterior ends while the lateral margins are shown in the round. The junctions of the incised lines and the sides give an octagonal appearance to the tablet (Plates 33-34).

The ventral surface of the tablet is flat. Into this flat surface three wide grooves had been worn. The longest of these grooves, 4.5 cm. long by 1.2 cm. wide and 0.25 cm. deep, extends from the body along the ventral surface of the extended neck of the turtle. The other two grooves are shorter and confined to the body area. Red ocher stains penetrate the grooves and appear on the surface.

Only the anterior two-thirds of the tablet was found. An old breakage line runs diagonally across the tablet from the front left leg to the rear right leg. This old breakage line had been worn smooth indicating that the object had been used long after it had been broken and before its being included in the mound feature. Enough of the tablet is present to make a reasonably accurate reconstruction.

Based on this reconstruction the tablet is 11.5 cm. long, 8.45 cm. wide, and 1.8 cm. thick. There probably was a short tail as shown in the illustration and the missing rear feet were most likely formed in the same fashion as the front feet. Additional ventral grooves may have been present on the missing posterior portion of the tablet.

2. *Rectanguloid tablet* (Carnegie Museum 3091. d.). This tablet is basically rectangular with rounded corners. It was made from a fine-grained, gray sandstone. The tablet was carefully fashioned and the edges and surfaces are smooth. Abrasion marks are present on both surfaces but there are no grooves. There are both red ocher stains and

Plate 33.   Top and bottom views of "kidney-shaped" tablet and turtle effigy
tablet found in Feature 6

Plate 34.   Reconstruction of the turtle effigy tablet based upon a supposed
symmetry of parts

small fragments of dark organic materials adhering to the surfaces. This tablet was 14.1 cm. long, 7.9 cm. wide, and 2.9 cm. thick (Plate 7).

3. *Rectanguloid tablet* (Carnegie Museum 3091. e.). This rectangular-shaped tablet with rounded corners was made from a fine-grained, gray sandstone. The tablet was carefully finished and the edges are rounded and smooth. On one surface of this tablet is a deep groove 4.0 cm. long, 1.5 cm. wide, and 0.35 cm. deep. In this groove is a deposit of red ocher of a pasty consistency which had been burned and fused to the surface of the tablet. On the other side of the tablet are several abrasion marks, but no grooves are present. Some red ocher stains are on this surface also. Dark organic stains are present on both surfaces. This tablet is 12.0 cm. long, 5.8 cm. wide, and 1.25 cm. thick (Plate 7).

4. *Kidney-shaped tablet* (Carnegie Museum 3091. f.). This tablet is kidney-shaped in general outline. It is of a fine-grained, gray sandstone which has been carefully shaped and smoothly finished on all surfaces and edges. On one face of the tablet are five grooves. The largest groove is 7.5 cm. long, 1.2 cm. wide, and 0.25 cm. deep while the smallest groove is 2.1 cm. long, 0.9 cm. wide, and 0.2 cm. deep. The other grooves are similar in size and configuration. The opposite surface also has five major grooves which are similar in form and dimensions to the grooves on the other face. The grooves tend to run in a parallel or oblique direction with the long axis of the tablet. Red ocher and dark organic stains are present on both surfaces of the tablet. This tablet is 10.2 cm. long, 6.8 cm. wide, and 3.0 cm. thick (Plate 33).

5. *Irregular-shaped tablet* (Carnegie Museum 3091. g.). This tablet was made from a flat irregular piece of fine-grained, gray sandstone. There seems to have been no intentional shaping of the stone, but the surfaces and edges are worn smooth. A shallow groove and abrasion marks are present on each face of the tablet. One face has red ocher stains over most of its surface, while the opposite face has several dark organic stains. This tablet is 8.9 cm. long, 5.6 cm. wide, and 0.85 cm. thick (Plate 7).

6. *Rectanglar tablet* (Carnegie Museum 3091. h.). This tablet is rectangular with only slightly rounded corners. The edges are rounded and smooth. Unlike the above tablets this tablet was made from a coarse brown sandstone. The surfaces of the tablet are carefully finished and

no grooves are present. Both faces show wear from abrasion. This tablet is 5.5 cm. long, 3.6 cm. wide, and 1.3 cm. thick (Plate 7).

7. *Rectangular tablet* (Carnegie Museum 3091. i.). This is a portion of a small rectangular tablet similar to No. 6 above. The surfaces and edges of the tablet are smooth and well executed. No grooves are present, but the faces are eroded from abrasion. This fragment is 3.7 cm. long, 2.7 cm. wide, and 0.9 cm. thick (Plate 7).

8. *Rectangular tablet* (Carnegie Museum 3091. j.). This is a broken corner from a small rectangular tablet similar to 6 and 7 above. It was made from coarse brown sandstone. The surface and edges are finely finished and smooth. No grooves are present but the faces show wear from abrasion. The fragment is 4.1 cm. long, 2.9 cm. wide, and 1.3 cm. thick (Plate 7).

9. *Rectangular tablet* (Carnegie Museum 3091. k.). This tablet is rectangular with convex ends. One end is slightly wider and thicker than the other. It is of a light-tan medium-coarse sandstone. The surface and edges are nicely finished and smooth. This tablet was found in two pieces, but the break is an old one as the edges are smooth and worn. Both pieces appear to have been used separately before they were thrown in the burned area at the top of the mound. There are no grooves, but both faces have been worn by abrasion. Red ocher and dark organic stains are present on the surfaces. This tablet is 18.2 cm. long, 9.1 cm. wide, and 3.5 cm. thick (Plate 7).

10. *A rectanguloid tablet* (Carnegie Museum 3092) was found 11.0 feet south, 9.5 feet east at an elevation of 9.35 feet above the mound floor and on the surface of the large inner mound. The surfaces of this tablet of coarse brown sandstone were plain, but both surfaces are slightly depressed from wear. The dimensions of this tablet are 12.5 cm. long, 7.65 cm. wide, and 2.3 cm. thick. The fine workmanship on this tablet is comparable to that present on the tablets found in F.6 above, and the position of this tablet indicates that it was placed in the mound at approximately the same time.

Feature 20. Subfloor tomb containing Burial 34. The following three tablets were near the burial (Plate 35, A-C).

Plate 35. Typical crude stone tablets from the Cresap Mound
A, B, C in Feature 20. D and E in Feature 15. F in Feature 29. G, H and I
with Burial 42

11. *Circular grooved tablet* (Carnegie Museum 3158. r.). This roughly circular tablet was made of a grayish-tan sandstone of fine texture. It is 8.3 cm. long, 8.3 cm. wide, and 1.2 cm. thick. There are four grooves on each face of this tablet. Within the grooves are stains of red ocher. The edges of the tablet show no special attention, being rough and irregular.

12. *Triangular-shaped grooved tablet* (Carnegie Museum 3158. s.). This crudely formed triangular tablet was made of a grayish-tan sandstone. It is 10.6 cm. long, 5.8 cm. wide at the base, 3.0 cm. wide at the apex, and 0.7 cm. thick. On one face is a long shallow groove 6.3 cm. long, 1.7 cm. wide, and 0.1 cm. deep which parallels the long axis of the tablet. On the other face is a groove 4.1 cm. long, 1.1 cm. wide, and 2.0 cm. deep which is at a right angle to the long axis of the tablet. In both grooves are remains of red ocher and a whitish material that appears to be ash.

13. *Irregular-shaped plain tablet* (Carnegie Museum 3158. t.). This irregular-shaped tablet of brownish-red sandstone is 7.8 cm. long, 7.7 cm. wide, and 0.7 cm. thick. One face is slightly depressed from abrasion and is covered with stains of red ocher and a white substance.

Feature 15. Crematory basin in the saddle formed by the adjoining sides of the south and west primary mounds. The following two tablets were on the floor of the basin (Plate 35, D-E).

14. *Irregular-shaped grooved tablet* (Carnegie Museum 3153. e.). This tablet of brown sandstone is 9.5 cm. long, 8.3 cm. wide, and 1.5 cm. thick. On one face is a shallow groove 5.8 cm. long, 2.3 cm. wide, and 0.3 cm. deep. This entire surface is slightly depressed from abrasion. The other surface has several shallow depressions but no distinct grooves. There are stains of red ocher and a whitish substance on the surfaces.

15. *Irregular-shaped grooved tablet* (Carnegie Museum 3153. f.). This tablet made of a brown flat sandstone river pebble is roughly circular in outline. It is 6.9 cm. long, 6.1 cm. wide, and 0.9 cm. thick. On one surface are two grooves, the larger being 4.3 cm. long, 1.4 cm. wide, and 2.5 cm. deep, and the smaller being 3.4 cm. long, 1.0 cm. wide, and 1.0 cm. deep. Encrusted in these grooves is a paste-like mass of whitish material mixed with red ocher.

Feature 16. An orange-red layer of clay containing Burial 29 just above the apex of the west primary mound at an elevation of 5.2 feet. The three fragments belonging to the same tablet were scattered over the surface of the layer.

16. *Irregular-shaped grooved tablet* (Carnegie Museum 3146. i., 3146. j. and 3146. k.). From the three gray sandstone fragments found of this tablet it was at least 9.0 cm. long, 6.4 cm. wide, and 0.6 cm. thick. On one surface of this tablet is a groove 5.5 cm. long, 0.8 cm. wide, and 0.2 cm. deep. Faint stains of red ocher are present.

Feature 29. Crematory basin containing remains of six burials at 0.4 foot above mound floor under the south primary mound. The following tablet was near the head of Burial 15 in this feature.

17. *Irregular-shaped grooved tablet* (Carnegie Museum 3116. c.). This irregular-shaped tablet of brown sandstone is 9.1 cm. long, 6.7 cm. wide, and 1.1 cm. thick. On one surface are two narrow grooves, the larger being 2.4 cm. long, 0.25 cm. wide, and 0.1 cm. deep. Several small scratches are in the groove. A sharp-pointed tool such as an awl may have made these marks. The surface of this tablet has a waxy appearance and feel. (Plate 35, F).

Burial 11. Extended adult male burial 0.4 foot above floor of mound. The following tablet was at the right knee of this burial.

18. *Irregular grooved tablet* (Carnegie Museum 3110. d.). This is a fragment of a crude grooved tablet of gray sandstone 5.4 cm. long, 5.1 cm. wide, ond 0.85 cm. thick. There is part of a shallow groove on one surface. No other parts of this crude tablet were found with the burial.

Burial 42. Extended adult burial found at an elevation of 0.9 foot above mound floor. The following three tablets were at the left side of the chest of Burial 42.

19. *Oval-shaped grooved tablet* (Carnegie Museum 3167. g.). This crude tablet of gray sandstone is 6.1 cm. long, 4.0 cm. wide, and 1.6 cm. thick. On one surface is a groove 2.7 cm. long, 1.0 cm. wide, and 0.4 cm. deep. On the other surface is a groove 4.4 cm. long, 1.2 cm. wide, and 0.4 cm. deep. In this groove was a whitish substance (Plate 35, G).

20. *Rectangular grooved tablet* (Carnegie Museum 3167. h.). This crude rectangular tablet of gray sandstone is 5.9 cm. long, 3.9 cm. wide, and 0.85 cm. thick. On one surface of this tablet is a shallow groove 2.9 cm. long, 0.8 cm. wide, 0.1 cm. deep. There are stains of red ocher on the surface of the tablet near the groove (Plate 35, H).

21. *Irregular grooved tablet* (Carnegie Museum 3167. i.). This crudely fashioned grooved tablet of coarse-grained, brown sandstone is 6.8 cm. long, 5.4 cm. wide, and 1.4 cm. thick. On one surface is a shallow groove 4.1 cm. long, 0.6 cm. wide, and 0.15 cm. deep. At one end of this groove are red ocher stains (Plate 35, I).

Feature 25. Burned area containing Burial 45 at an elevation of 0.2 foot above mound floor. The following tablet was found on the left side and near the waist of the burial.

22. *Irregular plain tablet* (Carnegie Museum 3168. h. and 3168. i.).
This crude tablet of coarse, brown sandstone is 12.1 cm. long, 7.8 cm.
wide, and 0.9 cm. thick. One surface had been extensively eroded by
abrasion but no grooves were present. On the opposite surface are
depressions made by abrasion. About 2/3 of the surface is stained by
red ocher. This tablet had been broken into two pieces. This breakage
appears to have been intentional.

DISCUSSION OF TABLET FORMS

The cache of tablets in Feature 6 at the top of the mound is of particular interest because it affords a number of insights into the manufacture, function, and chronological significance of tablets in Adena.

Two basic kinds of materials were used in the making of these tablets.
The effigy tablet (No. 1) and tablets No. 2-5 are all of a fine-grained,
gray sandstone identical with the Berea Grit sandstone found in Ohio.
In this group of tablets grooves are present on four of the five specimens.
The second group of tablets (No. 6-9) are all made from medium to
coarse grained sandstones probably of local origin. None of these tablets has grooves but all have surfaces worn by abrasion. Although both
groups of tablets show use as abrasive tools, their surfaces seem to indicate that they were used in a different fashion or for the abrasion or
grinding of different kinds of materials.

With the exception of tablet No. 5, all the ones of fine-grained Berea
sandstone are finely made and finished. This care in manufacture seems
to indicate clearly that these tablets had more than just passing importance to their owners. The fact that the effigy tablet and three of the
rectangular tablets were used after they had been broken indicates that
such items were not to be discarded but were still of sufficient significance to be retained for ceremonial purposes. The placement of tablets
with burials or with features, such as fire pits which appear to be associated with the rites which accompanied burial of the dead, clearly
suggests their direct use in such rites.

Webb and Baby in "The Adena People No. 2" (1957, p. 83-101) suggest that the finely made engraved Adena tablets and the well made
unengraved forms were important ceremonial objects. In speaking of
tablets similar to those just described from the Cresap Mound they state:

"These unengraved tablets also have carefully made edges, corners, and faces, showing the expenditure of considerable effort in their manufacture. They are sometimes found in grave associations, which suggests that they were deemed to have some value beyond the ordinary irregular grooved whetstones found in and beneath burial mounds. An illustration of such an unengraved, but carefully formed whetstone tablet in grave association was found by William C. Mills (1902, p. 470) in the original Adena Mound. It is important to note that this grooved tablet was found in the large central sub-floor tomb, obviously the first grave made, over which the large Adena Mound was later erected in stages as other tombs were added. This grave was the largest and most elaborately constructed and contained the largest number and variety of artifacts."

Webb and Baby (1957, p. 96) go on to cite the finding of similar tabular forms in association with a ceremonial fireplace beneath the Florence Mound and a circular stone plaque in association with a burial in the Niles-Wolford Mound in Ohio. Recently at the Ohio State Museum I examined these tablets and two well made rectangular tablets, one from the Clyde Jones Mound and one from the Dayton Mound in Licking County, Ohio. These tablets are of fine-grained Berea grit sandstone and are similar in every respect to those from the Cresap Mound. There can be little doubt that the unengraved tablets are related in use and importance to the tablets with engraved zoömorphic forms. Webb and Baby (1957, p. 97) state:

"There is the question why a number of the engraved tablets have on their reverse sides long shallow grooves. It will be recalled that similar but unengraved tablets are found in burial association in important graves. If the engraved tablets were used in cult ceremonies, as we have suggested, why not also the unengraved tablets? Certainly these unengraved tablets are not common whetstones, but seem to have all the properties and associations of burial cult objects save the engraving. Obviously these grooved tablets, engraved and unengraved, were designed to sharpen the points of bone awls with which they are found in grave association."

The finding of the turtle effigy tablet in direct association with well made plain and grooved rectangular tablets at the Cresap Mound illustrates a close relationship of the unengraved forms to those bearing zoömorphic designs. Since the turtle effigy tablet is the only effigy tablet known, it is impossible to compare it directly with any other tablet from an Adena mound. It seems to be most closely related to the engraved forms and it is possible that it represented a group or clan totem. Its design and execution, however, contrast sharply with the rectangular tablets which generally have a raptorial bird engraved on one face. The grooves, the type of material used, the degree of workmanship, the associations, and the repeated occurrence of these items in Adena mounds indicate that the engraved tablets, the effigy tablet, and the well executed unengraved tablet all have definite relationships to each other in the Adena burial cult. Their use was similar and, as will be shown, these particular forms were all used during a definite period in Adena.

Mention has been made in the above quotation from Webb and Baby that the grooved tablets were used for the shaping and sharpening of bone awls which these workers believe were used in "blood letting ceremonies" (Webb and Baby, 1957, p. 97). When Solecki (1943, p. 364) excavated the Natrium Mound a few miles down the Ohio River from the Cresap Mound in Marshall County, W. Va., he found a faceted lump of hematite lying directly in the grooves of a crude tablet. This find led Solecki to believe that such tablets were used for the grinding of red ocher pigment. Taking note of this find, Webb and Baby (1957, p. 97) make the following statement concerning the use of tablets for making pigments:

"Furthermore, if the participant in such a ceremony were a cult devotee, he would perhaps need some identification or record of his participation. What more natural way to accomplish this end than that the shaman at the time, should draw or stamp upon the body of the individual the appropriate symbols of the cult? He might use for this purpose some form of pigment like red ochre mixed with grease, or he might use some of the blood of the devotee to mix the small quantity of the paint. To grind a small quantity of pigment like red ochre the shaman might have used as a mortar the same whetstone which had sharpened the awl used in this blood-letting ceremony. Even if there was no blood-letting ceremony, a blunt awl would be effective in grinding pigment. If such possible operations are considered, it is easy to see why the whetstone, as well as the awls which it formed and sharpened, would become sacred paraphernalia and at the death of the shaman be buried with him."

The evidence from the Cresap Mound lends considerable support to the above statements. All nine tablets found at the top of the mound were stained in varying degrees with red ocher. In the lower levels 13 crude tablets were found associated with features and burials. Of these 13 tablets, 10 are grooved and three are plain. All of these tablets except two are stained with red ocher. In the grooves of some of the tablets there is a thick pasty deposit of red ocher mixed with a white ashy substance. Associated with most of these tablets were worked and faceted pieces of hematite. In the face of the evidence from Cresap Mound, Natrium Mound, and other sites there is little doubt that Adena tablets were used in the preparation of paint pigments of which red ocher was a major component.

The finding of these tablets associated directly with burials points to their importance in the interment rite. The question now arises as to their ownership. Did they belong to the individual with whom they were placed? Or, were they the property of the group which conducted the burial ceremony? Webb and Baby (1957, p. 96-97) have made the suggestion that the engraved tablets were used by the shaman "to stamp on the clothing or the body of a number of individuals on appropriate occasions the symbols and motifs of the cult to which those receiving the stamp were adherents." They go on to suggest that such a tablet would have been the express property of the shaman and would have been buried with him at his death and not passed on to another individual. Unfortunately, little is known about the situation and associations of the engraved tablets since most of these objects were found by collectors who kept no records of their finds. The only documented finds of tablets with burials all pertain to the unengraved type. Excellent examples of such association can be shown at the Cresap Mound, Natrium Mound (Solecki, 1953, p. 340-341), the original Adena Mound (Mills, 1902, p. 470), C. and O. Mounds (Webb, 1942, p. 324) and at other sites. It is possible that these tablets belonged to the individual with whom they were buried, but the presence of caked dried pigment on the surface and in the grooves of tablets found at Natrium Mound and Cresap Mound seems to indicate that the specimens were used by the individuals who conducted the burial. It also seems reasonable to suggest that pigments prepared on these tablets were actually used to decorate the body of the dead as well as the participants in the burial rite.

The disposition of the cache of tablets from the Cresap Mound appears indicative of a group activity centered around a large fire at the top of the mound. None of these tablets was directly associated with the extended burials which had been placed on the same mound surface around the fire. If the tablets were the individual property of a shaman among the burials we would expect them to be placed with his body. Since this is not the case, it seems reasonable to suggest these items were the sacred items of the cult group and not of an individual. At the end of the rite, after they had served their purpose, the tablets were consigned to the ceremonial fire. In such a situation the shaman may have been the keeper of the tablets and the director of the rite activities, but he was not the owner of the items used. In the Florence Mound excavated in 1938 by the Ohio State Museum, a number of unengraved tablets were found in a large fire pit at the base of the mound (Personal communication from Raymond S. Baby, March 31, 1959). No burials were directly associated with the fire pit or the tablets. This situation in the Florence Mound appears analogous to the find at the top of the Cresap Mound where the tablets were thrown into the fire rather than being placed with a burial.

From the data now available from mounds in Ohio, Kentucky, and West Virginia there emerges a picture of a long sequence of development of tablet forms in Adena. From the Cresap Mound alone there is an almost complete sequence in the development of the tablet. Beginning in the lowest levels and continuing to a height of 5.2 feet were tablets of irregular shape either grooved or plain. The well made tablets were confined to the top surface of the old inner mound at an elevation of 13.25 feet, but even there one irregular grooved tablet was included with the well made examples. Stratigraphically the finely finished tablets and the unusual effigy turtle tablet were the last items added to the Cresap Mound and were separated from the lower mound features by the well defined humus layer. These fine tablets were also associated with a well defined blade or point type, a wide, deep-shouldered, rounded-base, parallel-sided stem point, which appears to be confined to late Adena sites. The crudely formed tablets of the lower levels of the Cresap Mound were associated with slender, weak-shouldered, ovate-base, tapered-stemmed blades which characterize early and middle Adena periods. The crude tablets and other objects from the lower levels of the Cresap Mound are similar to the materials found in the Natrium Mound (Solecki, 1953), and the Beech Bottom Mound (Bache and Satterthwaite, 1930) in West Virginia, the Toepfner Mound (Baby, personal conversations) in Ohio, and the Fisher Site (Webb and Haag, 1947) in Kentucky. Radiocarbon dates from the Toepfner Mound in Ohio of 2780±410 to 2200±200 years ago indicate that this mound was one of the earliest Adena mounds in the Ohio Valley (Crane and Griffin, 1958, p. 1119). The subfloor pit burials and associated objects of the Cresap Mound bear a striking resemblance to those of the Toepfner Mound.

Several mounds in Kentucky and Ohio produced finely made tablets in association with wide, deep-shouldered, rounded-base, parallel-sided stem blades. The Wright Mound (Mm 6) (Webb and Haag, 1940), the C. and O. Mounds (Webb and Haag, 1942), and the Robbins Mound (Webb and Elliott, 1942) in Kentucky, the Clyde Jones Mound, Dayton Mound, and Florence Mound in Ohio (collections in the Ohio State Museum) are typical examples. The radiocarbon date of 1425±250 years ago (Libby 1955, p. 100) for the Florence Mound attests to the lateness of such items in Adena. The finding of an engraved tablet in the Wright Mound (Mn 6) in Kentucky (Webb and Haag, 1940, p. 115) indicates that the engraved forms were contemporary with the finely made unengraved tablets such as the ones from the Cresap Mound.

All of the above mentioned mounds are late Adena sites from bottom to top. Only the tablets and associated items from the topmost layer of the Cresap Mound are comparable to the items from these late mounds. In the light of the stratigraphy of the materials of the Cresap Mound, the statement by Webb and Snow (1945, p. 219) that "it is to be noted that there appears [sic] to be sites of both ages (early and late) in Ohio, and in Kentucky, but West Virginia sites seem to belong to Late Adena and Indiana sites to Early Adena" must be amended. A recent article by Ritchie and Dragoo (1960, p. 21) has suggested that many of the West Virginia sites are of Middle Adena origin and some may belong to the early period. The evidence from the lower levels of Cresap Mound suggests this position and indicates that when late Adena did appear at this mound it was clearly separated by a thick humus layer which shows a considerable time lapse between the middle and late occupation. This time lapse between the Middle and Late Adena occupations can best be accounted for by the encroachment of Hopewellian peoples on Adena late in the Middle Adena period. Evidence has recently been presented which shows that some Adena groups under Hopewellian pressure moved out of the Upper Ohio Valley to as far east as the Atlantic Coast at this time (Ritchie and Dragoo, 1959, p. 48). Although greatly influenced by Hopewell, Adena in Kentucky and portions of West Virginia appears to have been able to hold off direct Hopewellian invasion and continued its development into a late Adena period.

Since the peak in the development of Adena tablets was reached in the late Adena period when Hopewellian influences were at their strongest, it seems a logical assumption that the use of tablets would have been adopted by Hopewell along with many other burial and ceremonial traits of undisputed Adena origin (Webb and Snow, 1945, p. 327). This does not seem to be the case. In the collections from Hopewell mounds, tablets are conspicuously absent. The only well documented find of a tablet is the one from the Seip Mound now in the collections of the Ohio State Museum. With this small, thin, rectangular tablet were found a number of small bone awls. Even if we concede that this small tablet from the Seip Mound represents a similar usage of a tablet in Hopewell, the fact still remains that tablets are basically an Adena trait of great ceremonial significance which developed from crude forms in early Adena to finely fashioned engraved and effigy forms in late Adena.

MISCELLANEOUS POLISHED STONE ARTIFACTS

Hematite stones

Thirty-five hematite stones showing modification or faceting were found in association with other materials in the features and with the burials. The provenience and description of these stones are as follows (Plate 36).

Plate 36.   Typical examples from among the 35 worked and faceted pieces of hematite found in various features of the Cresap Mound

Feature 7. A large piece of worked and faceted hematite 11.6 cm. long, 5.2 cm. wide, and 3.0 cm. thick. There are abrasion marks over the entire surface and two large facets.

Feature 8. Two small pieces of hematite which fit together were found in opposite ends of this feature. When the two pieces are put together the piece is 5.8 cm. long, 2.7 cm. wide, and 0.9 cm. thick. A number of shallow grooves are present on one surface and a small facet is present on one edge.

A third piece of hematite from this feature is 2.7 cm. long, 2.1 cm. wide, and 1.2 cm. thick. There are two distinct facets.

Feature 15. Two faceted pieces of hematite were found in this feature. The largest is 5.2 cm. long, 3.1 cm. wide, and 2.4 cm. thick and has seven facets on its surface. The smaller is 4.2 cm. long, 3.1 cm. wide, and 2.2 cm. thick and also has seven facets on its surface.

Feature 16. One long semi-lunar shaped piece of hematite 10.3 cm. long, 3.15 cm. wide, and 1.8 cm. thick was found in this feature. There is a long facet the entire length of the stone.

Feature 25. Four pieces of hematite were present in this feature. The largest of these is 4.4 cm. long, 3.9 cm. wide, and 0.7 cm. thick, while the smallest is 2.4 cm. long, 1.2 cm. wide, and 1.2 cm. thick. All four pieces show effects of abrasion and have one or more facets on the surface.

Feature 28. Seven pieces of hematite were found in this feature. The largest is 7.3 cm. long, 4.1 cm. wide, and 2.4 cm. thick, while the smallest is 2.3 cm. long, 1.75 cm. wide, and 1.1 cm. thick. The surfaces of all these stones are covered with abrasion marks and each has one or more facets.

Feature 29. Eleven pieces of hematite were found near the head of Burial 15 in this feature. The largest of these is 6.9 cm. long, 4.3 cm. wide, and 3.2 cm. thick. The smallest is 2.2 cm. long, 1.4 cm. wide, and 0.6 cm. thick. All of these stones have abrasion marks and facets on their surfaces.

Burial 20. One small faceted piece of hematite 3.9 cm. long, 2.2 cm. wide, and 1.6 cm. thick was found with this burial. Four prominent facets are present on the surface.

Burial 32. One piece of hematite 5.3 cm. long, 3.8 cm. wide, and 2.7 cm. thick was found near the head of this burial. Fine facets are present on the surface.

Burial 39. One large piece of hematite 10.1 cm. long, 5.1 cm. wide, and 2.2 cm. thick was found near this burial. The surface is covered with abrasion marks and at one end is a smooth facet.

Burial 53. One faceted piece of hematite and two worked iron concretions were with this burial. The piece of hematite is 3.4 cm. long, 3.1 cm. wide, and 2.5 cm. thick. Fine facets are present on its surface. The two iron concretions show only slight abrasion and smoothing of the surfaces.

None of the hematite stones found in the above features shows any specialization in form. All appear to be raw materials used for the derivation of red ochre paint pigment. The facets common to these stones are the result of rubbing the stones on an abrasive material. The presence of grooved and plain stone tablets in association with the faceted hematite stones seems to point clearly to their use as the abrader in the paint-making process. The finding of a faceted hematite stone lying directly in the groove of a grooved tablet in the Natrium Mound clearly demonstrated this relationship (Solecki, 1953, p. 366). Many of the facets of the hematite stones from the Cresap Mound fit well into the grooves of the tablets in the same features.

Cup-stones

Five cup-stones of limonite and three of a sandstone impregnated with ferruginous material were found associated with features and burials as follows:

Feature 8. Two limonite cup-stones. The largest is 5.65 cm. long, 2.3 cm. wide, and 1.2 cm. deep, and the smallest is 4.2 cm. long, 2.9 cm. wide, and 1.3 cm. deep.

Feature 16. One limonite cup-stone 2.5 cm. long, 1.85 cm. wide, and 0.9 cm. deep.

Feature 21. One limonite cup-stone 2.7 cm. long, 2.3 cm. wide, and 0.9 cm. deep. Red ochre stains are on the surface of this object.

Feature 29. One sandstone cup-stone 4.6 cm. long, 3.4 cm. wide, 2.3 cm. deep.

Burial 21. One sandstone cup-stone 3.7 cm. long, 3.4 cm. wide, and 1.4 cm. deep.

Burial 41. One sandstone cup-stone 3.9 cm. long, 2.9 cm. wide, 0.9 cm. deep.

All of these cup-stones are of natural origin. The only modification occurs at the lips of the cup which have been smoothed and polished from use. The association of these objects with red ocher and faceted pieces of hematite seems to substantiate their use as paint cups.

Hammerstones

Two stones of natural shape were found in separate features. Included with the cache of tablets in Feature 6 at the top of the mound was a naturally faceted pebble of dense metamorphic stone with a slight depression on one face. Slight abrasion and smoothing appear on the facet with this depression. This stone is 5.4 cm. in diameter and 4.4 cm. in height. The same organic stains found on the associated tablets also cover the surface of this stone.

The second stone is a dense sandstone pebble with a natural basin-like depression on one surface found in Feature 15 in association with other artifacts. Some abrasion is present around the edges of the depression. This stone is 6.1 cm. long, 4.7 cm. wide, and 2.6 cm. thick.

Both of these natural stones could have been used either as hammers or abraders.

Drilled elliptical stone bars

Two unusual stone objects were found in association with the blades and gorget in the area adjacent to Feature 6. Both of these objects are elliptical in form with two large smooth holes drilled through them. Both were made of calcium carbonate which has weathered extensively. The larger of these pieces is 7.9 cm. long, 3.3 cm. wide, 0.7 cm. thick, and the diameter of the holes is 1.0 cm. The other stone is 6.9 cm. long, 2.5 cm. wide, 0.6 cm. thick, and the diameter of the holes is 1.0 cm. The holes in both these objects are worn smooth (Fig. 5).

Similar objects are unknown from any other Adena mound. A similar object was reported from West Virginia by Moorehead (1917, p. 58, fig. 34). This object, however, has three large holes and is rectangular in outline.

The use to which these objects were put by their aboriginal owners is unknown. The smooth margins of the holes indicate wear of a nature not common to objects generally classed as atlatl weights or gorgets. They may have been used only as ornaments, but it also seems possible that they could have been used in the spinning of cordage.

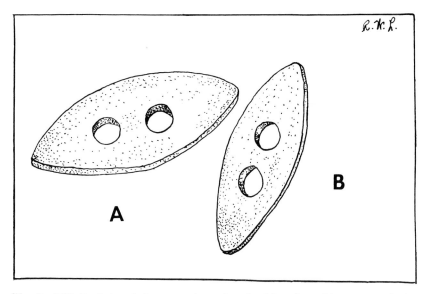

Fig. 5.   Elliptical, two-hole, stone bars found with other objects around the
burned area (Feature 6) near the top of the Cresap Mound
A is 7.9 cm. long, 3.3 cm. wide, and 0.7 cm. thick. B is 6.9 cm. long, 2.5 cm. wide,
and 0.6 cm. thick. The diameter of the holes in each object is 1.0 cm.

CHIPPED-STONE ARTIFACTS

In the chipped-stone category, there are 141 whole or fragmentary
specimens, including 93 blades or projectile points, nine drills, and 39
scrapers. The descriptions and associations of these objects are as
follows:

Leaf-shaped blades or knives

Nineteen specimens, all associated with burials or features, are
assigned to this group. The bases on eight of these blades are round,
while the bases on the remaining 11 blades are flat. Those having flat
bases appear to be less carefully chipped than those with the rounded
base, but none of these blades can be considered as crude. The maximum width of all the blades is near the midpoint, giving the blades a
true leaf-shaped appearance rather than a triangular outline. (Plate 37).
The blades range in length from 6.5 to 15.8 cm. The average length
is 10.65 cm. Thirteen of these blades are more than 10 cm. long. The

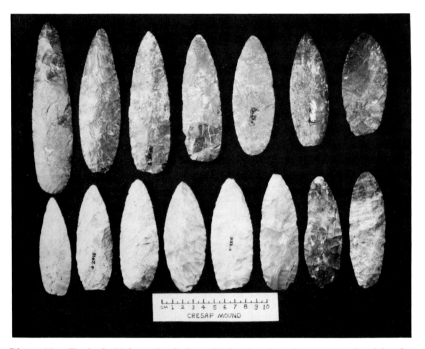

Plate 37.   Typical "Adena leaf-shaped" blades found associated with the various features and burials in the Cresap Mound

width of the blades ranges from 3.1 to 4.2 cm. with an average of 3.71 cm. They are all lenticular in cross-section, ranging from 0.7 to 1.3 cm. thick, with an average thickness of 0.98 cm.

All of the leaf-shaped blades found in the Cresap Mound have edges that have been worn and retouched by use. None of the blades is of the type that is generally considered an unused blank or one manu-factured especially for inclusion as a grave offering. Missing from the Cresap Mound are caches containing large numbers of leaf-shaped blades. The largest number in any single cache was seven in Feature 10. Since all the blades show extensive use as tools, it would seem that all these blades were taken directly from the deceased's or the burial rite participant's tool kits. The nature of the wear and smoothing present on these blades indicates their use as knives.

The materials used in the manufacture of the leaf-shaped blades are all of fine-grained flint ranging in color from blue-black to white. All

the flint is native to the Ohio Valley with most of the specimens having
been derived from the Flint Ridge, Ohio, quarries. Several of the blades
had been discolored and physically changed as the result of burning.
Chalky areas and fine fracture marks are present on the surfaces.
Patches of a black tar-like organic substance are present on some of
these blades.

With the exception of two specimens, one at 6.5 feet and one at 8.4
feet, the leaf-shaped blades were found with features near (below 1.0
foot) or below the floor of the mound.

Flat-base, tapered-stemmed blades (weak shoulders)

Fine blades with a flat base, tapered stem, and weak shoulders were
found distributed in three separate features in the mound. The bases
are thin and flat except on one blade which still has the remains of a
striking platform. The stem contracts slightly from the shoulders to
the base. The shoulders are weak in comparison with the other stem-
med-blade types found in the mound. In appearance these blades are
long and slender with fine flaking. They range in length from 6.2 to 10.7
cm., with an average of 8.45 cm. In width they range from 2.3 to 2.7 cm.
with an average of 2.5 cm. They are lenticular in cross-section with an
average thickness of 0.88 cm. (Plate 38,B).

These blades are distinctive both in form and in material at the Cresap
Mound. With the exception of two other blades in the collection, they
are the only blades of Kanawha black flint, a large flint deposit located
in the Kanawha Valley of West Virginia.

All these blades were found at or below the floor of the mound. Two
of these blades were with Burial 45 in Feature 25 on the floor of the
mound, and the other was with Burial 12 in Feature 4 at an elevation
of 0.6 foot above mound floor. All have worn edges as if used for knives.

A survey of the blades from many Adena mounds in the Ohio Valley
indicates that this type of blade is not a common form in Adena. A few
similar blades were examined in collections from village sites adjacent
to Adena mounds in the Moundsville, W. Va., area and the Kanawha
Valley. This blade form resembles certain stemmed blades from late
Archaic sites in the Upper Ohio Valley (Dragoo, 1959, p. 199, 208)
more than they do typical Adena forms. The intentional placing of these
blades in three separate features of the Cresap Mound can not be an
accident. It seems likely that this type is an Adena form which makes

Plate 38. Stemmed blade forms
A. Flat-base, straight-stemmed blades. B. Flat-base, tapered-stemmed "Cresap" blades. C. Flat-base, tapered-stemmed blades

its appearance early in the Upper Ohio Valley. It may have been derived from a late Archaic type in the area.

Flat-base, tapered-stemmed blades (distinct shoulders)

Two blades similar to those just described were found, one each in two features at the base of the mound. Although these blades have tapered, flat-base stems similar to the previous group, the shoulders are more distinct, the blades are wider, and the chipping is much cruder. The materials used in their manufacture appear to be crude varieties of Flint Ridge flint. (Plate 38,C).

One blade is 10.8 cm. long, 3.2 cm. wide, and 1.1 cm. thick. The other is 9.4 cm. long, 2.8 cm. wide, and 1.0 cm. thick. Both blades are diamond-shaped in cross-section. The edges of both blades are worn and smooth from use probably as knives.

Flat-base, straight-stemmed blades

There were eight blades with flat bases and straight stems found in the mound. The shoulders on these blades tend to be distinct but some are weak. With the exception of one blade, this group tends to be much shorter than the two previous stemmed types with the stem accounting for nearly one-third to one-half the length of the blade. These blades range in length from 5.3 to 9.8 cm. Six are less than 7.0 cm. long and the average is 6.65 cm. In width they range from 2.3 to 3.1 cm. with an average of 2.56 cm. They are lenticular in cross-section with a range in thickness from 0.7 to 0.9 cm., with an average of 0.766 cm. All these blades have edges worn from use. (Plate 38,A).

The flints used in their manufacture range from black to white in color. One blade is of Kanawha black flint while the others are of flint similar in color and texture to varieties of Flint Ridge.

Blades of this type were found from the base of the mound to an elevation of 5.1 feet. Four were below 1.0 foot while four were found above 2.5 feet. Six of these blades were associated with features and two were found in the fill earth of the mound. Both of the latter were near the floor of the mound.

All of the blades in this group can be duplicated from other Adena sites. As a group, however, they are less distinctively Adena than the ovate-base, stemmed blades to be described next. Some of the blades of this group are similar also to some late Archaic types in the Upper Ohio Valley (Dragoo, 1959, p. 199).

Ovate-base, tapered-stemmed blades

The dominant blade form at the Cresap Mound is one with an ovate base and tapered stem. It is a form often referred to as a "beaver tail." Thirty-seven blades of this type were found. They range in length from 3.40 to 15.0 cm. with an average of 7.65 cm. Only three blades were more than 10.0 cm. and there were seven blades less than 6.0 cm. The majority (27 blades) fall within the 6.0 to 9.6 cm. range. In width these blades ranged from 1.7 to 4.3 cm. with the average being 2.81 cm. They are lenticular in cross-section with a thickness ranging from 0.7 to 1.70 cm. and an average thickness of 0.96 cm. The shoulders on most of these blades are distinct. A few blades, however, possess weakly defined shoulders. The proportion of the length of the stem to the total length

Plate 39. Ovate-base, tapered-stemmed "Adena" blades. This form constitutes the dominant early-middle Adena blade type

of the blade varies from nearly one-half in the short blades to about one-fifth in the large blades. (Plate 39).

The degree of workmanship ranges from crude to fine with the finest craftsmanship present on the large examples. The material used in the manufacture of these blades was generally of good quality, fine-grained flint of the types found at Flint Ridge, Ohio. One blade, and perhaps a second, is made of the gray Harrison County, Ind., flint. One blade is of Kanawha black flint, and at least two blades of a whitish-gray flint with tan streaks are of flint from the Hughes River area of West Virginia.

All of the blades of this group have edges worn and smoothed by use. The finding of one of these blades in Feature 31 with the fragile remains of a bone handle still attached indicates that probably many of these blades were used as knives as well as for projectile points.

All of these blades were found in association with features except one found in the fill earth of the mound. The blades of this type were found in features below the mound floor up to a height of 8.2 feet. Their distribution was as follows: 11 blades (29.72%) in the major subfloor features, 11 blades (29.72%) in features on or less than 1.0 foot above the mound floor, six blades (16.21%) were found 2-4 feet above the mound floor in features associated with the small primary mounds, four blades (10.81%) were found at approximately the 5.2-foot level, four blades (10.81%) at the 6.5-foot level, and one blade (2.70%) at the 8.2-foot level. No blades of the ovate-base, tapered-stem type were found in the last addition made to the Cresap Mound.

The ovate-base, tapered-stem blade is a distinctive Adena type. It was the typical blade type from the beginning of the construction of the Cresap Mound until the mound was approximately two-thirds completed. During the final stage in the construction the blade gave way to the rounded-base, straight-stem, wide blade.

Rounded-base, straight-stem, wide blades

Scattered on the old mound surface around Feature 6 at the 13.5-foot level were 12 blades characterized by a rounded-base, straight-stem, wide blade with deep, well defined shoulders. In length these blades range from 5.70 to 10.00 cm. with an average of 7.80 cm. Width ranges from 2.90 to 5.50 cm. with an average of 3.68 cm. They are lenticular in cross-section with the thickness ranging from 0.65 to 1.00 cm. and an average of 0.78 cm. (Plate 40).

These blades are thin and finely chipped. The materials used in the manufacture of all these blades were fine-grained flints from the Flint Ridge, Ohio, deposits with a predominance of the light-colored varieties.

The shoulders on all these blades except one, tend to be deep and at a right angle with the long axis of the blade. On the largest specimen there are spurs on the shoulders which give them the appearance of notches. The edges on all these blades are worn and the bases are generally smoothed.

Blades of this type are known from many Adena mounds, especially those in Kentucky. At the Cresap Mound this type of blade is distinct in form and stratigraphic position from all other blade types found in the mound. They are associated with the finely made tablets found in

Plate 40.   Rounded-base, straight-stemmed, wide "Robbins" blades.   This
type was found in only the top zone of the Cresap Mound

Feature 6 which constitute the bulk of the items placed in the mound
during its final stage in construction. These blades were upon an old
humus layer that clearly seals off this material from all the earlier stages
in the mound. The importance of the stratigraphic position of these
blades will be thoroughly discussed in a later section.

Concave-base straight-stem blade

A blade 7.7 cm. long, 3.5 cm. wide, and 0.9 cm. thick was found in
Feature 4. The stem on this blade is wide and thinned at the concave
base. The shoulders are weakly defined. It had been made from a
grayish-tan flint containing small quartz inclusions. This blade is unlike
any of the others from the mound, both in form and material.

Side-notched blades

Three side-notched blades or projectile points were found in the excavation. Two of these points were in the earth fill of the mound and the third was associated with Burial 53. These points ranged from 3.3 to 4.6 cm. in length, from 1.9 to 2.3 cm. in width, and from 0.6 to 0.85 cm. in thickness. The materials used in the manufacture of all three of these side-notched points appear to be of local origin. This type of point is common on many of the Archaic sites in the area (Dragoo, 1959). Similar points indicative of an Archaic occupation have been found on the terrace adjacent to the mound. It appears that two of these points were accidental inclusions in the earth of the mound while the third probably had been picked up from the terrace by the Adena people rather than being one of their products.

Expanded-stemmed blade

One expanded-stemmed blade 5.1 cm. long, 2.4 cm. wide, and 0.95 cm. thick was found in the earth fill of the mound. This blade is also typical of the late Archaic and particularly the transitional culture of the Upper Ohio Valley (Dragoo, 1959, p. 212).

Triangular points

Two small triangular points were found associated with Burial 4 which had been intruded into the top of the mound long after the abandonment of the mound by Adena. The burial and the triangular points conform in all respects to the Late Prehistoric (Fort Ancient) Culture of the Upper Ohio Valley.

Miscellaneous blades

Three fragments of blades were found one each in Feature 10, Feature 15, and with Burial 28. One fragment was a mid-section of a blade while the other two were tips. None of these fragments is assignable to a specific type.

Drills

Of nine drills found in the mound, all, except one in the fill earth, were associated with features. Four of these drills were of the straight

Plate 41.   Drills and scrapers found in various features of the Cresap Mound
A. Drills. B. End scrapers. C. Side scrapers. D. Crude side scrapers. E. Crude,
heavy side scrapers

variety with dimensions ranging from 6.2 to 8.4 cm. in length, 1.65 to 1.85 cm. in width at the base, and 0.8 to 1.1 cm. in thickness.

Two drills have slightly expanded bases. One of these is 10.8 cm. long, 2.1 cm. wide at the base, 1.0 cm. wide at mid-section, and 0.7 cm. thick. The second drill of this type is 6.75 cm. long, 1.8 cm. wide at the base, 0.8 cm. wide at mid-section, and 0.8 cm. thick. The first drill was made of a grayish-tan flint while the second was of a dark blue-gray flint.

Two drills have rounded stemmed base. The first is 5.3 cm. long, 1.7 cm. wide near the base, and 1.0 cm. thick. It is of dark-gray flint. The second drill is 5.25 cm. long, 1.9 cm. wide near the base, and 1.0 cm. thick. It is of light-gray Harrison County, Ind., flint.

One drill has a flat stemmed base. It is 5.7 cm. long, 2.1 cm. wide at the base, and 0.8 cm. thick. It is of a dark-blue flint with white spots.

With the exception of two specimens which are rhomboidal, all the drills are lenticular in cross-section. They all show wear and smoothing from use. Drills of the above types have been found at most Adena sites. (Plate 41,A).

Scrapers and crude flint pieces

A total of 39 objects can be classified as either scrapers or crude blanks representing broken or incompleted objects. Some of the latter appear to have also been used as scraping tools although they show no special modification. This group of objects is divided into end scrapers, side scrapers, utilized flakes, crude scrapers, and crude blanks.

Of the four end scrapers, three were associated with features and one was found in the earth fill of the mound. All are of the plano-convex type with a rounded cutting edge at one end. They range in size from 2.7 to 6.7 cm. long, 2.1 to 3.4 cm. wide, and 0.6 to 1.2 cm. thick. Of three of these specimens, each has a stem-like projection opposite the cutting end, and the fourth is of the "thumb-nail" type. All are of fine-grained flints that have been worn from use. (Plate 41,B).

There are nine tools of the side scraper variety. They are lenticular in cross-section with both surfaces carefully chipped. The edges are worn and smooth from use. They range in size from 3.7 to 6.9 cm. long, 1.7 to 3.6 cm. wide, and 0.6 to 1.2 cm. in thickness. All are of good quality fine-grained flints. Six of these scrapers were associated with features or burials and three were found in the earth fill of the mound. (Plate 41,C).

There are nine scrapers made of irregular flakes of flint. They show no intentional shaping but the edges are well worked and show extensive wear from use. These items range from 3.2 to 5.5 cm. in length, 1.7 to 4.3 cm. in width, and 0.6 to 1.2 cm. in thickness. All except one are of fine-grained flints. All were associated with features. (Plate 41,D).

There are 12 pieces of flint that have edges showing wear and retouching from use as scrapers. These pieces tend to be heavier and cruder than the flakes mentioned above. Three of these crude scrapers have concave areas worn into their cutting surfaces. All are of fine-grained flint. Except for two scrapers in the mound fill, all were associated with features. (Plate 41,E).

In addition to the items described above, there are 5 pieces of worked flint where shape or broken condition made it impossible to classify into any specific category. All of these items show wear from probable use as scrapers.

SUMMARY OF CHIPPED-STONE TOOLS

The distinctive blade types and their stratigraphic position in the Cresap Mound are of extreme importance in the understanding of the chronological development of blade types in Adena. In no other Adena mound has such a definite sequence of types been found. Distinctive to the Cresap Mound are the flat-base, tapered-stemmed blades to which it seems appropriate to assign the name *Cresap Point*. This blade has been found on the surface at a number of sites in the Upper Ohio Valley having Adena components. The total distribution of the type is yet unknown. The finding of these blades in three separate features in the base of the Cresap Mound indicates that they were early in the Adena sequence in the Upper Ohio Valley.

The best known of all Adena blades is the ovate-base, stemmed type so common on most Adena sites in the Ohio Valley. In the literature this blade is usually referred to as the "Adena" point (Bell, 1958, p. 4). At the Cresap Mound blades of this type were found from the base of the mount to a height of 8.2 feet. They were not present among the materials found associated with the last structural stage of the mound. Such a distribution would suggest that they belong to the early and middle phases of Adena, but are replaced by the rounded-base, straight-stemmed, wide blade in late Adena.

The rounded-base, straight-stemmed, wide blades with distinct shoulders were confined entirely to features associated with the last stage in the construction of the Cresap Mound. They are clearly separated both by the form and provenience from all other types in the mound. This type has long been recognized as an Adena form; it is particularly common at sites in Kentucky, but the general tendency has been to lump this type with the Adena ovate-base, tapered-stemmed type. A survey made by me of the blade types in the collections from many Adena mounds in Ohio and Kentucky indicated that some mounds have only one of these two types; some have both. Certain other distinctive Adena objects seem to occur with one or the other of these two types of blade. For example, the finely made Adena tablets seem to be associated with the wide blade while crude tablet forms are present with the ovate-base, tapered-stemmed blades. The expanded center bar gorget also seems to occur more often when the wide blade is present. The cultural and chronological significance of the different associations of these two blade forms will be more thoroughly detailed in a later section of this report.

Important differences can also be seen in the manufacture of these two blades. The ovate-base, tapered-stemmed blades were made from slender, leaf-shaped blanks with thick cross-sections. More of the chipping seems to have been done by percussion than by pressure. The rounded-base, straight-stemmed blades were made from wide, thin blanks with a triangular or tear-drop outline. The chipping was carefully executed by a combination of percussion and pressure flaking. In certain details these blades approach the form and craftsmanship seen in blades from Hopewellian manifestations in Ohio. The late temporal position of these blades as indicated by their presence in only the last stage of the Cresap Mound suggests that such blades were made by Adena after their contact with Hopewell.

Since these two blades can be distinguished both in form and time, I feel that they should be given separate names. The lumping of these two types into one category is no longer satisfactory. For the ovate-base, tapered-stemmed blade that is present in Adena from its early to late phases, I suggest that the name Adena Point be continued. Since the rounded-base, straight-stemmed, wide blades have been reported in greater abundance at Adena sites in Kentucky, I suggest that the term Robbins Point be applied. Typical examples of these points were found by Webb (1942, p. 438-439) in his excavations at the Robbins Mound, the C. and O. Mounds (Webb, 1942, p. 335), and the Wright Mounds (Webb, 1940, p. 63). Any one of these names could be used, but the Robbins Mound seems to present a typical context within which these blades are found.

The remaining point types from the Cresap Mound are less distinctive in form and context. The flat-base, straight-stemmed blades occurred at the Cresap Mound in the same levels with the distinctive ovate-base Adena Point. This same association can be shown for other sites in the Upper Ohio Valley and Kentucky (Webb, 1941, p. 160, fig. 14). This blade may be merely a variation of the Adena Point. Its resemblance to stemmed blades found in some late Archaic sites suggests that it may have been derived from that source. Until the exact significance of this blade can be demonstrated in Adena, it seems unwise to give it a type name.

Plate 42.   The major blade types of the Cresap Mound
A. the "Cresap points" from features in the mound floor. B. "Robbins points"
from the top zone of the Cresap Mound. C. Flat-base, straight-stemmed blades
from lower and middle zones of mound. D. "Adena leaf-shaped" blades from
lower and middle zones. E. "Adena points" from lower and middle zones of
the Cresap Mound

The leaf-shaped blades of the Cresap Mound can be duplicated at most Adena sites and thus may be considered a typical form.

The three side-notched points found in the Cresap Mound, two in the earth fill and one with a feature, were probably not of Adena manufacture but belonged to an earlier Archaic occupation present on the same terrace. They are not Adena in form or choice of material.

All the other chipped-stone items such as drills, end scrapers, and side scrapers are not unlike those that have been found at many Adena sites. These items are non-distinctive in that they are not only common to Adena but also similar to items found in cultures older and later than Adena.

Copper gorget or breastplate

A copper reel-shaped (quadriconcave) gorget was found associated with skeletal remains and other items in crematory basin, Feature 15. The measurements of this gorget are 17.55 cm. long (max.), 16.9 cm. long (min.), 11.1 cm. wide (max.), 9.2 cm. wide (min.), and 0.3 cm. thick. Like the slate gorgets of similar design from the mound there are two holes 0.35 cm. in diameter drilled through the gorget near the middle. These holes are approximately 6.0 cm. from the side edges and 4.65 cm. apart. They lie on the approximate center-line of the gorget 4.6 cm. from the top and 4.45 cm. from the bottom. (Plate 13).

When the gorget was found there were clinging to its upper surface the fragmentary remains of a fabric and a thin layer of organic material which appeared to be skin. On the under surface was an impression in the patina 2.2 cm. wide and 16.9 cm. long running the length of the gorget through the center holes. Under this impression were the decayed remains of a strip of wood which seems to have been attached to the gorget. A thin layer of organic material, probably skin, was also present under the gorget. Both surfaces are badly oxidized and several areas near the outer margins have begun to crumble.

Copper strips

A small, thin strip of copper was found near Burial 7. This strip was 3.0 cm. long, 2.3 cm. wide, and 0.07 cm. thick. It had been folded twice and then beaten flat.

Another strip of copper was found in the burned area, Feature 6, at the top of the mound. It had been folded several times and then hammered flat. It was impossible to determine accurately its original size and form. From the fragment present it was at least 20.0 cm. long, 3.5 cm. wide, and 0.05 cm. thick. (Plate 7).

Copper beads

Copper beads were associated with six burials. The provenience and description of these beads are as follows:

Burial 8. Twenty-two small rolled copper beads were on a circular string 3.5 cm. in diameter. Their location at the wrist of the burial indicated their use as a bracelet. The beads are uniform in size with an average of 0.5 cm. in diameter, 0.4 cm. long, with a hole diameter of 0.2 cm. Lying over the bracelet was a small piece of tightly woven fabric 2.8 cm. long and 1.1 cm. wide.

Burial 11. One hundred and forty-eight rolled copper beads were found on a string attached to a skin sash that extended from the waist to the left knee of Burial 11. The average size of these beads is 0.5 cm. in diameter, 0.45 cm. long, with a hole diameter of 0.2 cm. These beads tend to be "barrel-shaped."

Burial 12. Twenty-four small copper beads were found on a string near the skull fragments of Burial 12. Their position indicated their use as a necklace. The beads varied in size with the largest being 0.8 cm. in diameter, 0.4 cm. long, and with a hole diameter of 0.3 cm. The smallest bead was 0.6 cm. in diameter, 0.3 cm. long, with a hole diameter of 0.22 cm. All were rolled from strips of copper. They are "barrel-shaped" in outline.

Burial 16. Forty-three rolled copper beads were on a string near the skull of Burial 16. The beads of this probable necklace were uniform in size with the average being 0.6 cm. in diameter, 0.5 cm. in length, and the diameter of the hole being 0.2 cm. They are "barrel-shaped."

Burial 26. Fifteen small rolled copper beads were found on a broken string with bundle Burial 26. These "barrel-shaped" beads averaged 0.3 cm. in diameter, 0.27 cm. long, with a hole diameter of 0.15 cm.

Burial 45. One hundred and twenty-eight rolled copper beads were found on a string wound around the right arm and wrist of Burial 45. These "barrel-shaped" beads ranged in size from 0.55 to 0.3 cm. in diameter, 0.5 to 0.32 cm. in length, with holes 0.35 to 0.15 cm. in diameter. (Plate 19).

All of the Cresap Mound copper beads were made by rolling a thin, narrow strip of metal. After the desired overlap of a quarter to a half of the circumference was obtained, each bead was smoothed and the rough edges dulled. The beads were then placed with the hole flat and hammered enough to bulge the sides slightly to give it a "barrel-shape." The variation in size and detail indicates that each bead was carefully handcrafted.

The process of manufacture of the Cresap Mound copper beads from narrow strips of metal of the proper size conforms with evidence of a similar technique at the Natrium Mound (Solecki, 1953, p. 370) and at Beech Bottom Mound (Bache and Satterthwaite, 1930, p. 14). Although Webb and Snow's (1945, p. 99-100) suggestion that sheet copper was first rolled into a cylinder and then cut into beads may be valid for certain sites, none of the beads from the Upper Ohio Valley Adena mounds seems to have been made in this fashion.

A microscopic examination of the Cresap Mound beads lends additional support to Solecki's (1953, p. 370) findings that some heat was used in copper working. As in the Natrium Mound specimens, the grains in the copper appear to be welded together and are not easily pulled apart even when small cracks are present in the surface.

The copper gorget and all the copper beads, except those with Burial 26, were found with features on or less than 0.9 foot above the floor of the mound. The two strips of copper and one string of beads were found with features above 6.5 feet in elevation. It thus seems that copper was used as commonly in the early phases of the mound as in the later. On the basis of Webb's (1941, p. 208) chronological chart of reel forms, the Cresap Mound reel falls within the simplest and presumably earliest category. The evidence is becoming increasingly clear that the mere presence of copper is not a good indicator of lateness in Adena.

BONE ARTIFACTS

The 23 objects of bone found in the Cresap Mound were all poorly preserved and extremely fragile. Some pieces were so broken and decayed that is was impossible to determine their original size or form. The description and provenience of these items are as follows:

Bone beads. Four small bone beads were found at the neck of Burial 54. They are of the tubular type with the average size being 2.5 cm. long and 1.2 cm. in diameter. They had been cut from the long bone of a large bird. The decayed and crushed condition of these beads made identification of the species used impossible. The presence of tiny, decayed, bone fragments adjoining the four above beads indicated that others may have been originally present.

Scapular awls. Two broken awls made from the scapula of the deer were found, one with Burial 54 and the other with Burial 26. The largest of these awls was 6.7 cm. long, 1.5 cm. wide, and 0.6 cm. thick. Most of the base and the tip are missing. Only a section of the tip 3.9 cm. long of the second awl was found. (Plate 43,A).

Bone splinter awls. Five awls, three with Burial 54 and two with Burial 21, were made from small splinters of unidentifiable bone. All were broken and poorly preserved. The largest of these awls was 4.9 cm. long, 0.7 cm. wide, and 0.5 cm. thick. All appear to have been carefully polished, and sharpened to a point.

Bone spatula. A bone spatula made from the split cannon bone of either the deer or elk was found near the head of Burial 21. It is 16.5 cm. long, 3.2 cm. wide, and 1.6 cm. in maximum thickness. The bit tapers to a rounded chisel-like edge. The surface had been polished.

Antler tip. The broken tip of a deer antler that had been sharpened and polished was found with Burial 54. This item could have been used as a punch or a flint-flaking tool.

Antler knife handles. Two worked sections of antler were found in such a position as to indicate their use as knife handles. One section of antler approximately 8.5 cm. long and 2.3 cm. in diameter was found in direct alinement with an ovate-base, stemmed blade associated with Burial 21. Although poorly preserved and broken, the handle appears to have been polished and carefully fashioned. The second handle was a similar section of antler found within Burial 11. It is 10.2 cm. long, and 2.3 cm. in diameter. A broken blade was found a few inches from this poorly preserved handle.

Turtle shell cups. Three cups made from the carapaces of small box-turtles were found in association with Burial 54. Two of these cups were found just above the left shoulder of the extended burial. Inside one of these cups was a mussel shell and a piece of worked flint. The third cup was at the right hip. The only modification of these turtle carapaces was a smoothing of the lips. All were poorly preserved, and broken. Since all had been carefully placed with the opening up, it seems possible that they may have contained food when placed in the grave.

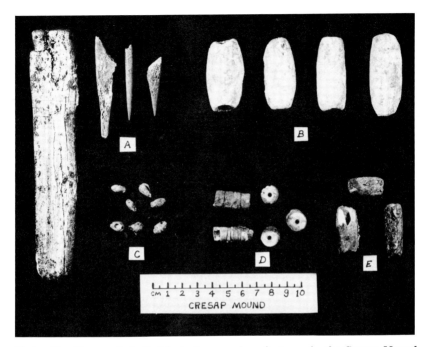

Plate 43.   Bone and shell objects from various features in the Cresap Mound
A. Bone spatula and awls. B. Large conch shell beads. C. Marginella shell
beads. D. Disk shell beads. E. Small conch shell beads

Elk antler head-dress. A unique item found in the Cresap Mound was
the fragile remains of an elk antler head-dress. It was located adjacent
to Feature 8 at an elevation of 6.5 feet above the mound floor. This
object consisted of the skullcap which had been carefully cut from the
remainder of the skull. Attached to the skullcap were the antlers from
which the distal prongs had been removed and the stubs smoothed. The
entire head-dress was so poorly preserved that it was possible to remove
intact only portions of it. Tiny roots growing through the bone had
broken it into small fragments. All observations had to be made as the
head-dress was uncovered. Fortunately, Dr. William S. Webb of the
University of Kentucky was present when this important object was
found. He was able to verify our identification of the nature of the
object and the kind of animal from which it had been made.

A head-dress made from an elk skull has not been previously reported
from an Adena mound. A copper antler head-dress, however, was

reported from the Fisher Site in Kentucky by Webb and Haag (1947, p. 76), and antler head-dresses are known to have been used earlier than Adena in the Archaic and later in Hopewell (Webb and Haag, 1947, p. 83).

Miscellaneous bone objects. One small, fragile piece of worked bone was found with Burial 21. Its fragmentary condition made it impossible to determine its form or use.

Deer antlers were found in three different areas of the mound without any definite featural associations. Because of their poor preservation, no intentional working was noted on these items.

SHELL ARTIFACTS

Disk shell beads. There are 51 shell beads of the disk type. Four of these beads were with Burial 12 and 47 were associated with Burial 54. The average size of these beads is 1.2 cm. in diameter, 0.45 cm. thick, and with a hole diameter of 0.3 cm. All of these beads were found at the neck of the respective burials where they were part of a necklace. (Plate 43,D).

Marginella beads. Forty-four of these beads made of marginella shells were found with Burial 54. Thirty-two of these beads were at the neck with the disk shell beads mentioned above. Twelve of the beads were around the right wrist. (Plate 43,C).

Large tubular beads. The large beads made from the columnella of the large conch were found in alinement over the pelvis of Burial 54. They appear to have been on a string either sewn onto a garment or held in the hands of the burial. These beads ranged from 3.2 to 4.8 cm. in length, and 1.5 to 1.7 cm. in diameter, and each had a hole diameter of about 0.7 cm. (Plate 43,B).

Small tubular beads. Six small tubular beads made from the columnella of the conch were in the string of beads at the neck of Burial 54. The average size of these beads is 3.1 cm. long, and 1.4 cm. wide, with a hole diameter of 0.6 cm. (Plate 43,E).

Mussel shells. Four shells of the fresh-water mussel were found in association with other items with three burials. One shell was in a turtle carapace cup with Burial 54. Two shells were at the skull of Burial

21, and one shell was near Burial 29. The one shell, and perhaps the others, in the turtle carapace cup was probably used as a spoon.

POTTERY

Only nine pottery sherds were found in the Cresap Mound. None of these sherds was found in direct association with a feature or burial. Eight of these sherds belong to the "Fayette Thick" type and one sherd may be classified as "Adena Plain." The description and provenience of these sherds are as follows:

"*Fayette Thick*" *pottery*. Three sherds of this type were found in the earth that filled subfloor tomb Feature 28. All three sherds are cord-marked on both the exterior and interior surfaces. They range in thickness from 1.0 to 1.7 cm. Two of the sherds have a crushed shale temper while the third was tempered with crushed igneous rock. A section of rim on one sherd has a rounded lip.

Four sherds of "Fayette Thick" were found at an elevation of 1.4 feet and just below Burial 41 and directly above subfloor tomb Feature 28. They are cordmarked on both surfaces and they are 1.4 cm. in thickness. The temper is crushed igneous rock.

One sherd of "Fayette Thick" was found at an elevation of 2.0 feet in the earth of the small mound covering Feature 29. The exterior is cord-marked but the treatment of the interior surface is unknown since it had crumbled away. The temper is crushed igneous rock. (Plate 44,A).

"*Adena Plain*" *pottery*. One rim sherd of "Adena Plain" pottery was found on the surface of the large inner mound that had its peak at the 13.25 foot level. It thus was in the earth that was added with the final addition to the mound. Both surfaces of this sherd are plain. The small section of rim has a flattened lip. The tempering is crushed igneous rock. (Plate 44,B).

Heavy, cordmarked pottery of the "Fayette Thick" type is the earliest known pottery in the Upper Ohio Valley where it has been found in stratified sites to a depth of eight feet. "Fayette Thick" is known from many Adena mounds and Griffin (in Webb and Snow, 1945, p. 244) has suggested that this type is associated with the early manifestations of Adena. At the Cresap Mound this type is confined to the earliest stages of the mound.

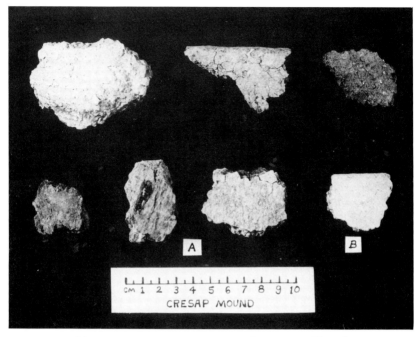

Plate 44.   Pottery types from the Cresap Mound
A. "Fayette Thick" sherds from the lower zones.   B. "Adena Plain" from the
top zone

The presence of the "Adena Plain" sherd in the last level of Cresap Mound seems to attest to its lateness and lends support to the belief that "Adena Plain" was most popular during late Adena times.

Miscellaneous Objects

Textiles and skins. Only one small fragment of textile that had been preserved by the copper salts from the string of copper beads with Burial 9 was found in the mound. This scrap of fabric, 1.4 by 3.9 cm., lay over the copper beads and is probably only the remnant of a larger piece of cloth. Although the specimen is poorly preserved, the type of weave appears to be plain twining. The warp and weft in the simple weave are of approximately the same size. Directly under the fabric and copper beads was a thin layer of organic material that looked like the remains of a hide.

Remnants of a thin organic material were also found in association with copper in two other features. The string of copper beads with Burial 12 appeared to have been sewn on a strip of skin. A similar organic material was found under the copper gorget in Feature 15.

Fragments of cords were found with all the beads. These cords seem to have been made of single narrow strips of hide that had been rolled and twisted. These cords average 0.15 cm. in diameter.

Basketry. The powdery fragments of a small shallow basket were uncovered in Feature 15. Little more than an impression remained of this interesting object and the few fibers that were still intact soon crumpled when exposed to the air. It was possible, however, to determine its size which was 21.6 cm. in diameter and 5.1 cm. in depth. It was of a shallow bowl shape. The weave was a simple basket-weave or plain plaiting where the weft movement is over one and under one warp strand. The weft and warp strands were small and tightly woven.

Mineral deposits. Several mineral deposits were found with features and burials in the mound. Although not strictly artifacts by the usual definition of the term, they are important, intentionally deposited items that have been in some instances modified by man. The following minerals were found in the Cresap Mound.

Red ocher. Red ocher was a common inclusion in 23 of the features and was present on or near 31 of the burials. Generally the ocher was sprinkled over the surface of the feature or around the burial. Occasionally, a small pile of ocher was present. None of these piles of ocher contained more than five ounces of the mineral.

Red ocher is an iron compound commonly derived from the earthy and pulverulent forms of hematite and limonite. Red ocher seldom occurs in nature in a condition where it can be used without modification. It usually must be washed, pulverized, and subjected to heat. Impurities such as oxides of other metals and argillaceous matter must be removed to obtain a pure red ocher. These impurities were nearly always retained in the red ocher prepared by the Indians. The color of the ocher obtained by the crude methods used varied with the impurities present and the amount of oxidation and hydration.

The color of red ocher may be varied by the heat to which it is subjected. All deposits of red ocher found in the Cresap Mound had been heated. All shades from dark red to brilliant crimson were present.

None of the ocher had the dark-brown color of the powder that would have been derived directly from the pieces of hematite found associated with several features in the mound.

In connection with the large red ocher deposits found in the Natrium Mound, Solecki (1953, p. 387) has called attention to the problem of whether or not the red ocher was intentionally roasted by the Adena people to change its color. It is possible that the intense heat that had been present in many of the features in the Natrium Mound and Cresap Mound contributed to the color change in the ocher without any specific intent on the part of the people involved. I believe, however, that the change was so obvious that it was consciously desired.

It is suggestive that a phenomenon in which a drab, dark-brown substance was suddenly transformed into a brilliant crimson would have mystical meaning to a primitive people. The presence of red ocher almost exclusively with the remains of the dead and the objects placed with them seems to indicate clearly that any special meanings attached to this substance pertained to the burial ceremonies. The actual content and significance of the belief held by these people will probably always be beyond the means of archeologists to ascertain.

The finding of roasted red ocher with burials or features where no evidence of heat was discernable would indicate that the ocher was either roasted in another feature, particularly a crematory basin, and then removed for redeposit, or the ocher was especially prepared in a fire made just for that purpose. Since no feature assignable to this latter purpose has been found in Adena, red ocher may have been prepared only in conjunction with the activities centered around the fires of the burial ceremonies.

Solecki (1953, p. 388), in his study of the red ocher found in the Natrium Mound, discovered that phosphate was often present in the red ocher. Phosphate was present also in several of the Cresap Mound samples tested. Since phosphate is not a normal contaminant of red ocher, it appears that this substance, which can best be derived from bone, became either accidentally or intentionally mixed with the ocher in the crematory fires. A mixture of red ocher and a whitish substance high in phosphate was present on some of the tablets found in the Cresap Mound (Dragoo, 1959, p. 141). This mixture was probably used as a paint to mark the participants in the burial rite as well as the body of the deceased. The blending of red ocher with the bone phosphates from the crematory fires seems to lend additional support to the contention that the ocher was primarily prepared in these fires.

Yellow ocher. This form of ocher was rare in the Cresap Mound. The only deposit of any size was found in Feature 15. It consisted of a small pile containing about two ounces. Faint traces of this substance were present in several other features where it seems to have been sprinkled sparingly over the feature's surface along with red ocher. The use of yellow ocher was probably the same as that of red ocher.

Graphite. This mineral was found in association with other items in two features below the floor of the mound and with an extended burial directly on the mound floor. In all three instances the deposits consisted of a small pile of the substance in the form of small grains or pebbles varying in size from 0.4 to 1.2 cm. in greatest diameter. No more than two tablespoonfuls of the substance were present in any of these deposits.

The deposit of graphite found in the north end of crematory basin Feature 10 was packed tightly in a mass with its height being greater than its width. Around the lumps of graphite was a dark, organic stain. Because of the unusual position of the grains and the organic stain, it seemed obvious that the graphite had been in a small skin container or bag that had held the grains in the odd position in which they were found. If the grains had been placed loosely in a pile on the bottom of the basin, their position would have been that of a small mound with its greatest dimension horizontally rather than vertically (Plate 11).

The other two graphite deposits were both associated with burials. One deposit was at the right shoulder of Burial 11, and the other deposit was at the left shoulder of Burial 54 in Feature 28. Both of these deposits consisted of tightly clustered grains of graphite with a dark organic stain around them, These grains seem to have been in bags also. All the grains were highly polished as if they had probably been rubbed against each other in the bags for a considerable time.

Webb and Snow (1945, p. 79) report the use of graphite for the painting of the wide band across the forehead of Burial 11 in Mound Be20 in Kentucky. No use of this substance as a pigment was noted for the Cresap Mound, but the finding of graphite in bags placed at the shoulders of two burials suggests that it may have been used for something besides pigment. It is certainly possible that graphite was carried by some individuals for use as paint, but the container of graphite may have served also as a medicine bag. That the bag and its contents had more than passing significance seems to be clearly indicated by its placement with the burials in an almost identical fashion.

Manganese dioxide. Two small deposits of manganese dioxide were found. One deposit was between the legs of extended Burial 11 and the other deposit was at the left side of Burial 54 in Feature 28. These deposits consisted of a few granules of bluish manganese dioxide and associated discolored earth. The only other reported occurrence of this substance in an Adena mound was a similar deposit in the Natrium Mound (Solecki, 1953, p. 386). This substance was probably used as a paint pigment.

ADENA IN THE UPPER OHIO VALLEY

DISTRIBUTION OF UPPER OHIO VALLEY ADENA SITES

With the picture of the Cresap Mound in mind, let us now turn our attention to the overall content and distribution of known Adena sites in the Upper Ohio Valley. Webb and Snow (1945, p. 132) recognized two major centers of Adena occupation, one along the Scioto River in southern Ohio and the second on the Kanawha River near Charleston, W. Va. Smaller centers were located in eastern Indiana, northern Kentucky, western Ohio, and northeastern West Virginia. The most eastern of these lesser centers was in the Upper Ohio Valley with its center at the great Grave Creek Mound at Moundsville, W. Va. (Map 2).

Within the immediate area of Moundsville, W. Va., 47 mounds and evidence of a wall of earth were recorded by De Haas (n. d.) and Hennen (1909, p. 12). Most of these mounds have been destroyed within recent years by the encroachment of industry along the banks of the Ohio River. Nearly all the available information on Adena in this area comes from this present report on the Cresap Mound and the reports of the excavations conducted at the Grave Creek Mound (Narona, 1957), Beech Bottom Mound (Bache and Satterthwaite, 1930), the Natrium Mound (Solecki, 1953), and the Half-Moon Mound (Fetzer and Mayer-Oakes, 1951). The Welcome Mound, located near Natrium, W. Va., excavated in the fall of 1957 by Dr. Frank M. Setzler (1960) was also of Adena origin. All of these mounds were typical Adena conical earth structures. The major features and the material traits of these mounds are summarized later in this section.

Moving north and east up the Ohio River from Moundsville, the number and size of earth mounds believed to be of Adena origin decrease as we approach Pittsburgh. A few small mounds have been listed (Mayer-Oakes, 1955) and several mounds have been reported by local residents of the area as having been destroyed many years ago.

There are several sites scattered along the Ohio River up to Pittsburgh, in addition to mounds, on which characteristic Adena traits have been found on the surface or eroding out of the banks of the river. Important among these items are fragments of blocked-end tubular pipes, reel-shaped gorgets, stemmed points of Adena type, and "Fayette Thick" pottery.

At the Watson Site in Hancock County, W. Va., "Fayette Thick" pottery was found stratigraphically below a Hopewellian burial mound

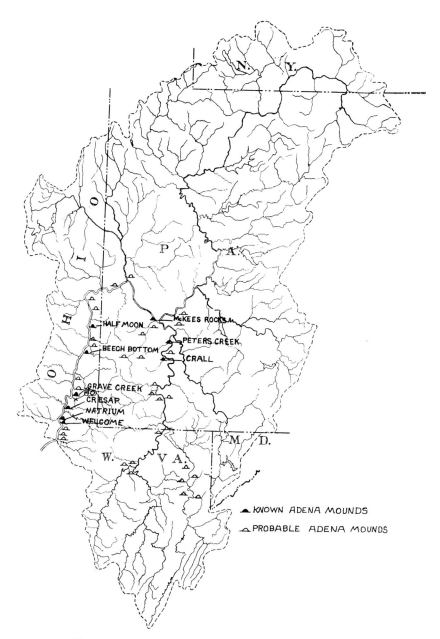

Map 2.   Major Adena mounds in the Upper Ohio Valley

constructed of stone (Dragoo, 1956). On the surface of this site were found stemmed points and fragments of gorgets drilled from one side only in the typical Adena fashion. A small earth mound was reported by the local residents to have been removed many years ago from the upper terrace of this site. A small conical mound approximately 30 feet in diameter and four feet in height similar to the one reported at the Watson Site still stands on the high terrace at the old Hewitt farm a short distance to the north.

Pottery of "Fayette Thick" type was found by Mayer-Oakes (1955, p. 178-181) at the lowest levels of the Georgetown Site in Beaver County, Pa. A radiocarbon date of 173±200 B.C. was obtained for the upper level of the deposit containing these sherds (Mayer-Oakes, 1958, p. 13). "Fayette Thick" sherds, or "Half-Moon Cordmarked", according to Mayer-Oakes's terminology, were found also to a depth of 18 inches below the dated carbon. The stratigraphic position of "Fayette Thick" pottery at the lowest levels at the Georgetown Site, Watson Site, and other stratified sites in the Upper Ohio Valley clearly indicates Adena priority as the first bearers of pottery to inhabit the area.

Along the Ohio River on the bluff at McKees Rocks just below the junction of the Allegheny and Monongahela rivers at Pittsburgh, was the largest Adena mound east of Moundsville. This mound was partially excavated by Carnegie Museum in 1896. Around this mound within a radius of 10 miles were several smaller mounds. All of these smaller mounds were destroyed by the expanding city of Pittsburgh before they could be properly excavated. The few notes on these mounds available in the files of Carnegie Museum are of little use in their cultural identification. Some of these mounds, perhaps most of them, were probably of Adena origin.

Assuming that Adena spread eastward up the Ohio Valley from the centers in Ohio and West Virginia, at Pittsburgh the Adena people were faced with the choice of either turning southward into the Monongahela Valley or northward up the Allegheny and Beaver valleys. The Monongahela Valley seems to have been more to their liking, but the northward routes were not completely ignored.

Thomas (1894, p. 494-499) in his survey of the Monongahela Valley reported seeing a number of small earth mounds, as well as several mounds constructed of stone. One of these mounds, the Crall Mound, was excavated by Thomas, and the mound structure and artifacts have been classified as typical of Adena by Webb and Snow (1945, p. 114).

We can only surmise that the other mounds were also of Adena origin since Thomas (1894, p. 494) stated that they had been repeatedly disturbed prior to 1894, and in recent years, industrial expansion in the Monongahela Valley has almost completely destroyed the remains. The Crall Mound and its contents are discussed more thoroughly later in this section.

In 1890, a small Adena earth mound known as the Peters Creek Mound was excavated in the Monongahela Valley some 20 miles south of Pittsburgh (Schooley, 1902). Several other small mounds in the surrounding area seem to have been Adena, but their contents were so meager that positive identification is impossible. Among these mounds are the Sheppler Mound (Engberg, 1930) and a small earth mound near Mapleton in Greene County, Pa., reported by Farabee (1919). Mayer-Oakes (1955, p. 94) reported that "a semi-keeled gorget of the Adena type" was found in a small earth mound, now destroyed, in Washington County, Pa. In the spring of 1955, a small earth mound at the north edge of the town of Washington, Pa., was bulldozed away for top-soil. Within this mound were the badly decayed remains of extended burials and bits of burned human bones. No artifacts were found, but the hill-top location of the mound and the scarcity of Hopewellian materials in the area would indicate that this mound was also Adena.

Some of the stone mounds in the Monongahela Valley appear to have been of Adena origin. The Pollock's Hill Mound reported by Cadzow (1933) and the Linn Mound reported by Dragoo (1955) are typical examples of small stone mounds containing Adena traits. As will be discussed in more detail in a later section, these stone mounds were probably constructed late in Adena times.

A number of stone mounds have been reported on the hilltops and along the terrace of the Cheat River, a major tributary of the Mononga-hela, in West Virginia (Hayden, 1941, p. 5-7; Dragoo, 1955). Some of the mounds are entirely of stone, while others contain more earth than stone. None has been scientifically excavated and reported. Surface collections taken by the author from village areas near these mounds contained items assignable to Adena. Some of the stone mounds are more than 125 miles south of Pittsburgh, but the most southerly earth mound of any size is located at Point Marion where the Cheat River enters the Monogahela some 60 miles from Pittsburgh. The contents of this mound are unknown.

No earth mounds are known for the drainage of the Youghiogheny, the major eastern tributary of the Monongahela, but small stone mounds, some of which may be of Adena origin, have been located as far east as Garrett County, Md. Stemmed points, gorget fragments, and pottery sherds similar to "Fayette Thick" have been found on village sites near these mounds. In Garrett County, Md., the drainage basins of the Ohio and Potomac rivers are separated only by a narrow mountainous ridge that can easily be crossed. The presence of Adena-like points and gorget fragments, some of the Ohio Valley raw materials, in surface collections from the Potomac Valley indicates that this route was used by some Adena peoples in their eastward movement.

Only a few mounds have been reported for the Beaver Valley in western Pennsylvania and eastern Ohio (Miller, 1878; Magrath, 1945; Mayer-Oakes, 1955). The materials found in these structures appear to be more closely related to Hopewell than to Adena. Several small stone mounds situated on hilltops overlooking village sites along the tributaries of the Beaver River have been located recently. The cultural affinity of these structures is unknown. On nearby village sites, especially those nearest to the Ohio River, both Adena and Hopewell materials have been found.

Among the important Adena traits found in surface collections from the Beaver Valley are blocked-end tubular pipes, reel-shaped gorgets, expanded-center gorgets, Adena stemmed points, and variations of "Fayette Thick" pottery.

The absence of any large Adena mounds in the Beaver Valley would seem to indicate that this area was peripheral to the settlements in the Ohio River Valley proper.

The Allegheny Valley is of considerable interest in tracing the distribution of Adena because it forms the most direct water highway from the Ohio Valley into New York and the Northeast where the Adena-like Middlesex complex has been found (Ritchie, 1944; Ritchie and Dragoo, 1959).

No earth mounds of definite Adena origin are known for the upper Allegheny Valley. The Oakmont Mound and the Darlington Mound, both located along the lower Allegheny near Pittsburgh, may have been Adena, but the information is so inconclusive that they could also be classified as of the later Hopewellian period. Several stone mounds have been studied in the middle and upper Allegheny Valley (Schmitt, 1952).

Plate 45. Tubular pipes of fireclay from the Allegheny Valley
A and B. Two unfinished. C. A finished blocked-end tubular pipe found as
part of a cache of six at Kinzua, Pa. (In the collection of Earl Parker at
Brookville, Pa.)

All of these structures have contained Hopewellian traits rather than
Adena.

Items assignable to Adena, however, have been found on several village sites scattered throughout the entire Allegheny Valley. Among the
most diagnostic of these items are blocked-end tubular pipes of fireclay,
"cigar-shaped" open-end tubes, and expanded-center bar gorgets.
(Plate 45).

One of the most interesting finds was a cache of six tubular pipes
found at Kinzua in Warren County, Pa. Three of these pipes now in the
collection of Earl Parker of Brookville, Pa., were illustrated by Mayer-
Oakes (1955, p. 63). Although these pipes were apparently with burials, there was no obvious mound covering them.

In a collection of artifacts recently donated to Carnegie Museum by
Walter Stein of Pittsburgh from site 36A119 was a cache of Adena
stemmed points and a crude grooved tablet found in the bank of the

Allegheny River at the suburb of Blawnox near Pittsburgh. No definite mound was present.

In summary, the distribution of Adena components in the Upper Ohio Valley is one of decreasing magnitude as we move eastward from the Moundsville, W. Va., area. Burial mounds decrease both in number and size with the McKees Rocks Mound near Pittsburgh representing the most eastern Adena structure of sizable proportions. Only in the Monongahela Valley to the south of Pittsburgh were there Adena earth mounds of any number. Even these mounds were relatively small when compared to the one located along the Ohio River. It is also of interest to note that the Monongahela mounds were within a radius of 50 miles overland from the concentration of mounds at Moundsville. Overland trails probably linked these areas. Stone and earth mounds, of probable Adena origin, along the Cheat and Youghiogheny tributaries of the Monongahela, have been found as far as eastern West Virginia and western Maryland.

Except in the area around Pittsburgh, no mounds of Adena have been found in the upper Allegheny or Beaver valleys. Adena traits are found, however, on a number of village sites along these streams as far north as New York state. The absence of mounds in these areas would indicate that no large numbers of Adena people ever lived in the Allegheny or Beaver valleys.

The specific cultural traits present in the Upper Ohio Valley Adena sites, in addition to those already presented for the Cresap Mound, can best be demonstrated by a detailed look at Grave Creek Mound, Beech Bottom Mound, Natrium Mound, Half-Moon Mound, and Welcome Mound in West Virginia, and McKees Rocks Mound, Crall Mound, and Peters Creek Mound in Pennsylvania. Of the information available on the contents of these mounds, only the report on the Natrium Mound gives full details of the complete excavation and findings.

Grave Creek Mound

The most famous Adena site in the Upper Ohio Valley is the Grave Creek Mound at Moundsville, W. Va. It is believed to be the largest of all Adena mounds. Its original dimensions as measured by road engineers in 1838 were 69 feet in height, 295 feet in diameter at the base and 60 feet in diameter at its flat top. The mound was a symmetrical cone with a flat top surrounded by a low parapet. The entire mound was surrounded by a ditch crossed by two passageways. Erosion caused by many partial attempts at excavation has reduced the mound's height and has completely filled the moat with earth. Within recent years the mound has been protected and erosion stopped by the joint efforts of the West Virginia Archeological Society and the state of West Virginia. The mound and a small museum at its base are now major tourist attractions in Moundsville. A book by Delf Narona (1957) traces the history of the mound and the depredations waged upon it. (Fig. 6).

Since our information on the internal structure of the Grave Creek Mound and its contents is confined to early accounts of the digging of pits and tunnels by amateurs, it is often difficult to assign specific materials to proper levels within the mound. Evidently the mound was built in several stages after the initial burial of a few individuals in a primary log tomb at or below the base of the mound.

Among the known objects removed from the Grave Creek Mound are over two thousand disk shell beads, several hundred marginella shell beads, an expanded-center bar gorget, a long diamond-shaped gorget, five copper bracelets found around the wrists of a burial, many fragments of mica found with a burial in the upper part of the mound, and an engraved stone tablet.

The expanded-center bar gorget and some of the beads were found in the lower burial chamber. The mica fragments, copper bracelets, and some of the marginella beads were found with a burial in an upper vault of the mound that was part of a late stage in the mound's construction.

The engraved stone tablet from the Grave Creek Mound has been the object of many discussions concerning its authenticity. Webb and Baby (1957, p. 33-37) in their study of the history of the tablet have shown that there were several versions by different people as to how the tablet was actually found. The inscription on this tablet sets it apart from all other Adena tablets for which sufficient documentation as to provenience can be demonstrated.

Although our picture of the interior of the Grave Creek Mound and its artifacts is sketchy, this mound was not only larger, but also seems to have been more elaborate in construction, than any other mound in the Upper Ohio Valley. The tombs were reported to have been of heavy crib-like construction in contrast to the simple pits with small log coverings found in the Cresap and Natrium mounds. The superimposition of tombs would clearly indicate multiple stages in the mound's construction. Most of the known traits, however, of the mound appear to be of

Fig. 6. A view of the Grave Creek Mound at Moundsville, W. Va., as published by Squier and Davis in 1848

late Adena origin. Among the traits that are indicative of this lateness are log tombs, the expanded-center bar gorget, the heavy copper bracelets, mica, the presence of a large ditch around the base of the mound, and the flattened top of the mound surrounded by a low parapet. The finding of some of these traits all the way to the base of the mound would indicate that even the initial construction was started in late Adena times. As will be discussed in more detail later in this report, the Grave Creek Mound seems more closely related to the late Kentucky mounds than to the nearby Cresap and Natrium mounds. Only the top level of the Cresap Mound would seem to be comparable in time.

Natrium Mound

The Natrium Mound in Marshall County, W. Va., was excavated by Ralph Solecki for the Smithsonian Institution during December 1948 and part of January 1949. This mound, approximately six miles down the Ohio River from the Cresap Mound, yielded a wealth of artifactual and osseous remains in its lower levels. The top of the Natrium Mound had been destroyed by previous digging.

The Natrium Mound was 65 feet in diameter at the base and 12 feet in height. Within it were 51 features, of which 22 were definitely burials. Several other features were also believed to have contained burials in which the skeletal evidence had disappeared (Solecki, 1953, p. 317). Thirty-six of the mound and burial traits of the Natrium Mound corresponded to those published by Webb and Snow (1945) for Adena. The more important of these traits were stratigraphy within the mound indicating a primary and secondary structure, primary purpose of mound to cover burials, simple horizontal log tomb built on bark-covered clay floor, subfloor pit, cremated remains in situ, redeposited cremated remains, artifacts burned with the body, extended burial in log tomb, extended burials in mound, intentionally mutilated artifacts placed with burials, and red ocher on both cremations and extended burials as well as on the artifacts.

Thirty-eight of the artifact traits of Natrium Mound were on the 1945 Adena trait list of Webb and Snow, while 11 new traits were found which have been added recently to the list by Webb and Baby (1957). Since the majority of these traits are typically Adena and similar to those of the Cresap Mound, our attention here will be only to the most significant ones as the total Natrium traits are also included on the trait list in this section (Fig. 7 and 8).

The effigy birdstone found at Natrium Mound was the first one definitely recorded for an Adena mound, although a similar birdstone was purported to have come from a mound in Kentucky (Webb and Baby, 1957, p. 28). This specimen of sandstone with conical perforations in its base is of the bust type representing only a small percentage of the total number of all types of birdstones. Webb and Baby (1957, p. 28) made the following statement concerning this birdstone:

"It can hardly be doubted that the placing of a bust-type birdstone with the remains of a cremation, re-deposited in an Adena mound, is a definite but rare

Fig. 7. Typical objects from the Natrium Mound, Marshall County, W. Va. A. "Cresap" stemmed blade; B and C. "Adena" ovate-base stemmed blades. D. "Adena" leaf-shaped blade. E and F. Drills. G. Modified tubular pipe. H. Slate pendant. I. Blocked-end tubular pipe. (After Solecki, 1953.)

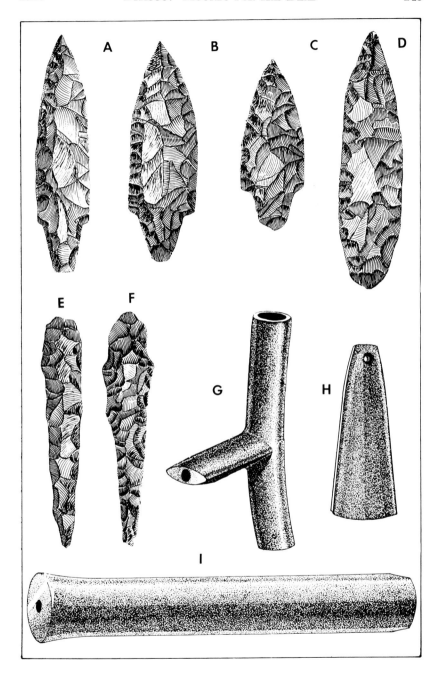

trait in Adena. This type of birdstone may well have been used on an atlatl, since it is perforated at the base. The evidences of the use of the atlatl by Adena people, as manifested by the occurrence of antler handles, expanded bar gorgets, and keel-shaped bar gorgets, increase as excavations are extended."

Although Webb and Baby have included the bust-type birdstone as an Adena trait, I am still rather skeptical of its Adena origin. The similarity of the Natrium specimen to those found in the Point Peninsula culture of New York State indicates that the bust-type birdstone may be derived from that area (Ritchie, 1938, p. 223). The study of birdstones made by Townsend (1959) indicates that these objects are more common in the areas just below the Great Lakes than in the Ohio Valley (Fig. 9).

A boatstone from the Natrium Mound was the first definitely known to have been in an Adena mound; although similar objects were reported from the Fisher Site in Fayette County, Ky., by Webb and Haag (1947). The keeled boatstone from the Cresap Mound is additional evidence for the presence of this type of object in Adena.

Three tubular pipes of the blocked-end type and one modified tubular pipe were recovered from the Natrium Mound (Solecki, 1953, p. 375). The blocked-end tubular pipes are similar to the specimens from the Cresap Mound and the Beech Bottom Mound, but the modified tubular pipe with a short stem set at right angles to the cylindrical bowl is more like specimens from Kentucky (Webb and Baby, 1957, p. 21).

Several other traits from the Natrium Mound are of particular interest. Among these are pearl beads, a copper reel-shaped gorget, celts with rectangular polls, hematite hemispheres, and crude grooved stone tablets. All of these items, except the pearl beads, were duplicated in the objects of the Cresap Mound.

There is a striking resemblance, both in the artifacts and the mound features, between the Natrium Mound and the middle and lower levels of the Cresap Mound. The importance of this resemblance is discussed in detail later in this section.

Fig. 8. Typical objects from the Natrium Mound, Marshall County, W. Va. A. Quadriconcave gorget of copper. B. Semi-keeled gorget of slate. C. Small celt of igneous stone. D. Large celt of igneous stone. E. Small celt of hematite. F. Hemisphere of hematite. G. Faceted lump of hematite. H. Natural ferruginous cup-stone showing aboriginal adaptation to use. I. Crude grooved tablet with associated piece of faceted hematite. (After Solecki, 1953.)

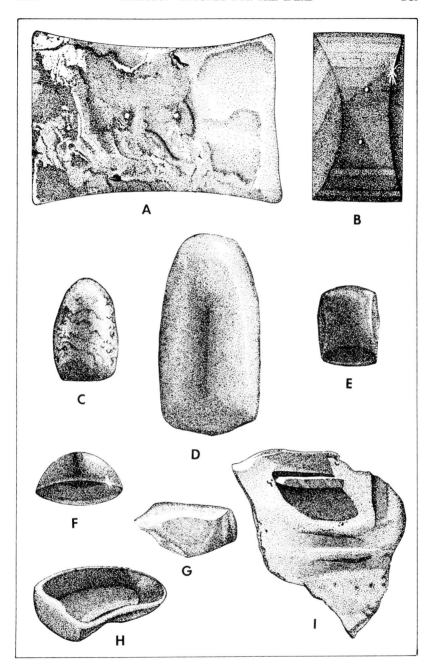

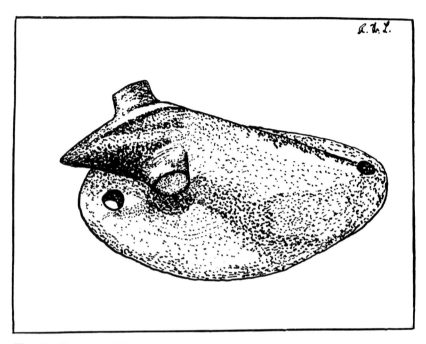

Fig. 9. Bust-type birdstone found in Natrium Mound, Marshall County, W. Va. Length 7.0 cm., width 4.1 cm., height 4.5 cm. (After Solecki, 1953.)

Beech Bottom Mound

The Beech Bottom Mound, partially excavated by Bache and Satterthwaite (1930, p. 133-187), contained a number of interesting objects and features. The number and types of objects found in this mound warrant a critical re-examination in the light of the information now known for the Cresap Mound and the Natrium Mound.

This mound, located 14 miles north of Wheeling, W. Va., along the Ohio River, was approximately 70 feet in diameter and 13 feet in height. Bache and Satterthwaite (1930, p. 156) believed that "the mound was built as a unit—if not at one time, at least according to one plan." In a subfloor pit near the center of the mound was found the only burial. They (1930, p. 157) stated that there was "little doubt that the mound and contents, so far as we excavated, pertains to the burial which we found." They felt certain that there were no other subfloor features, but they were uncertain as to whether other burials could have been present. It is unfortunate that the entire structure of the mound could not have been ascertained by complete excavation.

Bache and Satterthwaite (1930, p. 157-161) believed the sequence of events at the Beech Bottom Mound to be much as follows. A dark layer of earth had been spread in an irregular ring at the base of the mound. Through the dark layer of earth an oval pit 3.50 meters long by 1.30 meters wide was dug to a depth of 1.40 meters. The coarse sandy subsoil was thrown from the pit over the dark soil surrounding the pit. Near the south end of the pit there had been a fire on a smoothed area of the dark soil. The subsoil from the pit had covered this area indicating that the fire had been built there before the completion of the burial pit.

The burial pit was then lined with bark and the body of an adult male was extended in the grave on its back with the arms at the sides and the legs slightly bowed somewhat in the fashion of Burial 54 in the Cresap Mound. The head was towards the south. Three or four chains of discoidal shell beads and a string of tubular shell beads were placed across the face and neck. On the right shoulder was a bone flaking tool, and under the right scapula was a crude stemmed blade. Strings of rolled copper beads and tubular shell beads were laid across the chest and down the left side to the hip. Copper beads and discoidal shell beads were placed along the right side of the burial, and copper beads were across the waist and out over both arms, just above the wrists. Tubular shell beads had been down from the waist and out across the left femur. From the region of the left wrist down across the femurs up to the right wrist were looped strings of copper beads.

Between the femurs just above the knees were two strings of tubular and one of discoidal shell beads. Under these beads were a large blocked-end tubular pipe and the tip of a broken stemmed blade. From these beads between the femurs, two or three strings of copper beads led to a mass of all kinds of copper and shell beads that covered the lower half of the tibia and feet to a depth of 7.0 cm. Under this mass of stringed beads were large numbers of marginella and olivela shells that appeared to be in sheets rather than strings. Associated with these beads were two beaver incisors, an eagle claw, two tiny rodent jaws, and a broken bone "knife." These small beads were probably sewn onto a fabric or skin. The beaver incisor, eagle claw, and rodent jaws seem most likely to have been the contents of a medicine bag. Another sheet of small beads and strings of discoidal beads was found immediately to the right of the tibia on the bark lining of the grave.

Surrounding the body were a number of objects on the floor of the grave. Above the right shoulder of the burial was a cluster of 10 leaf-shaped blades and several broken pieces of blocked-end tubular pipes. Near and above the left shoulder were four rounded-base stemmed blades and one broken blade. To the west of these objects near the side of the grave were one blocked-end tubular pipe, one leaf-shaped blade, and one piece of worked stone. Near the right femur was one rounded-base stemmed blade, and lying across the right elbow was a modified tubular pipe (Bache and Satterthwaite, 1930, plate XIV, fig. 1). There were two celts, one near the left ankle associated with a broken tubular pipe and another near the right ankle. A bone handle was near the right shoulder, and close to a bone flint-flaking tool. Fragments of tubular pipes were found at the foot of the burial and at the right elbow. Deposits of graphite were located near the left elbow, left knee, and along the east side of the grave opposite the right knee. A deposit of yellow ocher was near the blades at the left shoulder and traces of red ocher occurred on some of the artifacts in the grave.

Bache and Satterthwaite (1930, p. 158-161) believed that, after the placement of the burial and the above objects the burial was then covered with a layer of yellow sand and the grave then filled with dark soil. In or on this dark soil were one hematite celt, four leaf-shaped blades, five stemmed blades, two notched points, four broken blade tips, 17 broken large sections and many small fragments of tubular pipes, and four animal bones, one of which was believed to be buffalo (Bison). On the basis of our present knowledge of animal remains at sites in the Upper Ohio Valley, I am inclined to believe that this bone was elk rather than buffalo. Bache and Satterthwaite conjectured that the above items had been tossed into the grave, since they seemed to be in no order except their slight concentration along the east side of the grave.

Pieces of charcoal and dark earth were found in the same area with the above items but Bache and Satterthwaite (1930, p. 158) stated that it "is hardly sufficient evidence of a fire having been kindled in the grave." The evidence of fire in subfloor grave, Feature 28, and in other features of the Cresap Mound would indicate that a similar situation could have existed at the Beech Bottom Mound.

Another cache of materials was found in the dark soil filling the grave near the top of the pit. In this cache were two complete and three broken leaf-shaped blades, and a long section of a broken tubular pipe. Twenty-four small tube fragments were nearby, placed close together in roughly parallel rows with the concave side up. Scattered about this cache on the same level were two tube sections, one leaf-shaped blade, one broken blade stem, one broken point, one celt, one piece of bone, and some mussel-shells.

Over the grave and the above items a thick layer of dark earth had been spread. This layer of earth seems to have been the beginning of a small primary mound to which additional objects and dark earth were gradually added until its apex was reached at about 2.60 meters above the base of the mound. Among the objects found in the upper portions of this small mound were caches of blades, single blades, celts, tubes, a slate gorget, and a slate pendant. Many of these items were associated with bark. There was a liberal use of red ocher to cover the artifacts and it was also deposited in lumps and scattered through the mound. On what seems to have been the top of this small primary mound, there were found a tubular pipe, 14 blades, and two lumps of red ocher. In a disturbed area dug by prior investigators down in the primary, six additional tube fragments were found. Bache and Satterthwaite (1930, p. 160) state that "the whole structure (the dark primary) was now covered with a thick layer of yellow surface soil and the mound was complete."

In summarizing the contents of the primary mound Bache and Satterthwaite (1930, p. 160) stated the following:

"There seem to have been four distinguishable periods when most of the objects were placed: the arrangement and decoration of the body, with careful placing of objects, yellow ochre and graphite about it, and with some breakages of tubes and blades; the period during which the grave was filled, characterized by much breakage, with but little careful placing of objects; and the periods when the cone had risen to the 1.25-1.50 level and again when it was about complete, each characterized by the careful placing of many objects and of red ochre, and probably not accompanied by ceremonial breaking."

In addition to the above quotation, I am particularly interested in Bache and Satterthwaite's (1930, p. 160) statement that the dark soil cap or primary mound over the grave "presented the aspect of a truncated cone resting on its base, with a large shallow funnel hollowed out of it at the centre, the bottom of the funnel plugged up with dark soil, its sides consisting of mixed earth, especially toward the bottom." In contrast to the orderly constructional sequence given by Bache and Satterthwaite, I believe that the above funnel-shaped depression and the lenses of soil seen dipping into the grave were caused by the collapse of a roof of small logs that originally covered the grave. In this event, the disorder mentioned for the materials found in the plug of earth in the grave becomes clear since this earth and the materials placed in it had shifted and collapsed downward. The order in which the artifacts in the upper portion of the primary were found would indicate that these materials were placed there after the collapse had taken place. I also suspect that most of these items, if not all, had been placed in definite features that had contained originally human remains that had completely decayed.

The subfloor grave and its contents and the primary mound and its contents compared very favorably with similar features found both in the Cresap and Natrium mounds. Among the most distinctive cross traits were leaf-shaped blades, rounded-base stemmed blades, blocked-end tubular pipes, rectangular poll celts, rolled copper beads, disk shell beads, marginella beads, columnella shell beads, graphite deposits, concretionary cupstones, crude tablet or abrading stones, barite hemisphere, slate pendant, and a reel-shaped gorget.

By far the most spectacular items from the Beech Bottom Mound were the blocked-end tubular pipes. The large number of these pipes present was very unusual. There were 32 identifiable pipes and sufficient fragments to indicate that even more tubular pipes were present. Most of the pipes had been intentionally broken in typically Adena fashion. The presence of so many pipes in this mound leads one to suspect that a particular cult group within Adena may have been involved in the mound's construction.

Two other pipes of different types from this mound are of interest. First, the modified tubular pipe found with the burial in the subfloor grave does not seem out of place in Adena since it occurred at the Natrium Mound (Solecki, 1953, p. 361) and at the Fisher Site (Webb and Haag, 1947, p. 56). The second pipe, a platform style, is most unusual. Unfortunately, the exact provenience of this pipe in the mound was unknown since it had been removed by the workmen after the departure of Bache and Satterthwaite. This pipe has generally been considered of Hopewellian origin, but its appearance is also similar to platform pipes reported for the Point Peninsula Culture in New York (Ritchie, 1944, p. 169). A crude birdstone found on the surface near the Beech Bottom Mound also resembles a similar specimen from the Point Peninsula component at the Oberlander Site, No. 2 (Ritchie, 1944, p. 153).

Several small notched points and a full-grooved ax found in the earth fill of the upper part of the Beech Bottom Mound were certainly not of Adena origin (Bache and Satterthwaite, 1930, plates XXI and XXIV). These items were all typical of the preceding Archaic culture that inhabited many of the areas in the Ohio Valley later built upon by Adena (Dragoo, 1959). The presence of such items in later Adena mounds should not warrant their inclusion as Adena traits (Webb and Baby, 1957, p. 27).

On the basis of the sequence of materials found in the Cresap Mound, I am inclined to place the Beech Bottom Mound towards the end of middle Adena times. The rounded base stemmed blades of the Beech Bottom Mound tended to be broader and have shoulders more distinct than those from either the lower levels of the Cresap Mound or the Natrium Mound. With the exception of one blade (Bache and Satterthwaite, 1930, plate XXIII, no. 4), none of the Beech Bottom Mound blades was as deeply notched at the shoulder or as wide as those from the late top level of the Cresap Mound. Except for this trend in blades, most of the other traits of this mound could be assigned from early to middle Adena.

Half-Moon Site

During the summer of 1940, Elmer W. Fetzer of Weirton, W. Va., excavated a small burial mound at the Half-Moon Site (46Br29) located along the Ohio River near Weirton, W. Va. A report of this excavation was made later by Fetzer and Mayer-Oakes (1951).

The mound excavated at the Half-Moon Site was one of a group of four. It was approximately 44 feet in diameter and 30 inches in height. The largest mound of the group, which had had many pits dug into it, was 60 feet in diameter and six feet in height. Two smaller mounds had been destroyed to make way for construction.

Near the center of the mound excavated by Fetzer was a subfloor pit that contained the decayed remains of an extended burial. On the chest of the burial were 252 rolled copper beads of various sizes (Fetzer and Mayer-Oakes, 1951, p. 5). A tip from a blade was also near the burial.

A small primary mound of dark earth had been constructed over this central burial pit. A layer of ash was present over the surface of this primary mound. This layer of ash may have resulted from the burning of a structure within which the burial and primary mound had been placed, but no post mold pattern was uncovered by the excavators. Covering the layer of ash was a thick layer of earth forming a secondary mound. In the soil of this layer were found a bundle burial and miscellaneous bone fragments.

Near the floor level of the primary mound was found a leaf-shaped blade and about one quart of red ocher. All other objects were found scattered in the mound fill and were probably scraped from the surface of the surrounding village area. Included among these items were a fragment of a banded slate gorget, two broken celts, a few notched and stemmed points, and several pieces of flint that had been used as scrapers. On the surface of the site near the mound, fragments of gorgets, hematite hemispheres, and blocked-end tubular pipes had been found. From this same site have come many sherds of typical Adena "Fayette Thick" pottery. This pottery has been called "Half-Moon Cordmarked" by Mayer-Oakes (1955, p. 184).

The structure and contents of the Half-Moon Mound and the items found on the surface near the mound are similar to those of other Adena sites in the Upper Ohio Valley. Webb and Baby (1957, p. 8) listed this mound as No. 216 on their recent additions to the list of Adena mounds.

Welcome Mound

The Welcome Mound was located near the Natrium Mound in Marshall County, West Virginia. During the fall of 1957, Dr. Frank M. Setzler (1960, p. 451-458) of the Smithsonian Institution performed a salvage excavation of this mound. The major find was an effigy tubular pipe of carved limestone found with a burial in the secondary mound several feet above the mound base. The pipe was made in the form of a shoveler duck with characteristic bill, eyes, and nostrils depicted in life-like fashion. (Fig. 17).

Near the center of the Welcome Mound and directly on the floor were two burials covered with bark and surrounded by logs. The skeletal material was almost completely destroyed and there were no associated grave objects. Except for a few stemmed projectile points recovered from the mound fill, no other objects were found.

Over the burials on the floor was a large primary mound constructed of dark humus-laden soil. Within this dark primary were lenses of burned soil. Over the primary mound was a covering of gravelly earth

Plate 46. McKees Rocks Mound at beginning of the Carnegie Museum
excavations in 1896

to a height of 15 feet and over 100 feet in diameter.

The meager content of the Welcome Mound in relation to its size
was unusual when compared to the wealth of materials from the adjacent Natrium Mound and the Cresap Mound only a short distance up
the Ohio River.

McKees Rocks Mound

The McKees Rocks Mound was located on the promontory overlooking the junction of Chartiers Creek with the Ohio River, about four
miles down-stream from the confluence of the Allegheny and Monongahela rivers at Pittsburgh. It was the largest mound up the Ohio River
and east of the great Grave Creek Mound at Moundsville, W. Va.
Before its excavation in 1896, the mound was 85 feet in diameter and 16
feet in height. (Plate 46).

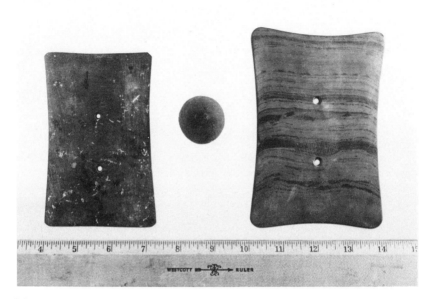

Plate 47.   Two reel-shaped gorgets and a hematite cone found during the Carnegie Museum excavation of the McKees Rocks Mound in 1896

The McKees Rocks Mound was partially excavated by Frank M. Gerrodette of Carnegie Museum in 1896. Several reports (Swauger, 1940; Carpenter, 1951; Mayer-Oakes, 1955; McMichael, 1956) based on Gerrodette's notes and the objects deposited in Carnegie Museum have been published in recent years. Since the mound was only partially excavated and the notes were often sketchy, our picture of the mound and its contents is none too clear.

The mound was apparently built in three phases. First there was a small primary mound of sterile clay that covered a central burial of an extended adult female of Adena physical type. It is not known whether or not the burial had been placed in a subfloor tomb or just placed on the floor of the mound. The depth of 15 feet 4 inches given in the notes for this burial indicates that the burial was probably near the floor since the apex of the mound from which the depth was measured was 16 feet. Over the primary mound was a distinct layer of charcoal and ash prob-

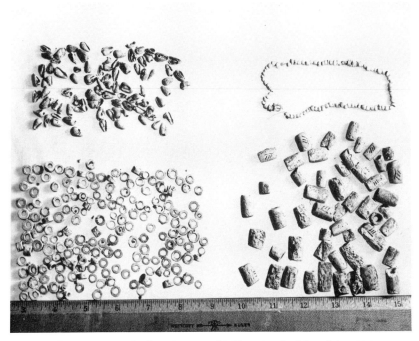

Plate 48.   Beads found in the McKees Rocks Mound in 1896
A. Marginella beads. B. Pearl beads from freshwater mollusks. C. Disk shell
bead. D. Tubular shell beads

ably resulting from the burning of a structure covering the primary.
Over this layer of ash was a secondary mound of earth scraped from the
surrounding village area. This secondary mound was not covered by the
final mound layer until a time sufficient for the development of a sod
line. The final step was the addition of the tertiary mound layer.

There were 33 or more burials scattered throughout the mound. Most
of the burials were extended, but bundle burials and cremations were
also present. Some of the burials were encased in cists of flat sandstones.
McMichael (1956, p. 136) has assigned one burial to the primary
mound, five to the secondary mound, and the remainder probably to the
tertiary mound. These latter burials may have all been placed on the
surface of the secondary mound at the same time and then covered by
the tertiary layer. There were stones associated with eight of these last
burials.

Plate 49. Imitation copper bear claw with fragments of cloth clinging to the surface, found in the McKees Rocks Mound. Actual size: 2-1/4 inches in length

Although there were 747 objects, supposedly from the mound, placed in the Carnegie Museum collection, only a few of these items can be directly associated with the burials. Among the items found with the central burial were one reel-shaped gorget, one grooved adz, one scraper, two blades, one copper sheath in the form of a bear canine tooth, 357 columnella shell beads, 153 marginella shell beads, antler and bone flaking tools, four deer or elk scapula awls, two bone flint flakers, and a piece of plain twined fabric found preserved on the copper sheath. A second reel-shaped gorget was found with a burial in the secondary mound. (Plates 47-49).

A number of artifacts was found in the secondary mound. In a number of places, there were apparently concentrations of these items, but there is no information available concerning their exact provenience or possible feature association. Some of these items are of Adena types, but many are more typical of the preceding Archaic and were probably scraped up in the earth from the surrounding village area that has upon it cultural remains from at least the Archaic to the Late Prehistoric periods.

In the tertiary mound some pearl beads were supposedly found with one of the burials. Near three other burials in this level limestone-tem-

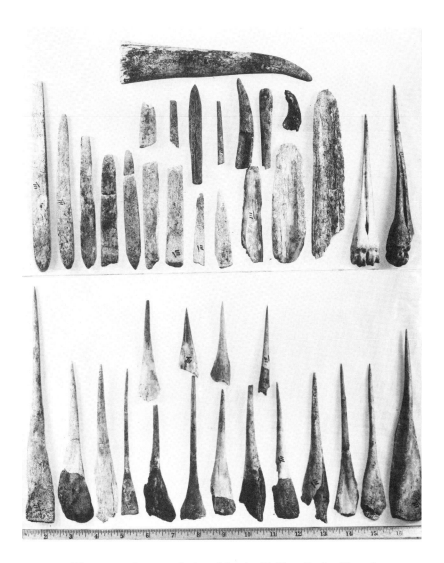

Plate 50.   Bone tools found in the McKees Rocks Mound

pered cordmarked pottery sherds were found. These sherds are of the "Watson Cordmarked" type associated with Hopewellian manifestations in the Upper Ohio Valley (Dragoo, 1956, p. 64). It seems quite possible that the entire tertiary mound and its contents were of Hopewellian origin (McMichael, 1956, p. 144).

Several pottery sherds were found in the lower levels of the McKees Rocks Mound. These sherds were of two basic Adena types—"Fayette Thick" (five sherds) and "Adena Plain" (79 sherds). The predominence of "Adena Plain" leads me to believe that the lower levels of the McKees Rocks Mound probably were constructed during late Adena times. "Adena Plain" pottery was found in only the top level of the Cresap Mound and seems to be a good indicator of lateness in Adena.

Perhaps the most important knowledge obtained from the McKees Rocks Mound concerned the clear picture of the types of bone tools used by Adena. In no other mound were bone tools so well preserved or so numerous. (Plate 50).

Peters Creek Mound

The Peters Creek Mound was located about 20 miles south of Pittsburgh, near the junction of Peters Creek with the Monongahela River. This mound was partially dug by amateurs in 1890, and a brief report of the findings was privately published in 1902 by one of the members participating in the excavation (Schooley, 1902).

The size of the mound in 1890 was near 80 feet in diameter and about six feet in height, but it had been plowed over many times in an attempt by farmers to level it. Any stratification in the upper levels of this mound would have been destroyed.

Within the mound, the excavators found a central burial area containing fragments of human bone and several important objects. The burial may have been in a shallow pit or placed directly on the mound floor. Since no mention of a deep pit was made in the report, I am inclined to believe that the burial was close to the mound's base. A layer of ash and charcoal was said to have covered the burial area and to have extended to near the margin of the mound. It seems quite possible that the central burial area had been made within a structure that had been burned upon the completion of the burial, and the building of a small primary mound to cover it. Areas of fire-reddened clay were also seen by the excavators. Some of these areas may have been definite features similar to those found in the Cresap and Natrium mounds.

Plate 51. Two copper gorgets found in the excavation of the Peters Creek Mound. The smaller gorget is 14 inches long and the larger one is 16-3/4 inches long. (These objects are in the Luther Higbee and Noah Thompson collection at the Fort Necessity Museum.)

After the completion of one trench across the mound and three much shorter trenches through the mound's center, Schooley (1902, p. 12) stated:

"The excavation or opening of the mound was considered thorough and complete. It occupied a whole day's time."

Since the excavation was done so rapidly and only a portion of the mound was investigated, the few notes published by Schooley gave a tantalizing hint of the mound's actual internal structure.

Among the artifacts found among the human bones in the central area of the mound were two round poll celts, one rectangular poll celt, one fully-grooved axe, one hematite hemisphere, 60 disk shell beads, 28 large columnella beads, two large copper gorgets, three small strips of folded copper, two copper sheaths (one covering a bear canine), one bear canine attached to a portion of mandible that had been cut and a hole drilled for attachment, and two large lumps of red ocher. The only other object reported found in the mound was one small piece of worked flint.

The copper objects found in this mound are of particular interest. The two copper gorgets are quite large, the largest being 16¾ inches long by eight inches wide, and the smaller being 14 inches long by six inches wide. Both are about one-eighth of an inch in thickness. They appear to have been roughly hammered into shape. The large gorget is basically rectangular with rounded corners, but the smaller gorget is reel-shaped (quadriconcave). Neither of these objects had been drilled as was the common custom. (Plate 51).

The small copper gorget, except for being undrilled, is very similar to the copper gorgets found in the Cresap Mound, Natrium Mound, and Crall Mound in the Upper Ohio Valley and mentioned in this report, and the Fisher Site in Kentucky (Webb and Haag, 1947, p. 73). The large rectangular gorget is unusual for Adena, but objects of similar outline have been found in Hopewell. The Hopewellian forms, however, are often embossed with designs or have curvilinear sections removed from one or more of the edges. The simple rectangular shape of this specimen may actually represent an early Adena form.

The two copper sheaths, one covering a bear canine tooth, and the other found near a bear canine, are similar to the copper sheath found in the McKees Rocks Mound.

The shell beads, celts, and hematite hemisphere are all typical items like those found in other Adena mounds of the Upper Ohio Valley.

Crall Mound

The Crall Mound was located within the limits of Monongahela City, Washington County, Pa. Thomas (1894, p. 495) stated that this mound was next largest after the McKees Rocks Mound in western Pennsylvania. It was 60 feet in diameter and nine feet in height. Several smaller mounds, including several constructed of stone, were found in the immediate area. Thomas (1894, p. 496) stated that nearly all of these mounds had been disturbed and that some had been completely destroyed.

Concerning the structure and content of the Crall Mound, Thomas (1894, p. 495-496) stated the following:

"Underlying the bottom of the mound was a tough gray clay, varying in thickness. On this the mound had been built up. At the center a hole measuring 3 feet across the top and 2 feet across the bottom had been dug down 2 feet into the original soil. In this were fragments of human bones too soft to be preserved. They indicated an adult of large size. The gray clay was unbroken over this hole. Directly over this, above the clay and resting upon it, were portions of another large skeleton, with which was found part of an unburned clay tube or pipe. About 5 feet southwest of the last mentioned skeleton, and on the same level, were a few fragments of bones, a copper gorget or breastplate, some small pieces of a gorget made apparently of stalagmite, and pieces of thin copperplate. The copper gorget was rectangular in form, 3x4¼ inches in size, with incurved sides, and had two holes on the long axis. It had been doubled over along this axis until the opposite sides were in contact and then hammered down flat. These, with some traces of charcoal and woody fiber, were lying flat upon the gray clay, extending over a space 2 feet across. The layer contained only traces of wood, as though the skeleton had been covered or surrounded by thin slabs of bark, there being no indication that logs or large pieces had been used. To the large piece of copper was adhering something like wood, which was rubbed off before its nature could be determined, and some fragments of a leather or buckskin string were preserved with it. On one of the smaller pieces was some kind of fur. Four feet west of the center, a foot above the bottom, were fragments of bones and skull."

"These four skeletons had either been buried in a sitting posture or doubled up on the side, or else only the bones had been interred. All the fragments were lying confusedly together. It seems probable that they were either buried in a sitting posture or doubled up, as the size of the hole at the center of the mound and the space showing traces of wood (where the copper was found) was more than would have been necessary to allow the interment of the bones alone."

"Over the center of the mound, 5 feet from the bottom, were a few pieces of bone and a tooth worn down nearly to the socket. Four feet west of this was the fragment of a femur, with its axis toward the tooth; by the femur lay a small chalcedony knife. These were no doubt remains of an intrusive burial. One other skeleton had been placed at full length, about 3 feet above the bottom and 6 feet southwest from the center, with head toward the east; only the leg bones were found. This, as its depth indicates, could scarcely have been an intrusive burial; yet none of those at a greater depth were buried in the same manner."

During the digging of another trench to intersect the first main trench, Thomas found another skeleton 20 feet from the center of the mound and close to the mound's surface. This burial was believed to have been intrusive along with several others that were reported to have been found earlier by the owner's workmen.

On the basis of Thomas's description of the Crall Mound,, Greenman (1932, p. 521) listed it as of Adena origin on his list of Adena sites. The general structure of the mound and the objects found in the lower levels are certainly typical of Adena. Most important of the structural traits were the bark-lined subfloor grave containing the central burial, a prepared clay base, a small primary mound covering the subfloor grave and additional burials on the mound floor, a layer of ash charcoal covering the primary mound that may have resulted from the destruction of a house, and a much larger secondary mound layer that covered all the primary features.

The tubular pipe, copper gorget and copper strip are like those previously mentioned for the Adena mounds in the Upper Ohio Valley. The finding of a piece of wood on the copper gorget is of particular interest since wood was also associated with the copper gorget found in the Cresap Mound. I am inclined to believe that these copper gorgets were attached to some kind of wooden object rather than being directly suspended by the holes in them. The intentional mutilation of the copper gorget was very similar to the folding seen on a gorget found in the Fisher Site (Webb and Haag, 1947, p. 60).

Discussion

In Table 1 are listed 122 traits that occur in the nine mounds in the Upper Ohio Valley previously described in this report. All of the traits except eight have been listed on the Adena trait lists published by Webb and associates. The trait numbers in the table are those assigned by Webb. The eight traits on this list that do not have numbers are either new traits or are traits that have been known to occur in Adena but not yet added to the Webb trait list.

The traits that appear for each site were derived through my interpretation of the information in the published reports augmented by personal observation of all or parts of the collections from the McKees Rocks Mound, Natrium Mound, Peters Creek Mound, Half-Moon Mound, and Cresap Mound. The location of each site was checked in the field for additional information.

The number of traits listed for each mound reflects the thoroughness of the original excavators and the detail with which their results were reported. Traits that were readily identified from the reports are marked in the list by an "X" while other traits that appear to have been present at a particular site but were not sufficiently detailed for positive recognition are marked with a "?".

Of the 122 traits on the list, 97 were present at the Cresap Mound and 87 at the Natrium Mound. Seventy-one of these traits were held in common by both mounds. Of the 60 traits listed for the Beech Bottom Mound, 57 were common to one or both of the above mounds. If the finely made tablets and wide blades from the top level of the Cresap Mound, the platform pipe of the Beech Bottom Mound, and the bust-type birdstone from the Natrium Mound are momentarily disregarded, the structure and artifactual contents of these three mounds are very similar. Each had been constructed over a simple subfloor grave containing an important burial with accompanying grave goods of the same basic types common in the lower levels of all three mounds. Only the number of types and the quantity of each type present in each mound varied.

Over the subfloor graves of the Cresap and Natrium mounds were constructed small primary mounds by the gradual addition of more burials and goods. Although no human skeletal material was found in the Beech Mound above the subfloor grave, I believe such remains were once present and the general sequence of events the same as for the other two mounds.

In the secondary mound layers of the Natrium and Beech Bottom mounds no materials of consequence were found. In the Cresap Mound, however, additional burials and objects were present in the secondary layer as well as in a tertiary layer that was distinctly separated from the layers by a dark humus zone representing an old sod line. The materials found in this tertiary zone are representative of a late Adena phase not present in the Natrium or Beech Bottom mounds. While the Cresap Mound had been used through early to late Adena, the Natrium and Beech Bottom mounds were abandoned no later than middle Adena.

Although our information is incomplete, the Half-Moon Mound with 34 traits, the Peters Creek Mound with 31 traits, and the lower levels of the Crall Mound with 21 traits appear to have been constructed from early to middle Adena times and are similar in structure and contents to the Cresap, Natrium, and Beech Bottom mounds.

Late Adena manifestations were present in the Grave Creek Mound and in the upper levels of the Cresap, McKees Rocks, and Crall mounds. The Welcome Mound may also have been constructed during this period. The presence of elaborate log tombs from top to bottom in the Grave Creek Mound indicates that the entire mound was constructed during late Adena. The heavy sod line separating the late Adena materials from the early Adena at the Cresap Mound, and similar old humus zones in the McKees Rocks and Crall mounds indicate that a considerable lapse of time occurred between the early and late periods at these mounds. The possible reason for this time gap is discussed in a later section of this report.

The traits of early and middle Adena in the Upper Ohio Valley mounds are not easily separated. There seems to have been little change in the structural or burial traits of the mounds during these periods. Small, shallow, burial pits lined with bark and covered by small logs laid across the pit opening were constructed continuously throughout early and middle Adena in the area. The use of logs to build substantial tombs was absent until late Adena when they occurred in the large Grave Creek Mound.

The most outstanding artifact traits of the early and middle Adena components in the Upper Ohio Valley are: 1. Blocked-end tubular pipes of fireclay or stone. 2. Reel-shaped or quadriconcave stone gorgets. 3. Hemispheres and cones of hematite or barite. 4. Leaf-shaped flint blades or knives. 5. Ovate-base stemmed points of the "Adena" type. 6. Rounded or rectangular poll celts. 7. Rolled copper beads. 8. Reel-shaped or quadriconcave gorgets of copper. 9. "Fayette Thick" pottery. 10. Crude tablet forms.

Of the above traits, Webb and Baby (1957, p. 112-113) have listed blocked-end tubular pipes, hematite cones and hemispheres, and reel-shaped gorgets as common to middle Adena, while copper reel-shaped gorgets were believed to be of late Adena manufacture. The stratigraphic position and association of these objects in the Cresap Mound and at other sites in the Upper Ohio Valley indicate that previous chronological ordering of these items warrants further clarification.

Blocked-end tubular pipes are a conspicuous item in the Upper Ohio Valley mounds. None of the pipes found at the Cresap Mound was associated with subsurface features. With the exception of the short, stone, blocked-end tube found directly on the clay floor of the mound, all the fireclay tubes were associated with features lying near the tops of the primary mounds or in features in the secondary mound. At the Natrium Mound tubular pipes were found in features near the mound floor while in the Beech Bottom Mound similar pipes were found with

the burial in the subfloor tomb and also in the primary mound covering
the tomb. If Webb and Baby's placement of blocked-end tubular pipes
of fireclay into middle Adena is basically correct, the Natrium Mound
and Beech Bottom Mound fall within that period at their beginning
while the absence of these pipes from the lowest levels of the Cresap
Mound would indicate the start of this mound in the early Adena
period. On the basis of pipes alone, the chronological sequence would
be Cresap, Natrium, and Beech Bottom.

Cones and hemispheres of hematite, barite, and occasionally other
stones, are common in the Upper Ohio Valley mounds. The presence
of hemispheres in features below the floor of the Cresap Mound indicates that they were early in this area and that they can not be taken as
an indicator of middle Adena as suggested by Webb and Baby (1957,
p. 113). Since cones and hemispheres were made from early to late
Adena and are present even later in Hopewell, they are of little aid as
a time marker. It is of particular interest, however, that cones and hemispheres are more abundant in the Upper Ohio Valley mounds of early
and middle Adena times than at Adena sites in Ohio and Kentucky.

Although stone reel-shaped gorgets were considered by Webb and
Baby (1957, p. 113) as associated with middle Adena, copper gorgets
were believed to belong to late Adena. The presence of a copper gorget
in a crematory basin lying between two of the primary mounds and
near the floor of the Cresap Mound clearly indicates that this object was
in use probably late in the early Adena period and certainly in the middle Adena period. The copper gorgets found in the Natrium, Peters
Creek, and Crall mounds were all in the lower levels and associated
with items of early-middle Adena. No copper gorgets have been found
in a late Adena context in the Upper Ohio Valley. The copper gorget
can no longer be considered a mark of late Adena. As will be shown
later, I believe that a number of Adena mounds have been erroneously
dated late because of the presence of copper gorgets and certain other
copper objects.

Reel-shaped or quadri-concave gorgets of stone did not occur in any
of the subfloor features of the Cresap Mound, but they were found in
all the major zones above the primary mounds. Similar gorgets were also
found in the Natrium, Beech Bottom, and McKees Rocks mounds. The
middle Adena context of this gorget form can clearly be shown for the
above mounds, and at the Cresap Mound there was a carry-over of this
gorget type into late Adena. Webb and Baby (1957, p. 113) seem to be

correct in their assignment of the reel-shaped gorget to middle Adena. It is possible, however, that this form may have made its appearance towards the end of early Adena.

Webb (1941, p. 192-215) made a study of reel-shaped gorgets in which he determined a chronological sequence in their development from an early rectangular form with only slight concavity in the sides to a late form with deep concavity in the sides giving a spoke-like appearance. On the basis of his finding, all the reel-shaped gorgets, of both stone and copper, of the Upper Ohio Valley mounds belong to his early forms.

In the lower and middle zones of Cresap Mound the ovate-base, stemmed "Adena" point was the dominant projectile and blade type. This typical Adena blade appears to be the major form throughout early and middle Adena. The flat-base, stemmed, wide blades, identified as the "Robbins" type in this report, were confined to the top zone at the Cresap Mound and are a distinct departure from the Adena type of the lower zones. As will be shown later, the "Robbins" type has been found at several late Adena sites in Kentucky. Only the earlier Adena type was found at the Natrium and Beech Bottom mounds and a variation of the type was present in the collection from the McKees Rocks Mound. The blade types from the other mounds are unknown.

On the basis of the above distinctive artifacts and their association with mound and burial features that can be demonstrated as stratigraphically of early to middle Adena in the Cresap Mound, and by comparison as of similar time to the materials of Natrium, Beech Bottom, and other mounds of the Upper Ohio Valley, there is now extensive evidence for the presence of early and middle components of Adena culture in the Upper Ohio Valley.

The presence of late Adena components in the Upper Ohio Valley can be also clearly defined both in terms of stratigraphy and artifact types. The distinctly separated top zone of the Cresap Mound, with its flat-base, stemmed, wide blades of the "Robbins" type associated with finely made plain and zoömorphic tablet forms, was most certainly of late Adena origin. The entire Grave Creek Mound seems to have been constructed during this late period. The large log-inclosed tombs, expanded-center bar gorgets, and mica cut into designs, all appear to belong to late Adena (Webb and Baby, 1957, p. 113).

Tertiary mound layers separated from the lower mound additions by humus or sod zones were also found in the McKees Rocks Mound

and the Crall Mound. On the basis of the presence of limestone-
tempered pottery, pearl beads, the use of stones around burials, and
the physical type of the burials, the tertiary layer of the McKees Rocks
Mound has been considered as of later Hopewellian origin (McMichael,
1956, p. 143). The general absence of distinctive artifacts of either
Adena or Hopewell in the tertiary layer of the McKees Rocks Mound
and also in the Crall Mound makes it difficult to assign these layers
accurately to either culture. Intrusive burials at both sites further complicated the picture.

The effigy shoveler duck tubular pipe discovered with a burial
several feet above the floor of the Welcome Mound is typologically
late Adena and similar to the pipes found in the Saylor Park Mound
in Cincinnati, Ohio. This pipe indicates that a late Adena component
was present in the Welcome Mound.

In the Upper Ohio Valley the following traits seem to be diagnostic
of late Adena: 1. The presence of log tombs. 2. Finely made plain or
zoömorphic stone tablets. 3. Effigy tubular pipes. 4. Mica. 5. "Robbins" blades. 6. "Adena Plain" pottery. 7. Expanded-center gorgets.

In view of the stratigraphic position of the materials of the Cresap
Mound and the above detailed structural and artifactual differences
found in the other mounds of the Upper Ohio Valley, it is necessary
to examine previous statements concerning the relationships and chronology of these mounds.

In his concluding remarks on the Natrium Mound Solecki (1953, p.
379-380) stated the following:

"Webb (Webb and Snow, 1945, p. 219) asserts that there appear to be sites
of both early and late Adena in Ohio and Kentucky, while West Virginia sites appear to be late Adena. To the hypothesis that West Virginia mound sites seem
to be late in terms of Webb's analysis, we offer Natrium Mound as further cor-
roboration. It sounds plausible to assume that Natrium Mound may have been
a culturally peripheral structure, both figuratively and literally. A cultural lag
seems to have carried it well into early Hopewell times. This is reflected in the
presence of such Hopewellian traits as the birdstone and the excavated boatstone,
occurring apparently contemporaneously with objects of patently Adena type (e.g.,
flat subrectangular stone celts, grooved stones) are also included in the list of
traits from Natrium. Granting that these may have been survival traits, we are
confronted here with the fact that we have a curious assemblage of mixed items,
all presumably within one temporal horizon. It is hoped that in the future we will
be able to make further assessments of this problem with more archeological exploration of the upper Ohio drainage."

It is obvious from the above statements that Solecki was disturbed by the traits he found in the Natrium Mound. However, the statement by Webb that only late Adena mounds were present in West Virginia and the finding of the birdstone and boatstone which he believed to be of Hopewellian types led Solecki to accept the lateness of Natrium Mound in spite of many early traits, these traits being considered as survivals from earlier times. As I have shown in previous sections of this report, all the traits of the Natrium Mound, except the birdstone, were directly comparable to those found in the lower and middle levels of the Cresap Mound of certain early to middle Adena origin. None of the traits that mark late Adena was present in the Natrium Mound.

The bust-type birdstone found in the Natrium Mound and a crude birdstone found on the surface near the Beech Bottom Mound are not necessarily an indicator of Hopewell. Birdstones were part of the Glacial Kame Culture located in eastern Indiana, southern Michigan, and northwestern Ohio long before the rise of Hopewell in Ohio. The bust-type birdstone also has been found in considerable numbers in New York and Ontario (Townsend, 1959, p. 315-696) where in certain instances it has been associated with the Point Peninsula Culture of that area (Ritchie, 1944, p. 152-160). A radiocarbon date of 2948±170 years was obtained from charcoal found with Burial 6 on the Oberlander component No. 2 at Brewerton, N. Y. (Libby, 1955, p. 92). A birdstone was directly associated with this Point Peninsula burial. The above date and others for Point Peninsula are earlier than any for Ohio Hopewell. This being the situation, I feel there is no longer need to look upon the birdstone as a Hopewellian object when found in an Adena mound in the Upper Ohio Valley where Adena and Point Peninsula were not only contemporary in time but also adjacent geographically.

Since a boatstone was also found in the middle zone of the Cresap Mound, the boatstone from the Natrium Mound appears less unusual in Adena and not necessarily a mark of Hopewellian influence. Boat-shaped barite bars have been found also in Adena mounds in Kentucky (Webb and Haag, 1947, p. 87).

The platform pipe found in the Beech Bottom Mound seems more closely related to those found in Point Peninsula than those common to Hopewell (Ritchie, 1944, p. 149, 169). When the possible Point Peninsula origin of this platform pipe, and also the birdstones of the Natrium and Beech Bottom mounds, are taken into consideration we are no longer faced with the "curious assemblage of mixed items" representing early and late Adena that disturbed Solecki.

In summary, the stratification of the Cresap Mound and the abundant artifacts of distinctive types found in association with the stratified zones have given us a key for the ordering of other Adena mounds in the Upper Ohio Valley. It is now apparent that there are sites ranging from early to late Adena in this area, contrary to the former opinion that only late sites were present. The distinct separation of the late Adena component from those of early-middle Adena at the Cresap Mound indicates that an interruption of Adena occupation may have occurred in this area. Changes in traits during early and middle Adena seem to be gradual, but rapid changes both in burial and artifact traits mark the late period.

In the following section of this report the relationships of the Upper Ohio Valley Adena to the general picture of Adena throughout its distribution in the Ohio Valley and adjacent areas will be investigated. The sequence and content of Adena components in the Cresap Mound and in other Upper Ohio Valley mounds enable us to draw some interesting comparisons to these other areas that were impossible before the Cresap Mound excavation. These comparisons also make possible a number of new insights into the origin, development, and downfall of Adena Culture.

TABLE 1. ADENA TRAIT LIST—UPPER OHIO VALLEY

No.	Trait	Cresap	Natrium	Beech Bottom	Grave Creek	Half-Moon	Welcome	McKees Rocks	Peters Creek	Crall
7	Mounds conical	X	X	X	X	X	X	X	X	X
8	Mound one of a gronp	X	?	X	X	X				X
9	Mounds in circular inclosure		?		X					
11	Mounds built on their own village	X	?	X	X	X	X	X	X	X
12	Mound on the site of burned house	X	?	?			?	?	?	?
13	Mound showing stratigraphy	X	X	?	X	X	X	X	X	X
14	Primary mound contains midden	X	X	X	X	X	X		X	X
15	Later mound sections built of sterile soils	X	X	X	X		X		X	X
18	Mound showing individual earth loads	X	X	X	X	?	X	X	?	?
19	Impression of grass, twigs, leaves	X	?	?	X		X			
20	Fired area at mound base	X		X			X	X		
21	Fired areas on mound surface	X	X				X	X	X	?
22	Primary purpose of mound to cover burials	X	X	X	X	X	X	X	X	X
23	Mound built by increments as burials were added	X	X	?	X	X	X	X	X	X
24	Constructional use of stone		X		X			X		
25	Horizontal log tombs built on bark-covered clay floor		X		X		?			
26	Single log rectangle about body		X							
37	Pit tomb dug below earth surface	X	X	X	X	X		X	?	X
38	Earth embankment around subfloor pit	X	X	X						
39	Subfloor tomb closed by log roof	X		?	?	?	?			?
40	Mound erected over subfloor pit	X	X	X	X	X	X	X	?	X,

TABLE 1. ADENA TRAIT LIST—UPPER OHIO VALLEY

No.	Trait	Cresap	Natrium	Beech Bottom	Grave Creek	Half-Moon	Welcome	McKees Rocks	Peters Creek	Crall
43	Post-mold pattern circular	X								
	Prepared clay floor	X	X	?	?	?			?	X
54	Circular fire basin	X	X	?			X			
55	Fire basins with burned stones	X	X							
56	Clay fire basins, raised clay rim	X								
59	House burned intentionally	X		?		?			?	
61	Cremation partial, in situ	X								
62	Cremation total, in clay basin									
63	Cremation total, in situ		X					X		
64	Cremation partial, in bark-lined pit	X								
66	Cremation, remains redeposited	X		?						
70	Cremated remains deposited with extended inhumation	X	X							
72	Communal deposit of cremated remains	X	X							
73	Artifacts burned with the body	X	X							
74	Unburned artifacts placed with redeposited cremations	X	X							
75	Artifacts intentionally mutilated when deposited with cremations	X	X	X			X		?	
76	Cremated remains accompanied by red ocher	X	X							
77	Body extended, no tomb	X	X	?	X	X	X	X	X	X
79	Body extended in log tomb, singly	X	X		X					
81	Multiple extended burials in same grave		X		X					
82	Important central graves	X	X	X	X	X	X	X	X	X
83	Use of bark in graves	X	X	X	X	X	X	X	?	X
84	Use of puddled clay in graves	X	X			X				

TABLE 1. ADENA TRAIT LIST—UPPER OHIO VALLEY

No.	Trait	Cresap	Natrium	Beech Bottom	Grave Creek	Half-Moon	Welcome	McKees Rocks	Peters Creek	Crall
85	Red ocher on skeleton	X	X							
86	Red ochre in mound	X	X	X		X	X		X	
87	Red ocher on artifacts	X	X	X		X			X	
89	Graphite in graves	X	X	X						
91	Separate skull with burial "Trophy"	X								
92	Burial of isolated skulls	X	X							
96	Skeletons bundled	X	X			?		X	X	X
	Artifact traits									
97	Blanks, flint	X	X	X		X		X		
98	Celts, flint		X							
100	Gravers, flint	X								
101	Leaf-shaped blades or knives	X	X	X		X	X	X		
102	Leaf-shaped blades deposited in cache	X	X	X						
103	Stemmed blades deposited in cache	X	X	X						
104	Projectile points, stemmed	X	X	X		X	X	X		
105	Stemmed blades with smoothed bases	X	X	X		X	X	X		
106	Projectile points, side-notched	X	X	X		X		X		
107	Drills and reamers	X	X			X		X		
108	Scrapers, flint, hafted	X								
109	Scrapers, thumb-nail, flint	X		X				X		
110	Scrapers, side, flint, flake	X	X	?		X		X		
111	Gorget, bar, expanded center				X					
112	Gorget, reel-shaped	X	X	X				X		
114	Gorget, semi-keeled, rectangular base		X			X				
115	Gorget, flat, various forms	X	X	X		X				
116	Gorgets conically perforated from one side only	X	X	X	X			X		

TABLE 1. ADENA TRAIT LIST—UPPER OHIO VALLEY

No.	Trait	Cresap	Natrium	Beech Bottom	Grave Creek	Half-Moon	Welcome	McKees Rocks	Peters Creek	Crall
117(220)	Pipes, tubular, blocked-end	X	X	X		X				X
118(219)	Pipes, modified tubular		X	X						
120	Pipes, platform			X						
122	Stone balls	X	X					X		
123	Celts, granite, and other igneous rock	X	X	X		X		X	X	
124	Celts, hematite	X	X	X		X				
126	Hammerstones	X	X				X			
127(230)	Abrading stones—Crude tablets	X	X	X				?		
130	Hemispheres, limestone, sandstone	X	X							
131	Hemispheres, barite	X	X	X						
132	Hemispheres, hematite	X	X			X		X	X	
133	Boatstones	X	X							
134	Pestles		?							
137	Concretions or fossils	X	X	X						
138	Stones with incised characters				?					
139	Geodes, cup-like	X	X	X						
142	Tablets, rectangular	X	?							
145	One side of tablet grooved	X								
	Effigy tablet, zoömorphic	X								
157	Awls, cannon bone							X		
158	Awls, scapula bone	X						X		
159	Awls, bone splinters or antler	X						X		
160	Beads, bone	X	X							
162	Flaking tools, antler or bone	X		X				X		
163	Teeth, animal		X	X					X	
164	Claws, animal			X						

TABLE 1. ADENA TRAIT LIST—UPPER OHIO VALLEY

No.	Trait	Cresap	Natrium	Beech Bottom	Grave Creek	Half-Moon	Welcome	McKees Rocks	Peters Creek	Crall
166	Spatula, metapodial bone of elk	X								
167	Spatula, flat bone sections		X					X		
168	Animal jaws, worked							X	X	
169	Cut antler sections	X						X		
171	Handles, bone or antler	X	X							
172	Spoons (containers) carapace of terrapin	X								
173	Shell spoons	X	X	?						
175	Beads, shell, circular disk	X		X	X				X	
176	Beads, *marginella*	X		X	X			X		
177	Beads, pearl		X					X		
178	Beads, cylindrical shell	X	X	X	?			X	X	
179	Bracelets, copper					X				
181	Beads, rolled copper	X	X	X		X				
185	Copper strips	X							X	
186(221)	Gorget, copper	X	X						X	X
189	Mica, fragments of designs					X				
191	"Adena Plain" pottery	X						X		
200	"Fayette Thick" pottery	X	X				X	X		
210	Textile, plain twining	X	X					X		
	Basket	X								
	Faceted and abraded pieces of hematite	X	X							
231	Ax, grooved		X	X					X	
234	Birdstone, bust-type		X	?						
	Worked coal	X	X							
	Deposit of manganese dioxide	X	X							
	Deposit of yellow ocher	X	X	X						
	Pipe, zoömorphic, tubular						X			
	Copper sheaths over bear teeth							X	X	
122 Traits		97	87	60	31	34	25	46	31	21

DEVELOPMENT OF ADENA CULTURE IN THE OHIO VALLEY

The stratified sequence of features and artifacts found in the Cresap Mound and the contents of the other Adena mounds of the Upper Ohio Valley are of importance in the understanding of Adena development throughout the Ohio Valley and of Adena's extensions into surrounding areas (Map 3). In order to fit the Upper Ohio Valley Adena into the general picture, I undertook an extensive study of collections and reports at major institutions in the Adena area. In this endeavor I received the full co-operation of many people including Dr. William S. Webb of the University of Kentucky, Dr. Raymond S. Baby of the Ohio State Museum, Dr. Glenn A. Black of the Indiana Historical Society, Mr. Ellis Crawford of the Behringer Museum of Covington, Kentucky, and Dr. William A. Ritchie of the New York State Museum. These individuals, and many others, gave not only their time but also their most valuable ideas and suggestions. To them, I am most grateful.

The comparative study of Adena components in the various areas of the Ohio Valley was a difficult and often frustrating task. The information available concerning the early excavation of Adena mounds is scant and in some cases so inadequate as to be useless. With a few exceptions, only the work conducted in the last 25 years, using modern archeological methods and techniques, is sufficiently detailed and accurate for comparative studies. The excavations and reports of Webb and his associates in Kentucky represent the best in field methods and reporting. A relatively comprehensive picture of Adena can now be given for that state.

In Ohio the story of Adena still remains somewhat obscured among the ruins of Hopewell. Most of the Adena mounds in that state were excavated many years ago and were inadequately reported. In recent years Raymond S. Baby has made a valiant effort to clarify the story of Adena in Ohio, but his work, however, has been greatly hampered by the partially destroyed mounds on which he has been forced to work. Most of these mounds were raided by vandals years ago and many have been nearly, or completely, leveled, first by farming activities and more recently by the expansion of industry and housing developments. Rarely in his salvage excavations has Baby had the opportunity to recover the entire contents of an undisturbed Adena mound. In many cases he has had to be contented with only a small fraction of the original contents. Nevertheless, he has already added important new information on the life of the Adena people, and the future publication of his complete site reports will be welcome additions to the literature.

Although abundant evidence of Adena has been found in Indiana, only a few mounds have been thoroughly excavated by modern methods, often with meager results. Sufficient information is available, however, to draw interesting comparisons with eastern Adena sites.

During my study of the collections, reports, and sites throughout the Adena area, it became obvious that it was impossible to attempt a complete trait by trait comparison of all the known Adena mounds for the following reasons: 1. The available reports and records of the majority of the early mound excavations described both the structure of the mound and its contents so inadequately that precise trait identification was impossible. 2. The collections of materials from many mounds often consisted of only one or two major traits and many contained no distinctive artifacts. 3. Inadequate report descriptions of objects and the failure to break major classes of objects down into distinctive types made specific type-to-type comparisons of most sites impossible.

In view of these conditions, it became necessary first to concentrate the study on sites for which extensive reports had been written and from which objects are still available for observation. The second task was to examine the literature and collections pertaining to less well known mounds in the hope that specific traits could be correlated with the controlled findings of recent years. The third objective was to determine whether or not specific traits could be assigned to definite time periods within Adena. The last and major objective was to determine the origin, distribution, and function of specific traits in the general development of Adena Culture and the relationships of these traits, if any, to cultures that preceded or followed Adena.

Distinctive Adena traits

Although 243 traits now appear on the Adena trait list (Webb and Baby, 1957), many of these traits are so general in nature and distribution as to make them useless in seeking cultural and temporal differences among the various Adena components. Also, some of the traits on the list represent a class of objects rather than specific types within the class. However, in the collections from Adena mounds

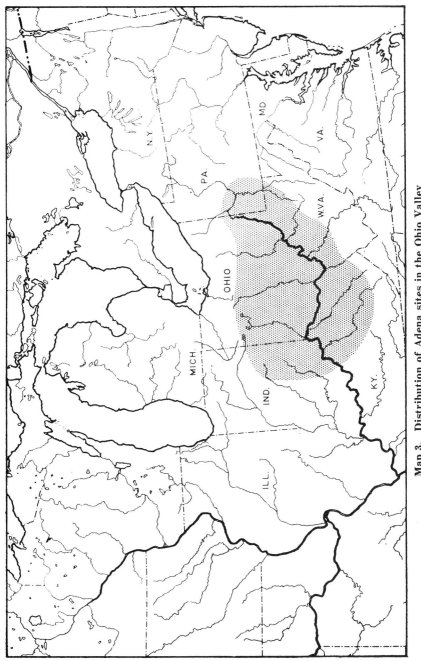

Map 3.   Distribution of Adena sites in the Ohio Valley

there are several groups of traits that stand out as distinctive of Adena Culture. These traits represent the most important material expressions of Adena arts and crafts such as flint blades, tablets, gorgets, pendants, pipes, copper objects, mica objects, and pottery. Within each of these classes are distinctive categories or types that seem to have distributional and temporal limitations. To these classes of material traits can be added those pertaining to burial practices and the construction of houses as known from the presence of post-mold patterns found at the base of some mounds.

In the comparisons of the Upper Ohio Valley Adena materials with those from other areas in the Ohio Valley, I have used the above classes of objects and their constituent categories or types as the basis for comparison. To prevent any misunderstanding of the nature of these categories, each is described below and illustrated in Fig. 10 and 11. These categories are keyed to the comparative trait charts that accompany the discussions of the major Adena areas that follow the descriptions.

1. Flint blades

Category A. "Cresap blade." A slender, lenticular cross-section blade with a tapered stem and straight base. The stem usually tapers directly from the shoulders with little or no indentation present. The chipping was carefully done by a combination of percussion and pressure. Generally made of Kanawha black flint this blade occurs mainly in the Upper Ohio Valley (Cresap Mound, Natrium Mound, Beech Bottom Mound).

Category B. "Adena blade." The typical ovate-base, stemmed, lenticular cross-section blade generally associated with Adena in the literature. The blade is slender with rounded shoulders forming a slight indentation at the juncture with the stem. This percussion chipped blade of good flints is found throughout the Adena area.

Fig. 10. Diagnostic Adena blade, tablet, gorget, and pendant forms
1—Flint blades: A. "Cresap" stemmed; B. "Adena" ovate-base stemmed; C. "Robbins" stemmed; D. "Adena" leafshaped; E. "Robbins" leaf-shaped.
2—Stone tablets: A. Irregular. B. Formal. C. Engraved. D. Zoömorphic.
3—Gorgets: A. Quadriconcave. B. Reel-shaped. C. Semi-keeled. D. Expanded-center bar. E. Rectangular. F. Elliptical. G. Bow tie.
4—Pendants: A. Trapezoidal. B. Bell-shaped with flat base. C. Bell-shaped with rounded base. D. Rectangular

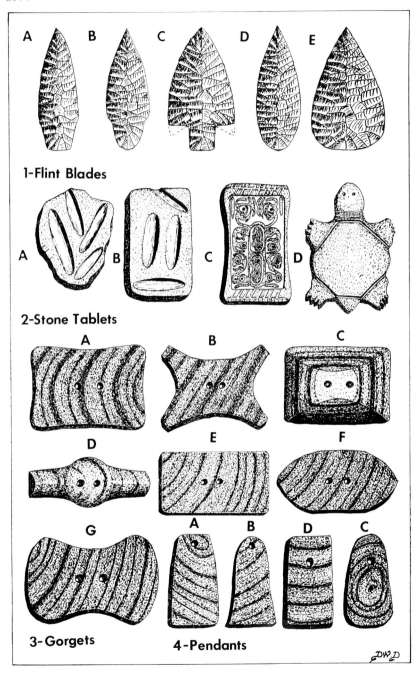

1-Flint Blades

2-Stone Tablets

3-Gorgets   4-Pendants

Category C. "Robbins blade." A wide, thin cross-section blade with a straight stem and straight or slightly rounded base. A deep horizontal notch or indentation is present at the juncture of the stem and blade. Carefully chipped of fine flints this blade has been found at many Adena sites, especially those in Kentucky.

Category D. "Adena leaf-shaped blade." A slender, leaf-shaped, lenticular cross-section blade that has its widest point near the middle of the blade. The base is usually rounded, but occasionally a narrow straight base occurs. Type B "Adena blades" appear to have been made from blanks of this shape. This blade form is common throughout the Adena area and they are often found in caches.

Category E. "Robbins leaf-shaped blade." A wide, leaf-shaped, thin cross-section blade that has its widest point near the base, which is rounded. Type C "Robbins blades" appear to have been made from blanks of this shape. This blade form is best known from the Adena mounds of Kentucky but it occurs at other sites throughout the Adena area. This blade was generally made of fine flints.

2. *Stone tablets*

Category A. Irregular tablets. Tablets of irregular shape made usually from sandstones and siltstones that were used for the preparation of red ocher paint and the sharpening of bone awls. Some have deep, wide, grooves worn into their surfaces while others have only traces of abrasion on the surfaces. These items have often been called grooved stones or abrading stones. They have been found throughout the Adena area.

Category B. Formal tablet. A carefully shaped tablet usually made of sandstones or siltstones with either grooved or plain surfaces. These tablets are generally rectanguloid in outline but kidney-shaped and oval forms have been found. Tablets of this type have been found at several Adena sites.

Fig. 11. Diagnostic Adena pipe, copper, and pottery forms
5—Pipes: A. Cigar-shaped. B. Straight tubular. C. Constricted tubular. D. Modified tubular. E. Flared tubular. F. Effigy tubular. G. Elbow. 6—Copper objects: A. Quadriconcave copper gorget. B. Rolled copper beads. C. C-shaped copper bracelet. D. Copper finger rings. 7—Pottery types: A. "Fayette Thick". B. "Adena Plain". C. Decorated ("Montgomery Incised").

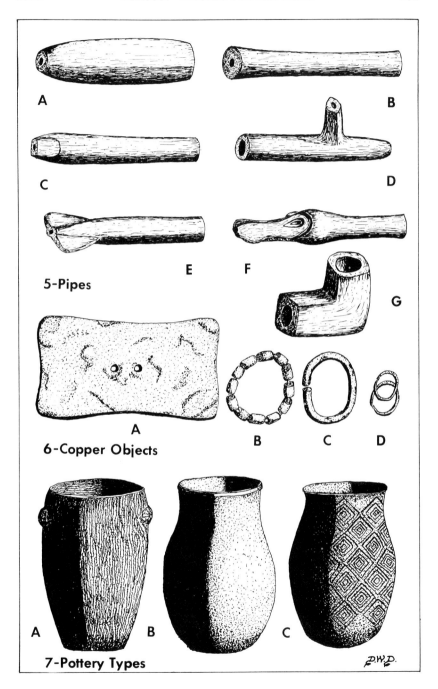

5-Pipes

A

B

C

D

E   F

G

6-Copper Objects

A

B   C   D

7-Pottery Types

A   B   C

D.W.D.

Category C. Engraved tablet. This tablet form is similar to type B except that upon one surface there is engraved in bas relief a conventionalized zoömorphic or geometric design. Twelve of these tablets have been reported from Adena sites in Ohio, Kentucky, and West Virginia. (Webb and Baby, 1957, p. 82-101).

Category D. Zoömorphic tablet. A tablet of siltstone carefully carved in the form of an animal. The only known example of this form is the turtle effigy tablet found in the Cresap Mound in West Virginia and described earlier in this report.

3. Gorgets

Category A. Quadri-concave. This gorget form of slate or siltstone is generally rectangular in outline with slightly concave sides. The corners may be rounded or pointed. Two holes near the middle of the gorget are usually drilled from one side only. This form, often called "reel-shaped," has been found at sites throughout the Adena area.

Category B. Reel-shaped. This gorget type is similar to type A except that the sides are deeply concave giving the corners a spoke-like appearance, hence the name reel-shaped. Reel-shaped gorgets found at certain Adena sites have less deeply concave sides than similar reels found in the later Hopewell Culture. (Webb, 1941, p. 204-215).

Category C. Semi-keeled. Rectangular in outline, this gorget is flat on the bottom and convex on the upper surface. Two beveled planes running parallel with the long axis are present on the convex surface. Two holes are drilled from the bottom or flat surface near the middle of the object. Gorgets of this type were usually made from slate but other materials were occasionally used. This type is not common in Adena, but has been reported from the Hartman Mound in Kentucky (Webb, 1943, p. 543-545), the Natrium Mound in West Virginia (Solecki, 1953, p. 359), and Mound 3 in Ohio (Greenman, 1932, p. 430).

Category D. Expanded-center bar. A rectangular bar form flat on under surface and convex on upper surface with semicircular protuberances at the center. Two holes are drilled near middle of bar usually from underside only. This type was usually made of slate but other materials were also used. Expanded-center bars have been found throughout the Adena area. (Webb and Snow, 1945, p. 84).

Category E. Rectangular. The gorget type is rectangular with square to slightly rounded corners. The two holes drilled near the middle of the gorget may be drilled from either one or from both sides. This type, usually made from slate, is not common on Adena sites.

Category F. Elliptical. This gorget is similar to Category E except that ends are rounded.

Category G. Bow tie. This gorget form appears to be related to types A and B. In this type the sides are concave and the ends are convex, thus giving the appearance of a bow tie. The two holes are usually drilled from one side only. Although usually made from slate, other materials were sometimes employed. This type is not common.

4. *Pendants*

Category A. Trapezoidal. This type of pendant has an elongated trapezoidal shape. The hole may be drilled from only one side or from both. Pendants of this type were usually made of slate but other materials occur. Pendants of this type were found at three major Adena sites in the Upper Ohio Valley (Bache and Sátterthwaite, 1930, plate XXIII; Solecki, 1953, plate 26).

Category B. Bell-shaped with flat base. Similar to type A except that the suspension end is rounded and the sides tend to be more concave.

Category C. Bell-shaped with rounded base. Both the top and the base are rounded in this form. The hole tends to be farther from the top than in types A and B. Shales and sandstones were used in the manufacture of this type (Webb, 1943, fig. 12).

Category D. Rectangular. This pendant form is rectangular with the hole drilled approximately ⅓ the distance below the top. The material used was generally slate. This type appears to be rare.

5. *Pipes*

Category A. Cigar-shaped. A tubular form with bulging barrel and a blocked end. Both stone and pottery clay were used in the manufacture of this type.

Category B. Straight tubular. A straight-barreled tubular pipe with a blocked end. The blocked end is flat. On some specimens there is a slight flare, or trumpet-shape, to the blocked end. These pipes were generally made of fireclay, but stone was occasionally used. This type is common in the Upper Ohio Valley.

Category C. Constricted tubular. This is similar to type B except that a beveled constriction occurs at the blocked end. This type appears to be most common in the Kentucky Adena mounds.

Category D. Modified tubular. This is a specialized tubular form with a short stem set at right angles to a long cylindrical bowl. This form is not common (Webb and Baby, 1957, p. 21).

Category E. Flared tubular. Another specialized tubular form has a flattened and flared bit at the blocked end. This type is rare.

Category F. Effigy tubular. This is a tubular form with a zoömorphic effigy head forming the blocked end. Only a few specimens of this type have been found.

Category G. Elbow pipe. A heavy elbow, usually equal-armed, pipe of stone has been reported for Adena (Webb and Funkhauser, 1940, p. 222). Although pipes of this type are often seen in surface collections, their distribution in Adena is not well known.

6. *Copper objects*

Category A. Quadriconcave copper gorget. Gorgets of copper similar to type A stone gorgets have been found in Adena, especially in the Upper Ohio Valley and Kentucky.

Category B. Rolled copper beads. These beads were rolled from sections of copper sheets.

Category C. C-shaped copper bracelet. A bracelet of rolled sheet or bar copper. This type of bracelet has been found at a number of sites in Kentucky and Ohio (Webb and Snow, 1945, p. 99).

Category D. Copper finger ring. Finger rings were made in a fashion similar to the copper bracelets.

Category E. Unusual copper forms. For our purpose here, this category includes any unusual object of copper such as strips of copper, celts, copper antler head-dresses, etc., that has been found in an Adena mound.

7. *Pottery*

Category A. "Fayette Thick." A thick ware tempered with either grit or limestone and covered on the interior and exterior by the impressions of a cordwrapped paddle (Griffin, 1943, p. 667).

Category B. "Adena Plain." A grit- or limestone-tempered ware with a plain surface. Some vessels of this type are thick while others are thin. The thick vessels have often been classified as belonging to type A, "Fayette Thick," while only the thin vessels were called "Adena Plain." I am opposed to the lumping of the thick cordmarked and plain vessels under the "Fayette Thick" type merely because both forms are thick and heavy. If a separation of the plain vessels must be made on the basis of thickness, I would suggest that "Fayette Thick" be divided into two types: "Fayette Thick Cordimpressed" and "Fayette Thick Plain," and that the type "Adena Plain" be used to include the thinner varieties. Since this separation has not been made in the past, I have used surface treatment only as the major factor in the division listed on the tables in this section. *See* Haag, (In Webb, 1940, p. 75) for original type description of "Adena Plain."

Category C. Decorated. Incised and stamped decorations have been found on some Adena vessels. In the table I have grouped such types as "Montgomery incised," "Paintsville Simple Stamped," and related types into one category (Webb and Snow, 1945, p. 102).

8. *Mica*

Category A. Crescent. Thin sheets of mica were cut in crescentic shape. Such crescents were apparently attached to cloth (Webb and Snow, 1959, p. 59).

Category B. Worked mica. Included here are worked pieces of mica of unknown form. The intent here is to note the presence of mica.

9. *Burial traits*

Category A. Subfloor pit. This is a simple pit grave, usually lined with bark and covered by small logs, below the floor of the mound. No major constructional use of logs present (Fig. 4).

Category B. Log tomb. In this category are tombs, either below or above the mound floor in which there was extensive use of large logs to form a crib or structure around the burial. Such construction may be elaborate (Fig. 12).

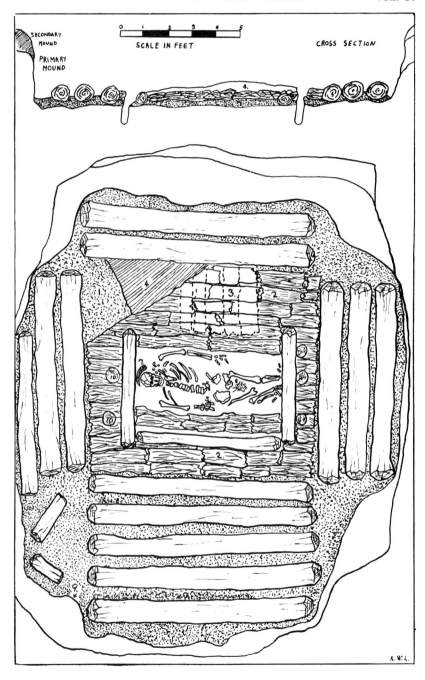

Fig. 13. Reconstruction of an Adena house with paired post wall construction. (After Webb, 1941.)

Category C. Extended burial. A burial extended on the back either in a tomb or anywhere else in a mound.

Category D. Cremation. A deposit of cremated human bones either in situ or redeposited with other burials or features.

Category E. Bundle Burial. The burial of bundled disarticulated bones anywhere in a mound.

Fig. 12. A typical Adena log tomb. Feature 23, Burial 17 in the Wright Mound (Mm6), Montgomery County, Ky.
1. Prepared clay floor. 2. Bark flooring over prepared clay. 3. Postulated bark covering for burial area. 4. Postulated prepared clay cap for central area. 5. Two copper bracelets. 6. Shell beads. 7. Copper crescent head-dress. 8. Infant bones. 9. Outline of pit in primary mound. 10. Vertical post molds. (After Webb, 1940.)

10. *Houses*

Category A. Single post-mold pattern. A circular house having evenly spaced wall posts.

Category B. Paired post-mold pattern. A circular house having the wall posts set in pairs (Fig. 13).

Category C. House pattern absent or not recorded.

On the basis of the above categories representing specific types or units of closely related traits, it is now possible to proceed to the direct comparison of the Upper Ohio Valley Adena remains with those of other areas.

ADENA IN KENTUCKY

Webb and his associates have listed 28 mounds that they knew or believed to be of Adena origin in Kentucky (Webb and Snow, 1945, p. 110-136; Webb and Baby, 1957, p. 1). Many more mounds present in Kentucky were probably also constructed by Adena. In Table 2 I have listed the major traits of 13 Kentucky mounds that were carefully excavated and reported by Webb and his associates. These mounds represent a good cross-section of Adena for that area.

It is obvious from the traits listed in Table 2 that there are a number of significant differences in the categories or types found at the Kentucky sites when compared to those found in Upper Ohio Valley sites. The majority of Kentucky mounds are characterized by the presence of "Robbins" stemmed and leaf-shaped blades (Categories C and E), formal tablets (Cat. B), expanded-center bar gorgets (Cat. D), constricted tubular pipe (Cat. C), copper bracelets (Cat. C), copper finger rings (Cat. D), "Adena Plain" pottery (Cat. B), mica (Cat. A), log tombs (Cat. B), and paired post-mold house patterns (Cat. B). The Robbins Mound (Be3)ʻpresented a typical example of this combination of traits and the C and O Mounds (Jo2 and Jo9), Dover Mound, Drake Mound, Wright mounds (No. 6 and No. 7), and Ricketts Mound contained comparable but less complete inventories of these same traits (Fig 14).

The stemmed, wide blades, formal tablets, and "Adena Plain" pottery found in the upper zone of the Cresap Mound are typologically similar to the items in the above mounds. The distinct stratigraphic and typic

SITE	BLADES					TABLETS				GORGETS						PENDANTS				PIPES							COPPER						POTS			MICA			BURIALS					HOUSE		
	A	B	C	D	E	A	B	C	D	A	B	C	D	E	F	A	B	C	D	A	B	C	D	E	F	G	A	B	C	D	E	F	A	B	C	A	B	C	A	B	C	D	E	A	B	C
Cresap Bottom	7	36	12	18		13	1	8		3	1	1	1			1	2				3		1				1				1	1	X						X		X	X	X	X		
Cresap Top		14		196		1				2	1			1							3	1	1		1			X			1	1		X							X	X	X			
Natrium	4			33		13				1	1							1			32						1	X	3				X							X						
Beech Bottom	1	36				1				1							1			1																				X						
Grave Creek		X	X	X		X							1														1	X									X		X	X		X				X
Half Moon		X																										X											X		X	X		X		
Welcome		X																										X												X		X			X		
McKees Rocks		X																									2													X	?					X
Peters Creek																											1													X						
Crall										2										2																			X							
Dover		3	3		2		3						1										2				2	2			1	1	X			5+	2			X		X	?	X		X
Drake (Fall)		1	1							2											?		2													2					X	X	X	X		
Crigler (Be20)	1	1					2			2			2								1	1					2	X	5	1	1	1									X	X	X	X		X
C. & O. (Jo2)			6				4			2			9								4							X	12					X		2				X	X	X	X		X
C. & O. (Jo9)	4	17		85	11	11	2							1									2				2	X	26		8	11				2				X	X	X	?		X
Fisher	93	2	2			1						5			1												2												X	X	X	X	X	X		X
Robbins (Be3)		7	2				5																																X	X	X	X	X	X	X	X
Wright (No.6)	4						3																			2			3										X	X	X		X	X	X	X
Wright (No.7)																												X	18		2					2			X	X	X	X	?		X	X
Hartman	3	3								1		5	2														X												X	X	X			X		
Riley (Be15)	3	X			7	7					1		1																					X		2				X						
Landing (Be17)		X																								2	X		3	4		2									X		X			
Ricketts	1		6			6	1			1																	X		18				X							X	X	X	X			
Adena*		1	11	X	11	11	2			1	1										1					2								X								X				
Clyde Jones	X	X	X		X	X				X																	X													X						
Toepfner	X	X		1						X				1														X	8		2									X			X			
Wm. H. Davis		X			7	7																																		X		X				
Sayler Park		2									3		1				1																						X		X					
C. L. Lewis			2	1	X								1															X											X	X		X				
Cato Site		2	X				1																						8										X							
Nowlin	X		X										1											1				X	1	1		1								X						
Fudge*		2		X		11	1			1				1															8					X						X	X	X			X	X

Region groupings (left margin):
PENNSYLVANIA AND WEST VIRGINIA — Cresap Bottom, Cresap Top, Natrium, Beech Bottom, Grave Creek, Half Moon, Welcome, McKees Rocks, Peters Creek
KENTUCKY — Crall, Dover, Drake (Fall), Crigler (Be20), C. & O. (Jo2), C. & O. (Jo9), Fisher, Robbins (Be3), Wright (No.6), Wright (No.7), Hartman, Riley (Be15), Landing (Be17), Ricketts
OHIO — Adena*, Clyde Jones, Toepfner, Wm. H. Davis, Sayler Park
INDIANA — C. L. Lewis, Cato Site, Nowlin, Fudge*

*Type G gorget in Adena Mound and Fudge Mound.

TABLE 2.

separation of these traits from those found in the lower levels of the Cresap Mound indicated a close relationship of this upper zone material to that common to most of the Kentucky mounds.

Of the other Upper Ohio Valley mounds with traits related to the above Kentucky sites and the upper zone of Cresap were the Grave Creek and Welcome mounds where logs were used in the construction of tombs in both mounds and where copper bracelets and an expanded-center gorget were present in the Grave Creek Mound. The effigy tubular pipe of the Welcome Mound also appears to accompany the above late traits.

The contents of the Fisher Site in Kentucky contrast sharply with the items of the "Robbins" Mound and the other mounds similar to it. At this mound, "Adena" stemmed (Cat. B) and "Adena" leaf-shaped (Cat. D) blades were the dominant types. These blades resemble closely those of the lower zones of the Cresap Mound, Natrium Mound, and Beech Bottom Mound in the Upper Ohio Valley. It is of interest to note that "Adena" blades occurred in far greater abundance in these mounds than did the "Robbins" blades in the mounds where they were the dominant types.

Among the other important traits of the Fisher Site were a crude tablet (Cat. A), a straight tubular pipe (Cat. A), two modified tubular pipes (Cat. D) two copper quadriconcave gorgets (Cat. A), one copper bracelet (Cat. C), eight unusual copper objects (Cat. E) [including two celts, three "eared" or "horned" objects, one copper boatstone, and two copper antlers], and one sherd of "Adena Plain" pottery (Cat. B). No elaborate tombs were found in this mound. All burials, including extended burials and cremations, were either in shallow pits or scattered through the mound (Fig. 15).

In their conclusions on the Fisher Site, Webb and Haag (1947, p. 100-102) stated their belief that this site was a late Adena burial mound. Because of the presence of modified tubular pipes and copper boat-

---

Fig. 14. Major artifact traits of the "Robbins" Mound, Boone County, Ky. A. Log tomb. B. Circular house pattern with paired posts in each hole. C and D. "Robbins" leaf-shaped blades. E-G. "Robbins" stemmed blades. H. Expanded-center bar gorget. I. Constricted tubular pipe. J and K. Formal tablets. L. Copper C-shaped bracelets. M. Small copper pendants. N. Antler flaking tool. O. Mica crescents. P. Spoon made from turtle carapace. Q. Antler handle. (After Webb and Elliott, 1942.) Objects not to scale

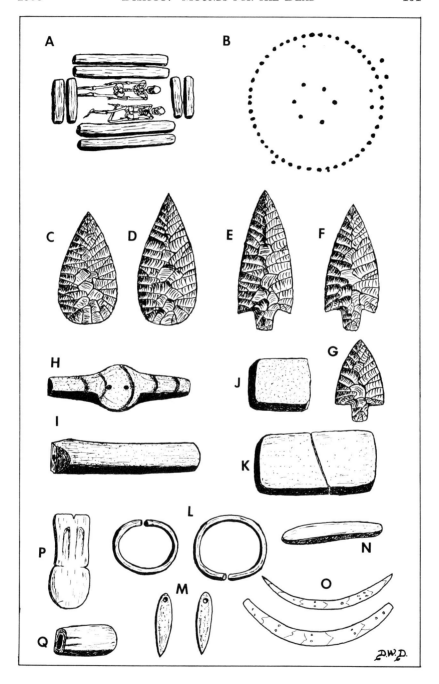

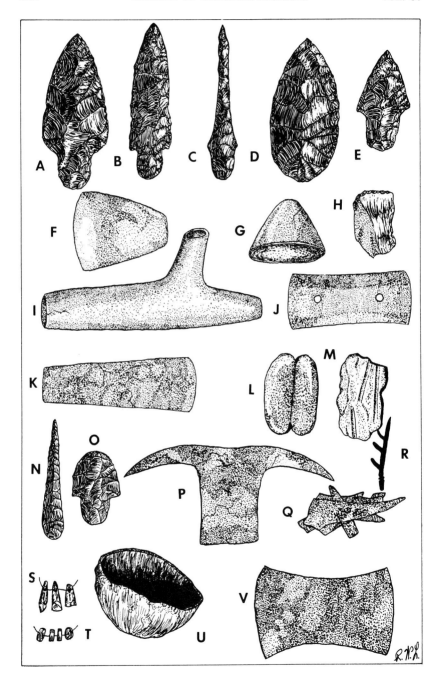

stones in the Fisher Site they suggested that there was a "demonstrated affinity of Late Adena as exemplified by the Fisher Site, and Early Hopewell as exemplified by the Tremper Site." When Solecki (1953, p. 376) wrote his report on the Natrium Mound in the Upper Ohio Valley, he noted the resemblance and probable contemporancity of the Natrium Mound materials to those of the Fisher Site and accepted Webb and Haag's assessment of lateness and possible "close cultural association with the Tremper Mound, an early Hopewell site." Because of the evidence now available from the Upper Ohio Valley, the lateness of the Fisher Site and its possible relationship with Hopewell must be reviewed.

As was demonstrated in a previous section of this report, the traits of the Natrium Mound and Beech Bottom Mound were shown to be typologically similar to those traits found in the lower and middle zones of the stratified Cresap Mound. The close correspondence of the traits in these mounds are also indicated in Table 2. It is obvious from the same table that the traits of the Fisher Site were more like those of the Cresap, Natrium, and Beech Bottom mounds than like those of the majority of Kentucky mounds, as typified by the Robbins Mound. Since there was clear stratigraphic and typological evidence for the lateness of "Robbins"-like traits in the upper zone of the Cresap Mound, it seems most unlikely that both the complexes of traits as represented at the Robbins Mound and at the Fisher Site can be equated with late Adena. The relationships of the Fisher Site are most certainly with those of Middle Adena in the Upper Ohio Valley.

The modified tubular pipes and the copper boatstone were particularly singled out by Webb and Haag (1947, p. 101) as demonstrating the close relationship of the Adena Fisher Site to the Hopewellian Tremper Mound. The presence of modified tubular pipes in the Natrium and Beech Bottom mounds in association with other typically

---

Fig. 15. Typical artifacts from the Fisher Site Mound, Fayette County, Ky. A, B and E. "Adena" ovate-base blades. C. Ovate-base drill. D. "Adena" leaf-shaped blade. F. Celt of igneous stone. G. Hemisphere of hematite. H. Flint scraper. I. Modified tubular pipe. J. Boatstone or bar weight of barite. K. Copper celt. L. Grooved stone. M. Irregular tablet with grooves. N. Straight drill. O. Stemmed scraper. P. Unusual winged copper object. Q. Folded and flattened copper antlers. R. Form of copper antlers shown in Q. S. Perforated human teeth. T. Shell disk heads. U. Human skull bowl. V. Copper gorget. (After Webb and Haag, 1947.)

early and middle Adena traits, as demonstrated at the stratified Cresap Mound, indicates that this form of pipe was used in the Upper Ohio Valley perhaps late in early Adena and certainly during middle Adena times. The straight tubular pipe found in association with the two modified tubular pipes at the Fisher Site was unlike the constricted tubular pipes found associated with mounds containing the late "Robbins" complex. The Fisher tubular pipe is of a type that had its earliest prototype in the shell mounds of the Archaic in Alabama. (Webb and De Jarnette, 1942, plate 37; Webb and Haag, 1947, p. 93). Raymond S. Baby (1959, p. 95) found in Ohio, associated with Archaic burials under the Davis Mound, a similar pipe that appears to be early Adena. Thus, tubular pipes had a long history that began late in the Archaic and continued through Adena with a number of changes. Since both modified tubular pipes and straight tubular pipes were not only used during late Adena but also in early and middle Adena, the Fisher specimens need not have any relationship with similar objects found at the Hopewell Tremper Mound where such pipes could have been picked up from earlier Adena occupations or from perhaps actual contact with late Adena peoples having the "Robbins" complex, since modified tubular pipes were also present at the Wright Mound (Mm6) belonging to this complex (Webb and Haag, 1947, p. 94).

Although the copper boatstone and the cones or hemispheres found at the Fisher Site were suggested as link traits from late Adena to Hopewell by Webb and Haag (1947, p. 88), I doubt their value as time markers. The history of the boatstone, like that of the tubular pipe, can be traced back into the Archaic. In such a case, the boatstone seems to be of little use as a chronological marker for the Fisher Site in this situation since Hopewell could have received this trait either early or late.

The boatstone found in the Cresap Mound was removed from the zone attributed to middle Adena and not from the upper zone with typical late Adena "Robbins" materials. Also, no late Adena items were associated with the boatstone found in the Natrium Mound (Solecki, 1953, plate 25). Most boatstones found in Hopewell (Mills, 1916, p. 364-367) are highly evolved and ornate forms in contrast with those of the Fisher, Cresap, and Natrium mounds. Cones and hemispheres were found in all these mounds containing boatstones. As I have pointed out in an earlier section of this report, cones were present throughout the early and middle zones of the Cresap Mound where they had definite stratigraphic priority in time to the late "Robbins" complex in the upper zone. I would agree with Webb and Haag (1947, p. 88) "that these traits [boatstones and cones] may have come to Tremper by way of Adena," but on the basis of the close similarities of Fisher Site materials to those of the lower zones of the Cresap Mound and to the items of the Natrium and Beech Bottom mounds, I can not see the Fisher Site as either contemporary with or the donor of these items to Tremper.

Another important link trait of the Fisher Site with the Upper Ohio Valley mounds was the copper antler head-dress (Fig. 16). A head-dress made from the skull-cap and attached antlers of the elk was a prominent item removed from the middle zone of the Cresap Mound. Antler head-dresses often associated with Hopewell also seem to have been used over long periods of time by various peoples. In their discussion of the simple, hammered, sheet, copper antlers of the Fisher Site Webb and Haag (1947, p. 85) stated:

"The present authors, while not presuming to fix any boundaries or attempting any interpretation of 'the Middle Woodland period of Hopewell domination,' would express the belief that antler headdresses were used in the early Archaic manifestation as represented by the deep shell middens. From this source Adena man may have learned the significance of this practice and was lead [sic] to make the first and simplest representation of antlers in copper, leaving to the later, richer, and more highly developed Hopewell the production of elaborate copper antler headdresses of varied form. Certain it is that the use of copper headdresses as a trait in Hopewell does not seem to have a sudden and unique origin."

The antler head-dress from the Cresap Mound, strikingly similar to the one found in the Archaic Flint River Site in Alabama illustrated by Webb and Haag (1947, p. 84), lends additional support to Webb and Haag's contention that antler head-dresses did not have a "sudden and unique origin" in Hopewell. The copper antler head-dress of the Fisher Site was a simple attempt by Adena peoples to fabricate a head-dress by hammering thin sheets of copper much in the same fashion as they made quadriconcave gorgets. The style and technique of manufacture of the Fisher Site head-dress was still a long way from the elaborate antler head-dress of Hopewell (Webb and Haag, 1947, p. 81), but it was an important step in the long evolution of this form from Archaic times.

The copper, quadriconcave gorget found in the Fisher Site also had its counterpart in the Cresap, Natrium, Peters Creek, and Crall mounds of the Upper Ohio Valley where nearly identical specimens were found. However, the copper celts and "eared" copper objects from the Fisher Site are unique as comparable items have not been reported either from Adena sites in the Upper Ohio Valley or in Kentucky. Although copper axes have been found at several Ohio Hopewell sites (Mills, 1907, p. 156; 1909, p. 296; 1922, p. 528), these objects do not closely resemble the Fisher specimens which approximate the typical Adena stone celt in form. The total complex of items associated with the copper celts of the Fisher Site bears little resemblance to the elaborate complex of traits associated with the Hopewell copper axes. On the basis of typology, the Fisher copper celts and "eared" objects appear to resemble tools of the Archaic Old Copper Culture (Ritzenthaler, *ed.,* 1957, p. 185-327) more closely than they do any of the Hopewell items. Again we are faced with the possible derivation of items in Adena from an earlier Archaic Culture. Such a possibility also casts doubts upon the use of these copper artifacts as good chronological markers in the development and relationships of Adena to Hopewell since it is impossible to confine the use of copper artifacts to any specific period in Adena.

In the preceding paragraphs I have, perhaps, dwelt upon the more unusual items of the Fisher Site to the point of boring the reader, but since these items have been cited as representative of late Adena and used to link the Fisher Site with Hopewell, a contention I believe to be invalid, the long exposition has been necessary. As brought out in the preceding discussion, it seems apparent that most of the unusual traits of the Fisher Site, those that have been used to link it with Hopewell, can be shown to have a long history reaching back into the Archaic. I do not deny that these traits in Adena could have eventually influenced Hopewell but I do not believe the evidence proves that the Fisher Site was contemporaneous with the Tremper Mound or any other nearby Hopewell site. To the contrary, the assemblage of traits found at the Fisher Site can best be assigned to the early and middle periods of Adena as demonstrated by the typological similarity of these traits to those of the lower and middle zones of the stratified Cresap Mound, by the presence of ancestral forms of these traits in the Archaic, and by the obvious differences in the total trait assemblage of the Fisher Site when compared to the traits of the sites assigned to the "Robbins" complex that can be equated with the top, late, zone of the Cresap Mound.

As of now, the Fisher Site appears to be the best example of early-middle Adena in Kentucky, but it is by no means the only site. Webb's (1943, p. 640-665) reconstruction of the Tarlton Mound (Fa15) from old notes and collections in the Smithsonian Institution indicated that the contents of this mound, adjacent to the famous Mt. Horeb Earthworks, were closely related to those of the Fisher Site. Among the typical items of this mound were many large "Adena" leaf-shaped blades, and "Adena" stemmed blade, fragments of crude grooved tablets, a broken slate pendant, and a small diorite celt (Webb, 1943, p. 661-665).

Webb in his many reports has recorded objects from many sites that are typologically similar to the Fisher and Tarlton specimens. There is little doubt that many more early Adena sites are present in Kentucky. It is hoped that future excavations will produce evidence that will enable us to define more clearly the extent and content of early Adena in Kentucky. The extensive occupation of Kentucky during late Adena times, as represented by the "Robbins" complex, seems to have masked the early development there. The close similarity of the Fisher Site and of vestigial early traits in late Adena sites to traits of the Cresap Mound suggests that the early history of Adena in Kentucky was not unlike that of the Upper Ohio Valley.

Adena mounds in Ohio.

In Ohio, as in Kentucky, the overwhelming majority of the excavated mounds seems to have been constructed during late Adena times. We have little difficulty in finding materials similar to those recovered from the top zone of the Cresap Mound in these structures that equate both in content and time with the "Robbins" complex of Kentucky. Mounds similar in structure and content to the lower zones of the Cresap Mound, the Natrium Mound, and Beech Bottom Mound in the Upper Ohio Valley appear to be poorly represented among the mounds of Ohio. This situation may, however, be more apparent than real because of the inadequate nature of the available information.

Although 134 mounds in Ohio have been identified as of Adena origin in the lists compiled by Webb and Snow (1945, p. 110-131) and Webb and Baby (1957, p. 1-9), detailed information concerning structure and content has been recorded for only a small number of this total. Webb and his associate found that in the old reports of Cyrus Thomas, Gerard Fowke, Warren K. Moorehead, W. C. Mills, and other early workers in the Ohio Valley there were few, and in some cases no, descriptions sufficiently detailed to permit the breakdown of classes of objects into specific types so necessary for accurate comparative studies. This same problem confronted the present study and as a result it was possible to include only a few Ohio Adena mounds in Table 2. Many other mounds were excluded from the table because so few traits were recorded for them as to make their listing meaningless. In spite of many difficulties, a number of interesting comparisons of Ohio Adena can be made with that of the Upper Ohio Valley and other areas.

Certainly the most famous of all Adena mounds was the Adena Mound excavated by William C. Mills (1902, p. 452-479) near Chillicothe, Ross County, Ohio, in 1901. Not only did the Adena culture receive its name from this mound, but also from this structure was gained the general concept of the content of Adena Culture still prevalent in many people's minds yet today. From the listing of major traits of the Adena Mound in Table 2, it is obvious that the contents of this mound were quite similar to the items found in the Late "Robbins" complex of mounds in Kentucky and to the materials of the top zone of the Cresap Mound, and the Grave Creek Mound, and the Welcome Mound in the Upper Ohio Valley. Conspicuous items in the Adena Mound were "Robbins" stemmed blades, "Robbins" leaf-shaped blades, a formal grooved tablet, a bow tie gorget, expanded-center bar gorget, constricted tubular pipes, copper bracelets, copper finger rings, "Adena Plain" pottery, and cut sheets of mica. The unusual human effigy tubular pipe from this mound was unlike any other pipe reported from an Adena mound, but it equates in general form and time with the animal effigy pipes of the Welcome and Sayler Park mounds. The ear-spools worn by the dwarf depicted on the Adena pipe were the most suggestive indicators of Hopewell influence upon Adena yet found. The constructional use of logs to surround and cover important burials in the Adena Mound also reflected its close relationship to the "Robbins" complex in Kentucky. The almost complete lack of correspondence among the specific major traits of the Adena Mound with those of the Fisher Site in Kentucky and the Natrium, Beech Bottom, and Cresap (lower zones) mounds in the Upper Ohio Valley seems to support the great time differences demonstrated by the stratigraphy of the Cresap Mound.

The Coon Mound in Athens County, Ohio, excavated by Greenman (1932, p. 369-523) in 1930 graphically illustrates the paucity of artifacts found in some Adena mounds in Ohio. With the exception of two copper bracelets and 260 disk shell beads found with the extended burial in the elaborate log tomb, no other artifacts were found associated with features in this mound. On the basis of the elaborate tomb and the copper bracelets this mound appears to have been on approximately the same time horizon as the Adena Mound and of the "Robbins" complex in Kentucky.

From the list of Ohio mounds and their traits compiled by Webb and Snow (1945, p. 110-127) and Webb and Baby (1957, p. 2-7), it is apparent that the majority of Ohio Adena mounds was similar to the Adena and Coon mounds both in content and time. Although only a few traits are known for each of the many mounds on this list, in most cases the traits are of such a distinctive nature as to suggest their relationship in the general Adena developmental scheme and to sites in other areas. The most prominent and frequently recurring traits are "Robbins" stemmed blades, "Robbins" leaf-shaped blades, formal and engraved stone tablets, expanded-center bar gorgets, blocked-end tubular pipes, copper bracelets, copper finger rings, "Adena Plain" pottery, mica crescents, log tombs of elaborate construction, and house patterns with paired post molds. As examples of mounds having three or more of the above traits are the Adena Mound, Coon Mound, Cowan Creek Mound, Clough Mound, Baldwin Mound, Streitenberger Mound, Redding Mound, Burgh-Orr Mound, Clyde Jones Mound, and Elmer Williams Mound (Webb and Baby, 1957, p. 2-7). Many more mounds on the list appear to share the same complex of traits to a lesser degree but space does not permit their listing here.

Most certainly, the majority of known Adena sites in Ohio conforms to the general picture of the "Robbins" complex in Kentucky and its counterpart as shown in the upper level of the Cresap Mound, Grave Creek Mound, and Welcome Mound in the Upper Ohio Valley. To be sure, there were differences in the way this complex was expressed in the three areas. A type, for example, the constricted tubular blocked-end pipe, may have been more abundant in Kentucky than in Ohio, but these differences in details seem less important than the overall configuration of the complex. Not to be forgotten is the fact that a considerable period of time elapsed from the beginning to the end of late Adena and that most of the mounds and their contents have not, or can not, be specifically dated within the period. The great variability in the contents of the individual mounds and the unsystematic fashion in which the mounds have been selected for excavation presents an almost insurmountable problem when we attempt to draw fine lines in the chronology.

In some sites the only obvious changes from earlier times may involve no more than one or two major traits. For example, effigy tubular pipes and zoömorphic engraved formal tablets appear to be the only unusual items at the sites where they were found. All these sites seem to have had a basic "Robbins" complex of traits containing the general forms of which the unusual items were a modification. I suspect that the effigy pipes in Adena as known from the Adena Mound (Mills, 1902, p. 476), the Welcome Mound (Anonymous, 1958, p. 19), and the two from the Sayler Park Mound in the Cincinnati Museum of Natural History represent an important innovation that resulted from an outside stimulus, probably Hopewell, late in Adena. The introduction of zoömorphic representations to durable forms that were made simply and undecorated during a long period in Adena seems an event of important temporal and cultural significance that warrants extensive future study.

The isolation and definition of what constitutes early-middle Adena in Ohio presents much greater problems than the elucidation of late Adena as discussed above. No mound so far excavated in Ohio has contained the abundance of early-middle Adena traits found in the Natrium Mound, Beech Bottom Mound, and Cresap Mound in the Upper Ohio Valley and the Fisher Site in Kentucky. However, in the collections of the Ohio State Museum and of private individuals are many artifacts that on the basis of typology can be assigned to early-middle Adena.

In spite of their often meager artifactual contents, there are mounds in Ohio that contained distinctive early mound-building and burial traits. For example, the subfloor pit and depressions at the bottom of the Toepfner Mound were very similar to the pits under the Cresap Mound. The radiocarbon date of 2780 ± 410 years (Libby, 1954, p. p. 737) for charcoal found in a tomb 4.4 feet above the floor of the Toepfner Mound indicated that the subfloor pits were well within the early Adena period. However, the date 2377 ± 150 years (Libby, 1954, p. 737) for the charred logs from a tomb 7.5 feet above the floor of this mound seems to suggest that the upper portions were constructed during late Adena. Unfortunately, the number of artifact traits in this structure was too small to be of much value for assessment of time position on the basis of artifact typology.

During the summer of 1959 Raymond S. Baby of the Ohio State Museum excavated the William H. Davis Mound about 10 miles east of Columbus, Ohio, on U. S. Route 40 (Baby and Mays, 1959, p. 95-96). This mound not only seems to be early Adena but it also was constructed directly over an Archaic burial ground containing items associated with the burials that could be ancestral to certain forms found in Adena. Of particular interest in this category were two cigar-shaped, blocked-end tubular pipes not unlike a few examples that have been recovered from Adena mounds in Ohio. Two cylindrical copper beads were also associated with the Archaic burials.

The structure and disposition of the burials of the William H. Davis Mound were similar in many ways to that of the Cresap Mound. Of the 29 Adena burials, all but two were found in the mound fill and on the floor of the mound. The other two burials, both extended, were found in elliptical subfloor pits. Three of the 29 burials were cremations. Most of the extended inhumations had been placed on and covered with strips of bark in the same fashion as the extended burials of the Cresap Mound. Use of logs to surround or cover a burial seems not to have occurred in the Davis Mound. However, since 15½ feet had been removed from the top of this mound (originally 20 feet in height) by commercial gravel operations before Baby began his excavation, our knowledge is confined entirely to the 4½ feet remaining above the floor of the mound. We will always wonder if perhaps later Adena periods similar to the Cresap Mound were present in the 15½ feet removed from this interesting structure.

Since Ohio is generally considered the major center of Adena, at least in the number of mounds, we would expect to find the full range from early to late Adena in that area. The evidence from the Davis Mound gives us hope that eventually a comprehensive picture of early Adena can be made available for Ohio in spite of the inadequate excavations of the past and the destructive forces of man today.

Adena mounds in Indiana

When we turn our attention to Adena manifestations in Indiana ample evidence for the presence of late Adena sites can be found, but little is known of early Adena in this important area. In Table 2, I have listed the major mounds that have been excavated and reported upon in Indiana. Close similarities of the traits of these sites can be seen with those of the late "Robbins" complex in Kentucky and related sites in Ohio and in the Upper Ohio Valley. Setzler (1930, p. 466-500) described four mounds that had been excavated in the Whitewater Valley of eastern Indiana. Three of these mounds (Mound Camp, Stoops Mound, and Glidewell Mound) were believed by Setzler (1930, p. 500) to be Adena or early Hopewell, but the fourth, the Whitehead Mound, was difficult to identify definitely as Adena because of the paucity of artifacts. The distinctive items from these mounds were expanded-center bar gorgets, a constricted mouthpiece tubular pipe, copper bracelets, "Robbins" blades, rectangular slate gorgets (actually these appear to be pendants since only one hole occurred in each of these objects), and "Adena Plain" pottery. Since log molds and post molds were found at the bases of two of these mounds it seems likely that tombs and house patterns were present at these mounds.

Setzler's (1931, p. 27-37) excavation of the Fudge Mound in Randolph County, Ind., produced artifacts similar to those from the four Whitewater Valley mounds mentioned above. Among the distinctive objects were an expanded-center gorget, a bow tie gorget, a plain, formal sandstone tablet, copper bracelets, and "Robbins" points. A large subfloor pit lined with posts contained the disarranged (from soil shifting) remains of an extended adult male holding a trophy skull in his lap. This latter trait was similar to the extended burial and accompanying trophy skull found in the upper zone of the Cresap Mound.

Black's (1936, p. 201-342) careful execution of the excavation of the Nowlin Mound in Dearborn County, Ind., uncovered several elaborate log tombs. Although not numerous, the artifacts found in this mound were similar to the items discovered in the mounds excavated by Setzler in the Whitewater Valley. Conspicuous were "Robbins" blades, a copper bracelet, and a plain, formal tablet.

The structural and artifactual content of the Nowlin Mound and the closely related sites of the Whitewater Valley indicates that the late Adena "Robbins" complex was of considerable importance and extent in southeastern Indiana immediately adjacent to Ohio and Kentucky. Adena materials and sites, however, have been found in other areas of Indiana. Kellar (1960, p. 357-398) has reported upon the excavation of the C. L. Lewis Stone Mound, in Shelby County in the central portion of Indiana, which unquestionably was of Adena origin. Near this stone mound are two small earth mounds probably also of Adena origin since Adena artifacts have been found on the surface near the mounds (Dragoo, 1951). The expanded-center bar gorget, copper bracelet, copper finger ring, and large "Robbins"-like blade of the C. L. Lewis Stone Mound certainly indicate a close relationship of this mound to those of southeastern Indiana and, as Kellar (1960, p. 397-398) has suggested to the "Robbins" and similar mounds in Kentucky.

In Pike County in southwestern Indiana Black (1946, p. 18-22) reported upon the Cato Site which he believed to be of early Adena origin with possible relationships with the Archaic. In his summary he stated (1946, p. 21):

"This second table leads me to conclude that at the Cato Site we have either a late Shell Mound or early Adena occupation. That it is late Shell Mound would be suggested by the presence of small projectile points of stone and pottery. That it is early Adena is suggested to me by the presence of the tubular pipe, gorgets of stone, antler handles, and the association of these things with materials representative of the Shell Mound complex which, everywhere in the Ohio Valley underlies chronologically all other complexes. The minimum amount of shells evident at the site might reasonably indicate a drift away from a shell gathering mode of existence toward a fuller life."

During this present study I examined the specimens from the Cato Site now belonging to the Indiana Historical Society and I believe most of the Adena items can safely be placed in late Adena rather than early Adena as suggested by Black. The three gorgets from this site are all of the reel-shaped type Cat. B, (Fig. 10) with deeply concave sides and ends, unlike the shallow concave sides and ends of the quadriconcave gorgets Cat. A, (Fig. 10) associated with early Adena sites. The tubular pipe is of the flared mouthpiece type Cat. E, (Fig. 11), that also seems to occur only in late Adena. Both "Robbins" stemmed and leaf-shaped blades accompanied the above objects.

On the basis of typology the Adena items of the Cato Site are closely related to the materials of the southeastern Indiana mounds and in turn to the general late Adena "Robbins" complex of Kentucky, Ohio, and the Upper Ohio Valley where it was demonstrated by actual stratigraphic position to be late at the Cresap Mound. Because of the relationships of the Cato Site's Adena objects with the "Robbins" complex, I believe that there was no connection of the Adena component with the earlier Archaic items found on the same site. Unless the Archaic persisted up into late Adena times in southwestern Indiana there seems to be little chance that the Cato Site materials actually represented a transition of a people from late Archaic into early Adena as suggested by Black (1946, p. 22). I believe, however, that Black was perfectly correct in seeing the carry-over of certain Archaic traits into Adena, but this sharing or transfer of traits must have taken place earlier than the Adena component represented at the Cato Site.

As of this time the preponderance of evidence pertains to late Adena in Indiana, but I feel certain that there are sites earlier than those so far excavated. In many surface collections from southern and central Indiana I have seen objects such as "Adena" stemmed and leaf-shaped blades quadriconcave gorgets, and "Fayette Thick" pottery that appear to represent early Adena. Whether or not these objects are associated with a burial complex similar to that found in the lower levels of the Cresap Mound is a matter for future research and discovery. The late Adena sites in Indiana appear to have been closely related to the general "Robbins" complex of late Adena times. Hopewellian influences, however, seem to manifest themselves more strongly in these sites than at the sites in the eastern Ohio Valley. The exact nature of these Hopewellian influences on Adena will be discussed later in this report.

Discussion

In the preceding paragraphs the Adena manifestations of the Upper Ohio Valley and particularly the stratified Cresap Mound have been compared with those in the central Ohio Valley. In these comparisons only the distinctive, or outstanding traits were used as guides to similarity or dissimilarity of the various components examined. By this method it was possible to demonstrate important distinctions between early-middle and late Adena. It now seems impossible, however, to draw a fine line dividing early from middle Adena. Our information on early Adena, if indeed we have yet discovered the earliest Adena, is far too meager to draw a clear picture of its content. Consequently, in the following discussion early-middle Adena will be discussed as a unit, leaving to future research the elucidation of what may eventually be a clear-cut distinction between the early and middle phases of this culture.

It is now possible to add many of the general traits that accompanied the distinctive traits that were used as chronological markers in the preceding discussions. Some of these traits may be confined to early-middle or to late Adena exclusively but the majority persisted throughout Adena. The chronological outline of the content of Adena Culture that follows is by no means the first attempt to depict the development of Adena. Webb and Snow (1945, p. 213) listed 13 mounds which they believed to show a developmental sequence and Webb and Baby (1957, p. 112-113) presented an outline of what they considered to be the important trait markers for early, middle, and late Adena. The outline presented here differs from these previous schemes not only in the chronological placement of certain individual traits but also in some cases the placement of entire sites. These changes have resulted basically from the finding of the stratified sequence of traits ranging from early-middle to late Adena in the Cresap Mound and the relationships that have been shown for many mounds in the Ohio Valley to the Cresap Mound sequence.

Early-middle Adena

A. Burial customs
     1. Burial of the dead in a conical mound that occurred singly or in a group. Probably no earthworks such as sacred circles, etc., were associated at this time.
     2. Mound may or may not have been constructed over an area formerly occupied by a house.
     3. Simple extended inhumations on bark and covered with bark; a few selected individuals, generally singly, placed in shallow subfloor pits usually elliptical in shape and sometimes covered by small logs and lined with puddled clay; others scattered throughout the fill of the mound or placed directly on the mound floor.
     4. Reburial of parts of bodies and bones in anatomical order in mounds.
     5. Reburial of disarticulated bodies (bundle) in mounds.
     6. Cremation in oval or elliptical basins below or near the mound floor; bones sometimes left in situ.
     7. Cremated remains redeposited separately or placed near an extended inhumation.

   8. Burned and unburned artifacts often placed with cremated remains.

   9. Artifacts, intact or mutilated, or both, often placed with important burials.

  10. Extensive use of red ocher; sprinkled on burials and artifacts, deposited in lumps or granules with burials and artifacts or separately in mound.

  11. Evidence of fire near or above burials both in subfloor pits and in the mound fill; intentional or accidental partial destruction of bodies by these fires.

B. Houses

   1. Circular, with single wall posts.

C. Tools, implements, ornaments

   1. Flint projectiles and blades of the following types: "Cresap" blade, "Adena" blade, and "Adena" leaf-shaped blade.

   2. Flint drills with slightly expanded, straight, or stemmed bases.

   3. Flint end and side scrapers.

   4. Bone and antler handles for flint knives and for atlatl, or both.

   5. Bone awls made from bone splinters, deer or elk cannon bones, and deer or elk scapula bones.

   6. Antler-flaking tools.

   7. Celts with rounded or rectangular polls made of igneous stones or hematite.

   8. Clay or stone smoking tubes, cigar-shaped, straight cylinder with a blocked-end (some may be slightly flared or trumpet-shaped at the blocked-end), and modified tubular.

   9. Stone gorgets (usually of slate) of the quadriconcave type. The semi-keeled type may appear late in this period.

  10. Stone pendants (usually of slate), trapezoidal and bell-shaped with flat base.

  11. Crude stone tablets with either plain or grooved surfaces.

  12. Faceted lumps of hematite.

  13. Cones or hemispheres usually made of hematite, barite, or sandstone.

  14. Stone concretions used as paint cups.

  15. Copper gorgets of the quadri-concave type.

16. Rolled copper beads, usually short and barrel-shaped.
17. Head-dresses made from deer or elk skulls and antlers, or the antlers imitated in copper.
18. Large pottery vessels with flat circular bottoms, cordmarked exteriors and interiors, and occasionally with truncated lugs just below a plain rim—the "Fayette Thick" type.

D. Typical sites of this period—Cresap Mound, Natrium Mound (Solecki, 1953), Beech Bottom Mound (Bache and Satterthwaite, 1930), Fisher Site (Webb and Haag, 1947), and the William H. Davis Mound (Baby and Mays, 1959).

Late Adena ("Robbins" complex)

A. Burial customs
1. Burial of the dead in a conical mound that occurred singly or more often in a group. Earthworks such as sacred circles often associated with mounds late in this period.
2. Mound frequently placed over an area occupied by a house that was burned during construction of mound.
3. Extended inhumations, singly or in groups in elaborate log tombs frequently made in or on house floor at base of mound.
4. Extended burials scattered in mound fill.
5. Cremations in situ in clay basins sometimes accompanied by artifacts (usually burned).
6. Redeposit of one or more cremations in the mound.
7. Decapitation, head buried separately or placed with extended burial as "trophy" skull.
8. Artifacts, intact or mutilated, placed with important extended burials and occasionally with cremations.
9. Use of red ocher on burials and with artifacts.
10. Fired areas on mound base and on mound surface.

B. Houses
1. Circular, with paired wall posts.

C. Tools, implements, and ornaments
1. Flint projectiles and blades of the following types: "Robbins" blade and "Robbins" leaf-shaped blades.
2. Drills, celts, and bone tools similar to early-middle Adena.

3. Clay or stone smoking tubes, blocked-end with constricted mouthpiece, blocked-end with flared mouthpiece, and blocked-end with zoömorphic effigy at mouth end or on tube.

4. Stone gorgets (usually of slate or sandstone) of the following types: expanded-center bar, reel-shaped, bow tie, rectangular and elliptical.

5. Stone pendants (usually of slate or sandstone), rectangular and bell-shaped with rounded base.

6. Formal stone tablets with plain or grooved surfaces, effigy stone tablet, and engraved stone tablets.

7. Copper C-shaped bracelets and finger rings.

8. Sheets of mica cut into designs, usually crescents.

9. Pottery vessels of the "Adena Plain" and "Montgomery Incised," "Johnson Plain," and "Paintsville Simple Stamped."

D. Typical sites "Robbins" Mound (Webb and Elliott, 1942), the Wright Mounds (Webb and Haag, 1940), the C. and O. Mounds (Webb and Haag, 1942), the Adena Mound (Mills, 1902), Mound Camp (Setzler, 1930), Nowlin Mound (Black, 1936), and Cresap Mound (top zone).

In early Adena the expression of the burial cult was one of simplicity. A mound was usually started with the burial of an individual in a shallow elliptical-shaped pit lined with and covered by bark. In some instances this initial burial seems to have taken place within a house while in other cases the burial was made in an open village area. The actual construction of a mound appears to have been gradual as more burials were slowly added and covered with earth. While some individuals were extended in the flesh, others were cremated, and in some cases, the dry bones were bundled together and deposited in the mound. This latter trait indicates that bodies were probably placed upon exposed platforms until the flesh decayed and dropped from the bones, or perhaps a person died away from home and his bones were returned for placement in the ancestral burial mound. Some bodies were dissected before burial with only certain articulated portions buried. Other parts of these cut-up bodies may have been cremated.

Why so many different ways in which the bodies of the dead were treated and buried appears impossible to answer with our present information. It has been suggested that only important individuals received a tomb burial extended in the flesh while the lot of the common man was the crematory fire. Although this may be true in some cases, it is also difficult to explain why prized objects were often consigned to the crematory fires along with the bodies while some extended burials in tombs received no durable offerings. Even the very reason for beginning a mound seems obscured. Certainly, in the case of the Cresap Mound, the individual with the most grave offerings in his tomb was not the first buried since that burial was of a young male, or perhaps female, with the inclusion of a single utilitarian object, a celt. We can only speculate as to the relationships of the individuals buried in a mound, members of a ruling family? of a clan? of a class? or of some larger tribal unit? Although the identity of the individuals placed in a mound remains obscure, it is obvious that even in early Adena times there were a number of well developed practices concerning the burial of the dead and the rites that accompanied burial.

Fire seems to have been an important element in their rites. Aside from the use of fire to burn bodies in crematories, there is abundant evidence to indicate that fires were placed near extended flesh burials both in tombs and in the fill of the mound. Some of these fires were so close that portions of the burials were often accidentally cremated. As was noted in a previous section of this report, accidental burning was found on several bodies in the Cresap Mound. Webb and Snow (1945, p. 75-78) have presented evidence that Adena tombs and burials were left exposed for a considerable period of time before being closed and covered with earth. During this period of exposure the body was sometimes painted with colorful pigments, usually red ocher, and offerings of artifacts and food placed with it. Fires were perhaps lighted during these occasions with the result that sometimes the bark coverings of the burial caught fire and were partially destroyed along with portions of the burial. I doubt that this was any cause for concern to Adena peoples since so many bodies were consigned to crematory fires anyway.

Other fires, not directly associated with burials in the mounds, were perhaps used for warmth and light by the participants in the rites for the dead. Such fires may also have had a strong mystical significance.

During early-middle Adena there was an abundant use of red ocher and in small amounts other pigments such as yellow ocher, graphite, and manganese dioxide. Red ocher was often sprinkled over the burial and the surrounding area. At times it was placed in small piles in the grave and it commonly covered artifacts placed adjacent to the body. Red ocher used in the paint used to decorate the body of the deceased, and also probably of the participants in the rite, was prepared on crude stone tablets. During early-middle Adena these tablets were made from any convenient thin slab of limestone, siltstone, or sandstone. The wide grooves on many of these specimens were worn by the rubbing of pieces of hematite of which so many faceted lumps have been found in mounds such as Cresap and Natrium.

The number and kinds of artifacts placed with early-middle Adena burials are of particular interest. Most of the artifacts in the early mounds appear to be utilitarian rather than ornamental in contrast to the late Adena mounds where ornaments appear in greater abundance. In mounds such as Natrium, Fisher, and the lower zones of Cresap there were many flint blades of the "Adena" ovate-stemmed and leaf-shaped types that were worn from actual use. Drills and scrapers were also common at these sites. In conspicuous abundance were celts of igneous stones and hematite that also appear to have been used in the day-to-day work and not made just specifically for inclusion with a burial. When conditions have been favorable, bone awls and handles have been found with the stone tools. The nature of these tools and their placement with the burials seem to indicate that they were the property of the person with whom they were buried.

The major durable items of personal adornment found in early-middle Adena were strings of beads, gorgets, and pendants. Some of these strings were of small copper beads while others were made from shells, usually marginellas and the columnellas of large marine gastropods. Disk shell beads and tubular bone beads were also occasionally used. The quadriconcave gorget either of slate or copper seems to have been the major form of this object during early-middle Adena. How early it came into use is still unknown but certainly by middle Adena it was a well established item. Trapezoidal and bell-shaped pendants with flat bases were the basic pendant forms during this time. Some of these had geometrical designs cut into their surfaces but most were plain.

Probably the most distinctive burial association in early-middle Adena was the tubular pipe. The early pipe form seems to have been a straight or cigar-shaped tube of stone or clay with a blocked end. In the Upper Ohio Valley where the blocked-end tubular pipe was common, many examples of this form had a slight flare or trumpet-shape at the blocked end but there were several pipes where the tube was nearly straight or slightly rounded at the blocked end. Although these pipes were usually made of fireclay, occasionally the same form was executed in a dense sandstone. The modified tubular pipe in which the mouthpiece was located in a tube projecting at a right angle from the main tube appears to have been an adaptation of the common tube form that probably occurred late in middle Adena.

The reasons for and the significance of placing pipes with burials present an interesting problem. Usually a single pipe was placed with a burial as in the Cresap and Natrium mounds where it would seem that the pipe was the property of the deceased. In the Beech Bottom Mound, however, there were more than 32 pipes that apparently were all presented as an offering to one individual. Why? Was this man the pipemaker? Was this a way of paying tribute to a revered individual in which the men of the clan gave up their prized pipes? Was the pipe of special significance in their ceremonies? If so, why were pipes placed with some persons and not with others? Did only certain individuals have the rights to a pipe? These and many other questions goad the archeologist, but unfortunately, all too often the available information is insufficient to warrant positive answers.

The finding of antler head-dresses in the Cresap Mound and the Fisher Site indicates that the impersonation and deification of animals were important elements in their ceremonies, and that these were well developed by middle Adena. This practice, undoubtedly derived from the earlier Archaic, was strongly expressed in late Adena and seems to have reached a peak in the later Hopewell where animals were portrayed in most of their arts and crafts (Fig. 16).

Although many early-middle Adena traits carry over into late Adena, late Adena, as typified by what I have called the "Robbins" complex, was marked by many sweeping and seemingly abrupt changes. In their burial practice the simple pit grave gave way to large burial chambers, or inclosures containing one or more extended bodies, constructed below or on the floor of a house with paired-post wall supports. It is believed that these tombs were left open for a period of many days during which the body or bodies were painted with pigments such as red ocher and graphite (Webb and Snow, 1945, p. 77). While the body "lay in state," ceremonies were conducted in which offerings of goods and foods were placed in the grave. To protect the body from the elements a canopy sometimes was erected over the tomb and a platform of logs was placed around it. The disturbance of single bones from correct anatomical order and the application of paint directly to the bones seem to indicate that a tomb remained open until after the flesh had decayed before an earth mound was started. In many instances more log tombs covered by earth were added to a mound until the mound reached tremendous dimensions, as for example in the Grave Creek Mound.

In late Adena greater attention seems to have been lavished upon fewer individuals. A smaller number of burials was scattered in the mound fill outside of the log inclosures, and grave associations tended to be generally reserved for those persons placed in tombs in contrast to the early-middle Adena practice of placing items with many burials scattered throughout the mound. This change seems to suggest that class and rank distinctions had become well defined and more rigid by this time.

One of the interesting traits of late Adena was the placement of "trophy" skulls with burials (Webb and Snow, 1945, p. 79). These skulls seem to have been dry, clean skulls long before they were placed, often on the lap, of an extended burial. The "trophy" skull found on the lap of an extended burial in the upper zone of the Cresap Mound possessed a slightly polished surface like that seen on bone that had been handled by man over a period of time. Whether these skulls are truly "trophies" in the sense that they were conquered enemies, or whether they were members of the tribe, remains unknown. Physically these skulls appear to be the same as the other burials in the mound. Although isolated skulls have been found in early-middle Adena, the intentional placement of a skull along with other "property" seems to be confined to late Adena.

Before turning to the artifactual content of late Adena, the association of Adena mounds with earthworks, usually "sacred circles," must be mentioned. Webb and Snow (1945, p. 29-33) have amply demon-

---

Fig. 16. Adena and Hopewell head-dresses
A. Reconstruction of the elk antler head-dress from the Cresap Mound. B. Copper "antler" head-dress from the Fisher Site Mound, Fayette County, Ky. C. Reconstruction of wolf head-dress from the Ayers Mound, Owen County, Ky. D. Copper head-dress from the Hopewell group, Ross County, Ohio. (B and D after Webb and Haag, 1947; C after Webb and Baby, 1957.)

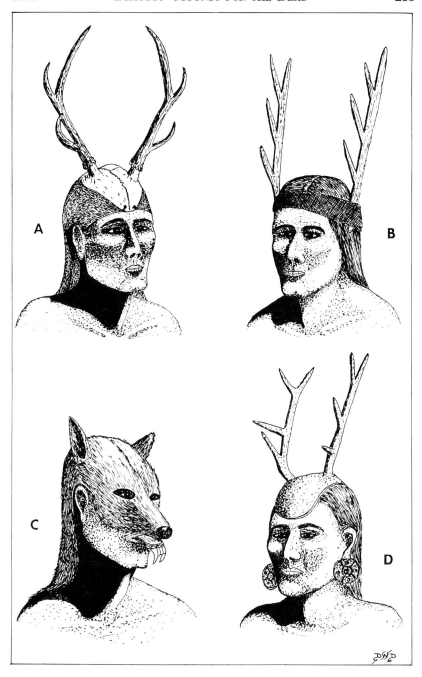

strated the Adena origin of many of these structures and they go so far as to state that "every 'sacred circle' is of Adena origin." The bulk of evidence gathered in this present study convinced me that "sacred circles" were constructed only during late Adena. An Adena mound containing the "Robbins" complex of traits was usually but not always one of a group of mounds constructed near one or more earth circles. Except for early-middle Adena mounds, for example the Fisher Site, that were present in an area of heavy mound concentration spanning the entire time range of Adena, early mounds were isolated or one of a small group of mounds without earthworks association. The suggestion that "sacred circles" were the meeting place of a phratry or other social subdivision of the tribe seems to be a valid one (Webb and Snow, 1945, p. 32). The presence of elaborate log tomb burials of certain individuals in the mounds near "sacred circles" is highly suggestive that these individuals were the leaders of the social and ceremonial activities of the group that used the earthwork. The finding of "sacred circles" in groups of two to eight also seems to indicate that Adena peoples were divided into formal and well established subdivisions, probably clans, with strong leaders during late Adena times.

Changes from early-middle Adena in the artifactual associations with late Adena burials are as striking as the changes noted for the actual disposition of the burials in the mounds. Not only were there changes in form but also in the selection of items to be included with burials. Some of these changes appear to be very important to the understanding of the internal development of Adena.

Flint blades continued to be placed with the dead but the "Robbins" blades of late Adena were markedly different than those of the "Adena" types found in early-middle Adena mounds. In contrast to the long, thick cross-section, weak shoulder, ovate base, stemmed "Adena" blade, the "Robbins" blade was wide in relation to length, thin in cross-section, deeply notched at the shoulders, and the stem was parallel-sided with a slightly rounded or nearly flat base. The chipping of the "Robbins" blades was more carefully executed and the flints, usually from Flint Ridge, Ohio, finer grained and more colorful than those chosen for "Adena" blades. The "Adena" leaf-shaped and the "Robbins" leaf-shaped blades were marked by the same basic differences as noted for the stemmed types. In contrast to the Adena blades that usually showed wear on the edges from use, the "Robbins" blades often showed little or no wear. This latter characteristic has led many people to suggest that these blades were made either only as offerings to the dead, or for ceremonial purposes.

I believe the "Robbins" blades reflected a basic change in Adena not only in chipping techniques but also in form. The early "Adena" blades appear to be modifications of techniques and forms present earlier in the Archaic but the "Robbins" blades can be closely linked with the techniques and forms that reached a high state of development later in Hopewell. The significance of this change in Adena will be covered later when Adena's relationships with Hopewell are considered.

Although drills, scrapers, celts, and other utilitarian objects have been found in late Adena mounds, these items were rarer than in the early-middle Adena sites and were overshadowed by the presence of other distinctive ornaments and implements that were not found with the earlier burials.

Of the objects of personal adornment, copper and shell beads of various types continued in use, but copper bracelets and finger rings appear to be an innovation of late Adena. In some late Adena mounds, for example, the Dover Mound in Kentucky, large numbers of copper bracelets have been found (Webb and Snow, 1959, p. 55-59). Coetaneous with copper bracelets and rings was the introduction of ornaments, usually crescents, cut from sheets of mica. At some sites rectangular pendants and a large bell-shaped pendant with a rounded base came into use.

During late Adena gorget forms became varied. The quadriconcave gorget of early-middle Adena was made with deeper concavities on the sides giving a more truly reel-shaped appearance. The "bow-tie" gorget with deep concavities on two sides and with ends convex also came into fashion in certain areas. At some sites, probably towards the end of late Adena, rectangular and elliptical gorgets made their appearance.

The most distinctive and diagnostic gorget in late Adena was the expanded-center bar. As already suggested by Webb and Snow (1945, p. 84-85) this object was probably not truly a gorget but actually an atlatl weight. When found in grave association, it generally was near the lower extremities along the side of the body rather than near or on the chest. A bone handle found in alinement with an expanded-center bar at the Ricketts Site (Funkhouser and Webb, 1935, p. 89) strongly supports the use as atlatl weights. In early-middle Adena there were several objects that probably served as atlatl weights. The barite and galena bars from the Fisher Site (Webb and Haag, 1947, p. 87) were undoubtedly so used, and boatstones like the one from the Cresap Mound were probably attached to throwing sticks. Cones and hemispheres of hematite and other heavy stones, long a mystery as to their function, may also have been lashed to the atlatl. The expanded-center bar, however, seems to have been made only in late Adena as part of the distinctive "Robbins" complex.

Smoking pipes underwent a number of modifications during late Adena. In Kentucky the blocked-end tubular pipe generally had a constricted mouthpiece, but on a few examples the mouthpiece was flared. No pipes of these types have been reported from mounds in the Upper Ohio Valley where the straight tubular pipe with blocked end may have persisted into late Adena. Certainly the most interesting modification of the tubular pipe was the addition of an animal effigy carved either into the mouthpiece as in the examples from the Welcome Mound in the Upper Ohio Valley and the Sayler Park Mound in Cincinnati, or carved into the entire tube as in the famous human effigy pipe from the Adena Mound in Ohio. The addition of zoömorphic designs to durable objects was a great advance over the plain and undecorated items of early-middle Adena (Fig. 17).

Stone tablets also came in for important modifications during late Adena. Any crude, flat stone no longer sufficed, for care was now taken in the selection of the stone and its shaping into a tablet. The usual shape of the finished tablet was rectangular, round, or kidney-shaped. Upon the surfaces of some tablets deep, wide, grooves were worn while on others the surfaces were slightly depressed from abrasion. Some tablets received special attention in that on one face a zoömorphic or geometric design would be carved (Webb and Baby, 1957,

---

Fig. 17. Effigy and tubular pipe forms of the late Adena "Robbins" complex. A and B. Top and bottom views of the shoveler duck pipe from the Welcome Mound, Marshall County, W. Va. C. Wolf effigy pipe from Englewood Mound near Dayton, Ohio. D and E. Duck and aquatic bird (duck?) effigy pipes from the Sayler Park Mound, Cincinnati, Ohio. F. The famous human effigy pipe from the Adena Mound, Ross County, Ohio. G. Constricted tubular pipe from "Robbins" Mound, Boone County, Ky. H. Flared tubular pipe from Cato Site, Pike County, Ind. Pipe A is 6-5/8 inches in length, Pipe D is 6-1/4 inches in length, and Pipe F is 8 inches in length (A-E after Setzler, 1960.)

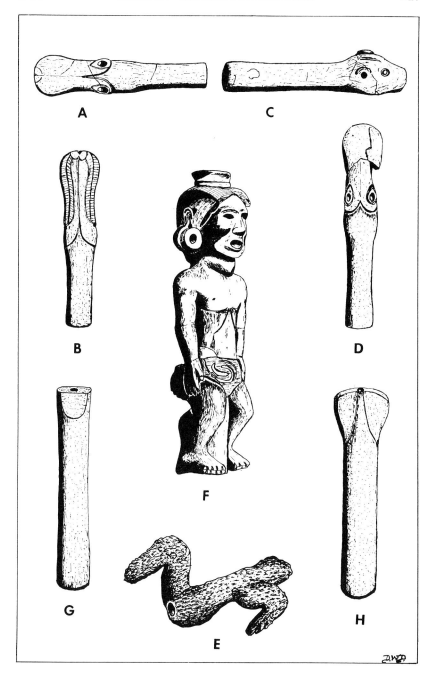

A   C

B   D

F

G   H

E

p. 83-101). The opposite face usually was grooved like the plain varieties of the formal tablets mentioned above. The typical zoömorphic representation was that of a raptorial bird, probably the carrion crow. The most unusual zoömorphic tablet in Adena was the turtle effigy found in the top zone of the Cresap Mound. In this example, the entire tablet was carved in the shape of a turtle rather than having the design cut into only one face of the stone (Fig. 18-19).

The finely made stone tablets of late Adena appear to have been the end product of a ceremonial practice that was as old as Adena itself. The preparation of paint pigments was an integral part of the ceremonies accompanying the burial of the dead. Webb and Baby (1957, p. 100) have suggested that the raptorial bird motif on the late engraved tablets indicated that the carrion crow was revered because of its aid in removing the flesh from bodies before they were placed in the crematory fires. If bodies had been exposed on platforms for a period of time sufficient to allow partial decomposition, the carrion crow and other flesh-eating birds certainly would have been attracted. It seems quite logical that these birds would have been considered as agents of the spirit world who assisted the people in the preparation of the dead.

The turtle depicted on the effigy tablet from the top zone of the Cresap Mound can not be as easily associated with the preparation of the dead as the raptorial bird. I am inclined to regard the turtle as a clan totem in this instance. If the turtle did represent a clan symbol, we are confronted with additional evidence of the clan organization of Adena as has been suggested in connection with the presence of "sacred circles" ranging in number from two to eight at some large Adena centers. This tablet may have been a sacred paint palette belonging only to the turtle clan. Could the animals depicted on the tubular pipes also be clan symbols or totems? Unfortunately, our evidence is still too fragmentary to draw any hard and lasting conclusions, but it does suggest lines to follow in future research.

Fig. 18. Design elements depicted upon recorded Adena tablets
A. Wright tablet. B. Gaitskill stone tablet. C. Allen tablet. D. Gaitskill clay tablet. E. Grave Creek tablet. F. Lakin B tablet. G. Cincinnati tablet. H. Wilmington tablet. I. Kiefer tablet (conjectural restoration). J. Meigs County tablet. K. Lakin A tablet. L. Berlin tablet. (After Webb and Baby, 1957.)

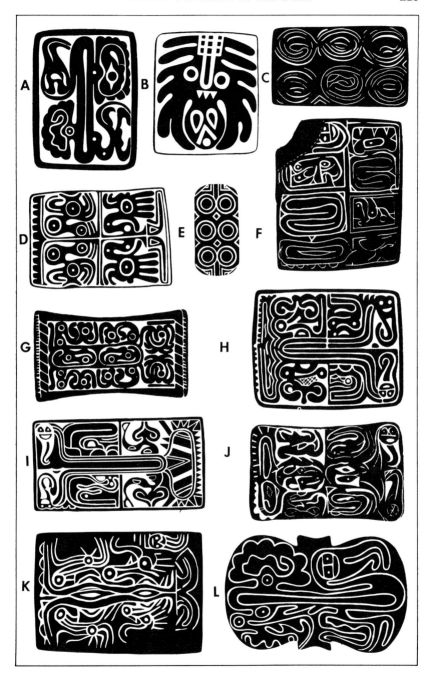

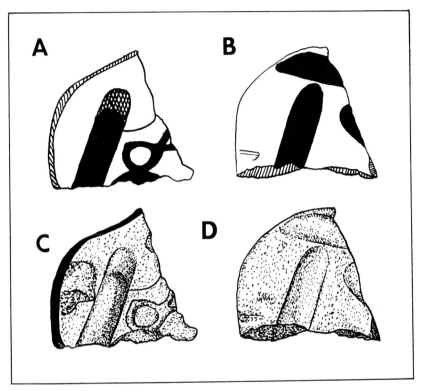

Fig. 19. Fragment of a previously unrecorded engraved tablet from the Castor Site, Muskingham County, Ohio. (In the collection of William Buker, Pittsburgh, Pa.)

Webb and Baby (1957, p. 61-71) have presented a well documented case for the use of animal masks by Adena. All known examples of such masks appear to have been found in mounds attributable to late Adena in time, but I suspect that masks were also used by early Adena and that the ultimate origin of these objects will be found in the Archaic. In the Wright Mound (Site 6) Webb (1940, p. 66) found the palate bone of a wolf that had been trimmed to a spatula shape with the incisors, canines, and first premolars still in place. Then in the excavation of the Ayres Mound (Webb and Baby, 1957, p. 62-64) a similar cut wolf palate was found in association with the skull of an adult

Adena male in which the upper lateral and medial incisor teeth had apparently been removed intentionally to permit the insertion of the cut wolf palate into the man's mouth. Webb and Baby's (1957, p. 70) reconstruction of this type of mask depicted the skin of the wolf's head worn over the man's head in association with the cut wolf palate and attached teeth. In light of George Catlin's (1860, p. 76) observations of similar masks worn by historic Indians in the West, Webb and Baby's reconstruction of the Adena mask seems to be a logical one. The cut jaws of the puma or cougar have been reported from the Westenhaver Mound (Mills, 1917, p. 227-266) and the Dover Mound (Webb and Snow, 1959, p. 65-66), but these jaws were probably left attached to the animal's head and not inserted into the wearer's mouth as were the wolf palates (Fig. 20).

What relationships, if any, the animal masks had with animals depicted on Adena pipes and tablets remain to be determined, but mounting evidence is beginning to indicate an important function in the portrayal of certain animals by late Adena peoples. If future investigations can demonstrate a pattern to the occurrence of specific animal representations, we may be able to determine whether or not they depict clan motifs or whether they are wide-spread ceremonial symbols used by the shaman throughout Adena society without regard to social divisions.

Aside from those changes in the burial and ceremonial complexes of late Adena from those of early-middle Adena, we have little evidence for other changes in Adena culture with the exception of pottery. During early-middle Adena "Fayette Thick" pottery seems to have been the dominant type. Some vessels of the "Fayette Thick" type probably were still made during late Adena but by this time "Adena Plain" had reached a peak in popularity. Throughout most of late Adena, pottery vessels were not decorated, but at the C. and O. Mounds at Paintsville, Ky., decorated pottery of the "Paintsville Simple Stamped" and "Montgomery Incised" types was found (Hagg and Webb, 1942, p. 341-349). These types, however, may have been trade items and not a development within Adena since only a few sherds of each type were found. I am inclined to believe that the C. and O Mounds were very late and that at these mounds we see the impact of new cultural influences from the South.

From the present evidence it is impossible to discern any time differences in Adena weaving techniques. Fabrics have been found in

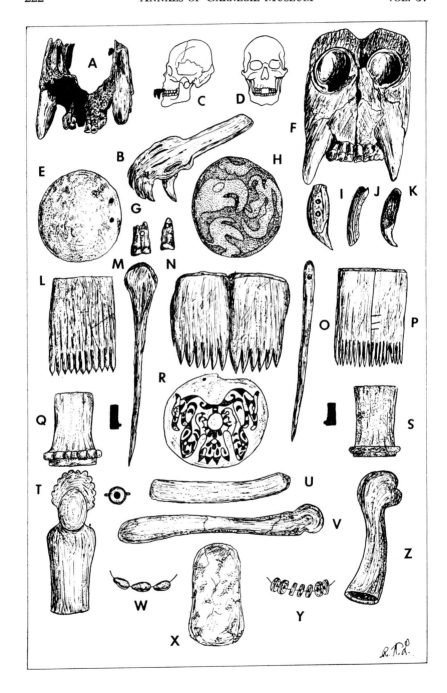

both early and late Adena mounds. It would seem that weaving was a well established craft that had its beginning back in the Archaic (Fig. 21).

Although we are able to discern marked changes in the burial customs and artifacts from early to late Adena, there is no conclusive evidence to indicate that any new and important innovations occurred in the living pattern. Robert M. Goslin (1957, p. 41-46) in his study of food remains from Adena sites concluded that Adena subsistence was based upon a combination of hunting, fishing, collecting, and a simple form of agriculture in which gourd, pumpkin, squash, and sunflowers were cultivated. The products of their agricultural pursuits furnished a very small percentage of the daily ration and probably was no more than the occasional addition of a little spice to the pot. To state that Adena was truly an agricultural society, as some have suggested (Griffin, 1958, p. 2), seems to be overstating the case. Such an assumption is based upon the belief that corn was grown along with squash, pumpkin, and sunflowers. There is no evidence that corn was grown by Adena, and pumpkin, and squash, have been reported from only two late Adena mounds (Goslin, 1957, p. 42). In the Kentucky rock shelters containing remains of Adena culture, corn has al-

---

Fig. 20. Bone, antler, and shell work from various Adena mounds
A. Cut upper jaw of mountain lion, Dover Mound, Mason County, Ky. B. Cut wolf jaw from Wright Mound, Montgomery County, Ky. C. Lateral view of human skull with cut wolf jaw (B) inserted in mouth. D. Front view of skull showing removal of incisor teeth to permit insertion of wolf jaw. E. Gorget made from skull from the Westenhaver Mound, Pickaway County, Ohio. F. End of the lower jaw of bear cut into an ornament, Westenhaver Mound. G. Perforated human teeth from Fisher Site, Fayette County, Ky. H. Human skull gorget decorated with raptorial bird motif, Florence Mound, Pickaway County, Ohio. I. Perforated bear canine, Streitenberger Mound, Ross County, Ohio. J. Beaver incisor, Westenhaver Mound. K. Bear canine tooth, Westenhaver Mound. L, N and P. Bone combs from the Wright Mound, Montgomery County, Ky. M. Elk scapula awl, Adena Mound, Ross County, Ohio. O. Perforated bone awl, Adena Mound. Q. Antler handle, Westenhaver Mound. R. Shell gorget with raptorial bird motif, Crab Orchard Spring Mound, Lincoln County, Ky. S. Antler atlatl handle, Dillard Stamper Rock Shelter, Wolfe County, Ky. T. "Whistle-like" object (handle?) of bone, Westenhaver Mound. U. Antler flaker, Wright Mound. V. Elk bone spatula, Westenhaver Mound. W. Marginella shell beads, Wright Mound. X. Shell spoon, Wright Mound. Y. Shell disk beads, Wright Mound. (A after Webb and Snow, 1959; B, C, D, H, I, R and S after Webb and Baby, 1957; G. after Webb and Haag, 1947; E, F, J, K, Q, T and V after Mills, 1917; L, N, P, U, W, X and Y after Webb, 1940; M and O after Mills, 1902.)

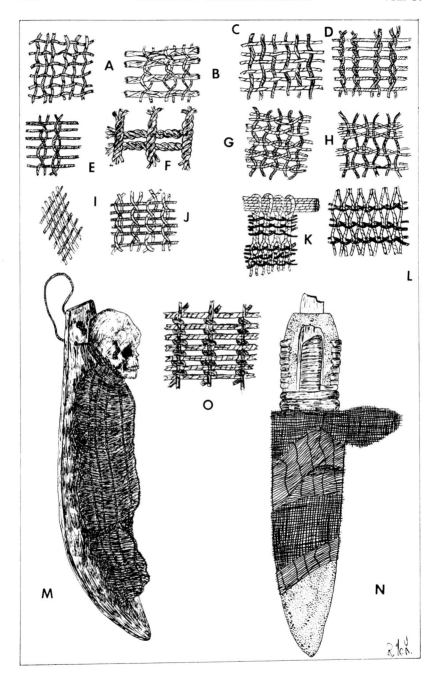

ways been located in, or associated with, the upper levels of occupancy attributed to cultures later than Adena (Goslin, 1957, p. 45). Since other plant remains were found in the Adena levels, the absence of corn seems highly significant.

On the basis of our present knowledge, it would appear that early Adena need not have been geared to an agricultural economy based on corn in order to have constructed mounds for the burial of the dead. The gradual build-up of a mound, for example the Cresap Mound, did not necessitate the expenditure of great amounts of labor at any one time. By the use of every source of food that was available from hunting, and gathering of wild plants, early Adena could easily have established the scattered pattern of settlement that marks the culture from the stable village life of later peoples with corn growing. The great shell midden deposits of the Archaic peoples amply demonstrated that peoples could concentrate their economic pursuits within a relatively circumscribed area without the need to range far and wide. If agriculture, and specifically cultivation of corn, did become an important factor in Adena, I feel that it must have been very late. Only during the late Adena "Robbins" complex did mounds become large and often associated with earthworks requiring the labor of many people to construct. The wide distribution and large number of mounds of the "Robbins" complex indicates that Adena's greatest internal expansion came at that time. Whether corn was, or was not partially responsible for this growth has yet to be demonstrated (Fig. 22).

In the preceding discussion I have deliberately omitted mention of radiocarbon 14 dates for certain Adena sites because it seemed to me

---

Fig. 21. Examples of fabrics and weaving techniques from Adena
A. Plain plaiting or basket weave. B. Plain twining. C. Twilled plaiting. D. Twilled twining. E. Chevron twining. F. Over-two-under-two twilled twining. G. Over-two-under-two twilled twining with zig-zag direction of the warp members. H. Twilled twining over-two-under-two weave of fine strands with pronounced zig-zag direction of the warp cords. I. Twilled plaiting over-two-under-one with warp and weft members crossing obliquely. J. Twilled twining over-two-under-one with straight warp elements. K. A piece of textile edge or selvedge. L. Twilled twining with zig-zag warp elements widely spaced. M. Reconstruction of an Adena cradle board with child wrapped in textiles. N. Copper dagger with textile covering from the Drake Mound, Fayette County, Ky. O. Lattice or bird cage twining technique used on fabrics in M and N (A–L from Morgan Stone Mound, Bath County, Ky. after Webb, 1941; M after Webb and Snow, 1945; and N and O after Webb, 1941.)

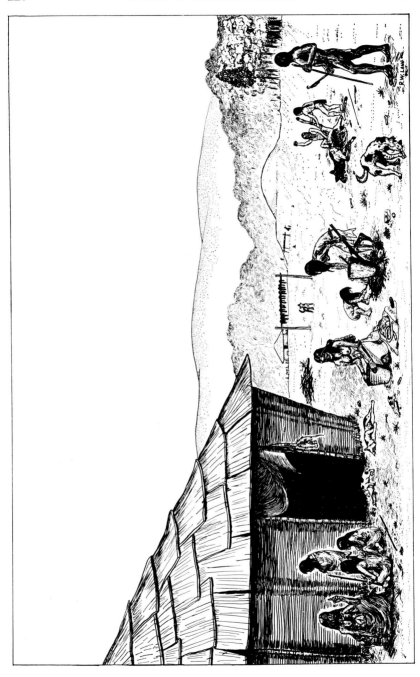

much more important to define the actual typological and stratigraphic evidence for Adena development in the Ohio Valley before introducing the presently available dates that tend only to confuse the picture. Before turning our attention to these dates later in this report, several important aspects of Adena culture first must be scrutinized in the hope that some insights may be gained into the reasons Adena culture developed as it did and not in some other direction. The next section of this report will be devoted to seeking answers, or the direction in which the answers may eventually lie, to the following questions:

1. What were the origins of Adena culture?

2. What were the relationships of early Adena with the preceding Archaic cultures and with other cultures in surrounding areas at the early Adena level?

3. What were the causes of the changes that made late Adena clearly distinguishable from early Adena?

4. What were the relationships of Adena to the Hopewell Culture?

5. What influence did Adena have on areas outside of the Ohio Valley?

6. What was the ultimate fate of Adena Culture?

Fig. 22. Artist's reconstruction of an Adena settlement showing the wide spacing of the houses along a major river valley. (Drawing by Richard W. Lang.)

THE ORIGIN OF ADENA CULTURE

When Webb and Snow (1945, p. 317) wrote "The Adena People" they made the following comment concerning the origin of Adena:

"The point of origin of Adena man with his mound-building traits cannot yet be demonstrated, but it is certain that he was the *first builder of earth-works* in this region and thus could not have derived these traits from any earlier occupants of the region. As a broadheaded individual, with head deformation, one would suspect a southern origin, and his mound-building traits would point to the Middle American Area as a possible source."

Albert C. Spaulding (1952, p. 260-268) accepted Webb and Snow's suggestion of a Middle American origin for Adena and presented several reasons why he believed this to be so. He stated (1952, p. 265-266):

"Adena traits which seem to suggest Circum-Caribbean affiliations in greater or lesser degree include the mortuary concept, with its tombs in earth mounds, multiple burials having a central inhumation with subsidiary inhumations or deposits of cremated remains (this practice considered by Webb to indicate actual killing of retainers to accompany the body of a chief), burial on or under a house floor with subsequent burning of house, use of a considerable amount of grave goods including trophy skulls (one of which was painted), and sharp social differentiation shown in burial practices, with simple cremation for ordinary folk. Head deformation, tubular pipes (probably tobacco pipes), and the large circular houses are also relevant. Although our information is not conclusive, we may suspect the presence of villages fortified by earthworks and palisades in Adena. In the field of arts and crafts, rather elaborate weaving and utilization of cold-worked sheet copper for ornaments can be mentioned. J. B. Griffin has pointed out to me that the carved Adena tablets of stone are a particularly interesting trait in this connection, as they resemble certain Mexican tablet stamps of unknown age, the resemblance extending even to design details. Webb has suggested, on the evidence of traces of paint on one of the Adena specimens, that the Adena tablets were also stamps. Perhaps significantly, the Mexican examples which most strongly suggest Adena are said to come from the Vera Cruz area. The Adena preference for the stone celt as opposed to the Archaic and Hopewell grooved axe has been mentioned above. The grit-tempered, flat-bottomed Adena Plain jar with its occasional tetrapod suports is at least not incongruous in this context. If there are Adena prototypes for Hopewell painted cloth, wrap-around shirts, copper ear spools, and copper panpipes, as seems possible, the case for connection is further strengthened. There is probably little to gain at this stage of our knowledge from a typological refinement and extension of this list of parallels; the purpose here is to bring this situation to the attention of Middle and South American specialists so that a more expert appraisal can be made."

Spaulding (1952, p. 266) goes on to state specifically that "it would seem that the Adena culture appeared in the Ohio Valley as the result of a migration from lowland eastern Mexico" and that "the migrants would have been essentially tropical forest peoples whose culture possessed strong Circum-Caribbean affiliations." He gave no reasons for this postulated migration of Mexican peoples to the Ohio Valley nor did he suggest a route by which these peoples arrived. Spaulding (1955, p. 21) in another and later paper admitted that "unfortunately, no one has yet discovered an unmistakable ancestor in the proper part of Mexico" but he continued to regard his "migration theory as less cumbersome" than other theories that looked elsewhere than Mexico for the origin of Adena.

In "The Adena People No. 2" Snow (1957, p. 56) stated "that nothing has developed since that time (the original publication of *The Adena People* by Webb and Snow, 1945) to change the basic conclusions, but much has been discovered which may be considered to increase the validity of the speculations." Basing his contentions primarily on the physical type of the Adena people and their practice of deforming the skull, Snow suggested that the physical type from the early Zacatenco levels of three sites (El Arbolillo, Ticoman, and Tlatilco) in the valley of Mexico "reveal contours of typical Adena-like skulls." He then suggested that perhaps the earliest advent of the Walcolid physical type to which Adena belonged could be traced to Tepexpan Man which has been dated as 10,000-12,000 years ago (De Terra, Romero, and Stewart, 1949). Thus, for Snow, the Adena physical type could be associated with well established Archaic cultures in Mexico.

Snow (1957, p. 57-60) placed considerable stress on the presence of artificial head deformation in Adena as pointing to the Middle American origin of these people. Snow (1957, p. 60) stated:

"Just now we place credence in the Middle American origin of the Adena People, since the very earliest skulls found in the Valley of Mexico have the same kind of head shaping deformation as Adena. When this cultural mark of head shaping, in addition to the same basic physical type, is added to the many distinctive and diagnostic cultural traits which have a definite relationship to the Middle American cultures, it would seem that the place of origin has been traced."

Let us now take a closer look at the evidence that has been used to link Adena with Middle America, for as Spaulding (1955, p. 21) has stated "the problem is an extremely important one because it deals with a fundamental cultural reorientation involving the establishment of a set of basic practices which persisted until the obliteration of Indian culture in the eastern United States." The relationships of Adena culture to Middle America are of crucial moment not only in the understanding of what happened in the eastern United States but are also important in tracing the migrations of peoples and their culture throughout much of the New World.

Disregarding the physical aspects of the problem for a moment, let us examine the cultural traits that have been advanced as indicating a close tie of Adena with Middle America. How do these traits fit into the picture of Adena development presented in the preceding section of this report?

Among the inhumation traits listed by Spaulding and quoted above were tombs (log) in earth mounds, multiple burials having a central inhumation with subsidiary inhumations or deposits of cremated remains, burial on or under a house floor with subsequent burning of house, use of a considerable amount of grave goods including trophy skulls, and sharp social differentiation shown in burial practices, with simple cremation for ordinary folk. All of these traits certainly belonged to Adena but they did not mark early Adena but were typical of the late Adena "Robbins" complex. As I have pointed out earlier in this report, the tombs of early Adena were merely shallow pits such as those found in the Cresap Mound. In such a grave generally only one individual with or without grave goods was buried. Not until the late stage of Adena were there large and elaborate tombs in which more than one individual was commonly placed. It was in these late tombs that social stratification became obvious with special attention in the form of grave offering being paid to some individuals and not to others. True "trophy" skulls appear to be associated with late Adena sites and have not been reported from the early sites. Fine artifacts and the destruction of these artifacts in the cremation fires of early Adena indicate that those persons so treated were not necessarily just the "ordinary" folk as suggested from the evidence of the late Adena mounds.

All the major burial traits mentioned as linking Adena with Middle America seemed to be confined to, or reached their fullest expression at, the end of Adena and not at its early stages. Likewise, earthworks other than burial mounds, such as "sacred circles", were also features of late Adena that seem to be lacking in early Adena. Although Spaulding (1952, p. 265) has suggested that the Adena earthworks may have been of a defensive nature, there has been no conclusive evidence to indicate that they were used for anything other than ceremonial inclosures. The very large Adena mounds such as the Grave Creek Mound which was nearly 70 feet in height, all seem to have been constructed usually in association with earthworks during late Adena when the "Robbins" complex was at its peak.

Spaulding (1952, p. 265-266) also stated that carved or engraved tablets of stone, "Adena Plain" pottery, and worked sheet copper were links with Middle America. Again, as with the burial customs and large earthworks, these items, except worked copper, were traits of the late Adena "Robbins" complex. Working of sheet copper need not have been introduced from Middle America since the practice was already well developed in the Archaic Old Copper Culture in the Great Lakes area immediately adjacent to the Adena homeland in the Ohio Valley.

If we are to find the origin of Adena must we not look at the early stages of this culture? How can we use traits that are present in the late stage of a culture, but not present in the early stage, as indicators of origin? Are we to believe that the Adena people had all these ideas with them when they arrived from Middle America but that they did not use them for several hundred years? On the basis of the evidence as I see it, those who have looked towards Middle America for the origin of Adena culture have done so with almost a complete disregard for the facts of the chronological development of Adena culture in the Ohio Valley. All too often the florescent stage of a culture has been looked upon as if it typified the culture throughout its history. In attempting to find the origin of a culture by comparing the end product seems to me to have been the prime fallacy in the Adena situation. Even if we accept a Middle American origin for certain traits in Adena we have not demonstrated that the ultimate origin of the culture can be traced there, for in reality these traits mark only a certain period in a cultural continuum that existed long before their appearance. Unless we can show that these traits were basic to the culture from its first appearance in a specific area and that these traits were also present in the areas of Middle America from which the culture was supposed to have migrated, we are only grasping at straws in suggesting that the origin of Adena has been found.

As I understand the picture of cultural development in Middle America I see little that can be equated with the basic foundations of early Adena that can not also be shown to have existed in areas much closer to the Ohio Valley on the proper time level. It is indeed true that the cultures of the Southeast and the Ohio Valley received many influences from Middle America at a later time, but it was these same influences that set the Mississippian cultures apart from the earlier cultures focused around a cult of the dead as seen in Adena. I seriously question any cultural relationships of Adena with the early sites of Zacatenco, El Arbolillo, and Ticoman in Mexico as suggested by Snow (1957, p. 59) on the basis of the presence of similar physical types with artificial head deformation. None of the basic elements of Adena burial practices were present at Zacatenco (Vaillant, 1930, p. 188 where the bodies were placed in graves in a cemetery area. There was no formal preparation of the graves, no grave goods, and the position of the body as to whether it was extended or flexed depended upon how difficult it was to dig the soil because of the presence of stones. I see no similarities of the material culture of Zacatenco, except those of a universal nature, with that of Adena; and in the case of pottery, the vessels of four major wares (Vaillant, 1930, p. 31) and the pottery figurines of Zacatenco bear no possible genetic relationship with Adena. The only major change in the burial practices at Ticoman was the inclusion of grave goods, among which pottery vessels were conspicuous, with the bodies (Vaillant, 1931, p. 316). Pottery vessels were never part of the grave offerings of Adena, and their absence seems to be a very important negative trait. Although additional information was gained on the burial habits of the early and middle Zacatenco populations at the El Arbolillo Site (Vaillant, 1935, p. 168-188), the placement of the burials in graves and the accompanying grave furniture, particularly the pottery, can in no way be considered as ancestral to Adena.

If, as suggested by Snow (1957, p. 60) and Spaulding (1955, p. 21) an actual migration of peoples from the Valley of Mexico was responsible for the establishment of Adena in the Ohio Valley, then we are faced with a situation in which these people left behind them the ideas for making their most distinctive cultural items. On the basis of pottery alone, it is difficult to believe that they would not have retained the basic techniques of manufacture and design used in their Middle American homeland. The radiocarbon date of 3310±250 years ago for the early pottery level of Zacatenco I (Arnold and Libby, 1951, p. 118) has indicated that pottery was already at that time a highly developed craft with distinctive types unlike any known for early Adena. The absence of a pottery type comparable to Adena "Fayette Thick" in the early levels of Middle American sites strongly indicate that the origin of this pottery is to be sought elsewhere. The rapidly emerging picture of Middle American prehistory now coming to light through extensive stratigraphic and typological studies, like those of McNeish (1958) for the Tamanlipas region of Mexico, indicates a cultural development quite unlike that of the Ohio Valley during Adena times. Although the theory for a Middle origin for Adena has been romantic and thought-provoking, the time has come for serious consideration of other possible sources for the roots of Adena.

In a recent study by Chard (1961, p. 21-25), The possibility of an Asiatic origin of the burial mound complex was considered unlikely. After weighing the evidence, Chard concluded that the burial mound complex was not in use in northeastern Asia at an early enough date to have been ancestral to the New World manifestations. Thus, the burial mound complex of the eastern United States was an independent development that owed nothing to the Old World.

If not to distant Middle America, where do we turn in our quest for Adena's beginnings? Certainly, the most obvious place to look would be in the homeland of Adena, the Ohio Valley, and in the Archaic cultures that immediately preceded the rise of Adena.

It is of interest to note that in spite of their belief in the Central American origin of Adena, Webb and Baby (1957, p. 113-114) recognized that several important traits of Adena were similar to those of the Archaic. Among the most important they listed: 1. The use of red ocher in burials, 2. Cremation, 3. Animal masks and head-dresses. 4. Medicine bags. 5. Conical tubular pipes. 6. Grooved axes. 7. Atlatls and atlatl weights. Most of the above traits were present in the Archaic shell middens of the lower Ohio Valley and the Tennessee Valley (Webb and De Jarnette, 1942; Webb, 1950), but these and other traits related to Adena appear to have been most abundant in several important late Archaic manifestations in the lower Great Lakes area and in the Northeast.

Ritchie (1955, p. 1-135) suggested that the origin of the burial practices of Adena were to be found in several late Archaic manifestations in the eastern United States. His findings at Muskalonge Lake, Red Lake, and at other sites in New York indicated that a formalized burial cult had flourished in the Northeast near the end of the Archaic period. Among the traits of the New York sites were: 1. Presence of burials in graves on small, isolated, natural, sandy knolls. 2. Burial of bundled bones, cremations, and probably flexed bodies. 3. Prepared crematories. 4. Intentional destruction of artifacts in the crematory fires. 5. Inclusion of grave offerings such as weapons, tools, and ornaments with burials. 6. Extensive use of red ocher on burials and artifacts. 7. The employment of fire in burial ritualism.

In summarizing his views on the significance of the Northeast burial cult evidence Ritchie (1955, p. 78) stated:

"Thus from Archaic period cultures of the eastern United States, widely separated in space, although not in time, come suggestions of the presence of certain ideas possibly germinal to the development of the burial cult, whose oldest known, more or less full blown manifestation we have witnessed in the Indian River complex, and dated just beyond the upper limit of the presently established range of these Archaic cultures. Whether from this evidence we may legitimately infer the autochthonous rise of the cult pattern is at present indeterminable."

Ritchie (1955, p. 75), however, went on to suggest that a "basic core of religiosity" could be traced from these late Archaic manifestations, which included Red Ocher and Glacial Kame to be discussed later in this section, through early Point Peninsula, Adena, and into Hopewell.

With Ritchie's general thesis I am in basic agreement. The content and orientation around a burial cult of several manifestations, especially Red Ocher and Glacial Kame, and the similarities of these manifestations to those of the Northeast present evidence of great portent to the origin of Adena which was surrounded by these complexes. The spatial and cultural relationships of these complexes to Adena warrant a detailed examination (Map 4).

RED OCHER CULTURE

Remains of the Red Ocher Culture have been found in Illinois, Indiana, Michigan, Minnesota, Ohio, and Wisconsin, but the center of this culture seems to have been in Illinois (Cole and Deuel, 1937, p. 66, 225; Wray, 1952, p. 153; Morse, 1959, p. 193-207; Faulkner, 1960, p. 35-49). This culture is known only as a burial complex characterized by the placement of burials in shallow pits in natural ridges or in low artificial mounds situated on natural prominences. Although flexed burials predominate, semi-flexed, bundle burials, and cremations also

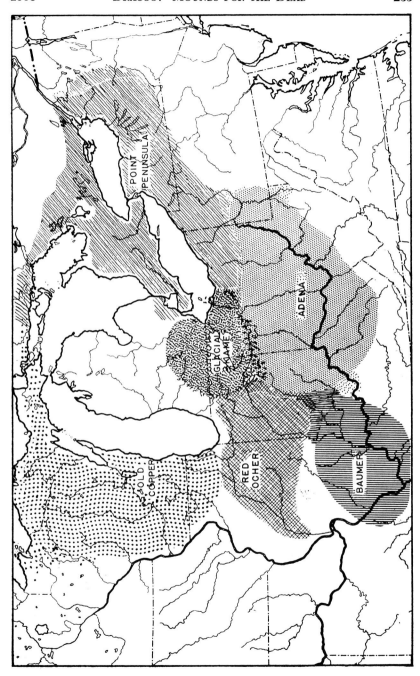

Map 4. Late Archaic and Early Woodland manifestations in the Great Lakes and Ohio Valley regions

have been found. The culture received its name from the practice of sprinkling red ocher, often profusely, over the burials and over caches of artifacts frequently placed with burials.

The distinctive blade form for the Red Ocher Culture was the side-notched, double-pointed "turkey tail" blade, but other types also have been found including the typical ovate-base, stemmed "Adena" blade and the "Adena" leaf-shaped blade. Other stemmed and notched blades and various types of scrapers and drills resemble earlier Archaic forms.

Among the other artifact traits of Red Ocher were several that resemble Adena such as celts, antler handles, faceted pieces of hematite, marginella shell beads, rolled copper beads, and a rectangular copper gorget with concave sides similar to the copper gorgets found in the early Adena mounds of the Upper Ohio Valley (Fig. 23).

In Indiana, burials covered with red ocher and accompanied by "turkey tail" blades have been discovered in natural elevations (Townsend, 1959, p. 190-196). In these sites celts and birdstones have also been found. This latter trait would suggest contact with the Glacial Kame Culture. At a Red Ocher burial site in Wisconsin were found a slate gorget and several copper awls in association with a variation of the "turkey tail" blade in which the notched, pointed base was enlarged to form a stem that on some specimens approached the "Adena" ovate-base stemmed blade in appearance (Ritzenthaler and Niehoff, 1959, p. 115-120). The copper awls were like those from Old Copper Culture sites and may indicate contact of these two cultures in Wisconsin.

The Red Ocher Culture was originally placed in the Woodland pattern mainly because of the presence of pottery and burial mounds (Cole and Deuel, 1937, p. 65). Recent studies, however, indicate that

---

Fig. 23. Typical traits of the Red Ocher complex
A. Burials in low mounds on natural ridges. B. Prepared crematory basin. C. Side-notched, double-pointed blade or "turkey tail". D. Leaf-shaped blade. E. Lanceolate blade. F. Stemmed, ovate-base blade of "Adena" type. G. Stemmed blade. H. Notched blade. I. Stemmed scraper or bunt. J. End scraper. K. Faceted piece of hematite. L. Cuboid of galena. M. Socketed antler handle. N. Expanded-base drill. O. Copper pin, square cross-section. P. Circular gorget of marine shell. Q. Copper beads. R. Marginella shell beads. S. Polished celt with rectangular cross-section. T. Copper plaque or gorget. U. Awl from deer metapodial. (After Cole and Deuel, 1937.)

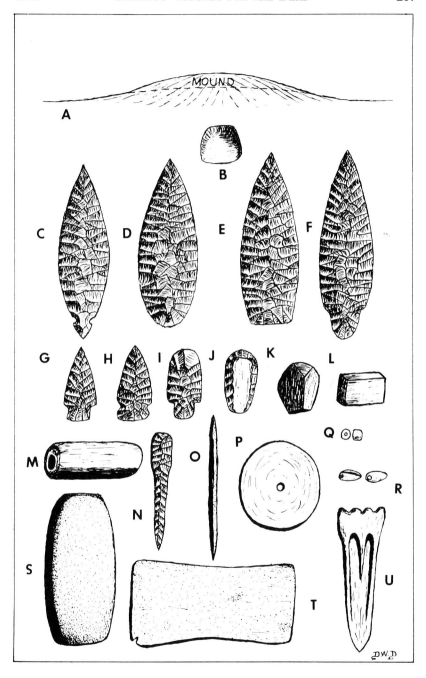

the Red Ocher Culture should be placed in the late Archaic since more traits of this culture are similar to late Archaic manifestations than to early Woodland cultures such as Black Sand and Morton that succeeded Red Ocher in Illinois (Morse, 1959, p. 204; Ritzenthaler and Niehoff, 1958, p. 120). Pottery also seems to have been absent from most Red Ocher sites and the few sherds that have been found represent a heavy, grit-tempered, cord-marked pottery similar to Adena "Fayette Thick." In Red Ocher we see the presence of several basic burial and artifact traits very similar to those of early Adena as manifested in the lower levels of the Cresap Mound in the Upper Ohio Valley. Perhaps of greatest importance, however, is the fact that Red Ocher burials have been found in natural mounds and in cemeteries as well as in small artificial mounds. Red Ocher seems to represent a people of basic Archaic orientation in transition from a non-mound to a mound-building burial complex. Since many of the basic burial traits such as the use of red ocher, the depositing of artifacts with burials, and the practice of cremation were already present before the construction of mounds, the idea that the burial mound complex moved or migrated as a unit is seriously challenged. The practice of erecting mounds seems to have begun only as an innovation upon an existing burial complex that would concentrate the dead in a specific area. Since natural elevations or mounds were already preferred as burial locations, it was a small step to add a little more earth to cover additional burials placed in an area already containing burials below the ground level. All the mounds of Red Ocher and probably most of the early mounds of Adena were small in size. It was not until late Adena times, long after the first small mounds had been erected, that mounds became large imposing structures.

Although the sample of measurable human remains from Red Ocher sites is quite small, the physical type found seems to be that of a brachycephalic group similar to Adena (Neumann, 1937, p. 262; Ritzenthaler and Niehoff, 1958, p. 116). Thus, not only were there many cultural traits shared by Red Ocher and early Adena but there also seems to have been a close physical bond. Since the closest resemblances of Adena to Red Ocher can be seen in the early Adena traits, I am inclined to believe on the basis of our present meager knowledge that Red Ocher and early Adena were physically related peoples, contemporary in time, and inhabiting contiguous areas. In Illinois Red Ocher was soon replaced by the Morton Culture which in turn played an important part in the development of Illinois Hopewell. In the central and upper Ohio Valley, however, Adena seems to have developed relatively undisturbed by outside influences for a much greater time before it eventually gave way to the Hopewell.

GLACIAL KAME CULTURE

The Glacial Kame Culture is known almost entirely from burials and associated artifacts found buried in glacial kames or knolls in northwestern Ohio, northeastern Indiana, southern Michigan, and southern Ontario (Cunningham, 1948, p. 1-45).

Burials were generally flexed, but extended, partially cremated and bundle burials have been found. Artifacts placed with burials were mainly ornaments rather than tools, and where grave offerings occurred they were restricted to a relatively few recurring types. Although red ocher was sometimes used on burials and artifacts, the practice was not common.

The predominant ornamental forms were made from conch shells. The characteristic form was a sandal-shaped shell gorget with three holes for attachment, but circular and rectangular shell gorgets have also been found. Barrel-shaped and disk-shaped beads cut from the columnella of conch shells were common.

Among the objects of stone were gorgets of banded slate similar to the forms in shell, birdstones of slate used as atlatl weights, celts, and simple tubular stone pipes.

Copper was used in the making of awls, spherical and tubular beads, and a copper gorget was found at one site (Cunningham, 1948, p. 5). At some Glacial Kame sites nuggets of galena have been found.

A few items of bone and antler including worked animal jaws, antler tines and antler flint-flaking tools were used by Glacial Kame peoples, but we know very little about their types of flint tools. Morgan (1952, p. 85), however, listed stemmed projectile points as the major flint tool (Fig. 24-26).

The exact relationships of the Glacial Kame Culture to other cultures in the same region have been the subject of much debate. Until recently most writers have suggested that Glacial Kame was basically a Woodland culture and on general typological grounds the complex should be assigned to the general Adena-Hopewell time period (Morgan, 1952, p. 86). It was suggested (Griffin, 1948, p. 50) that certain traits in

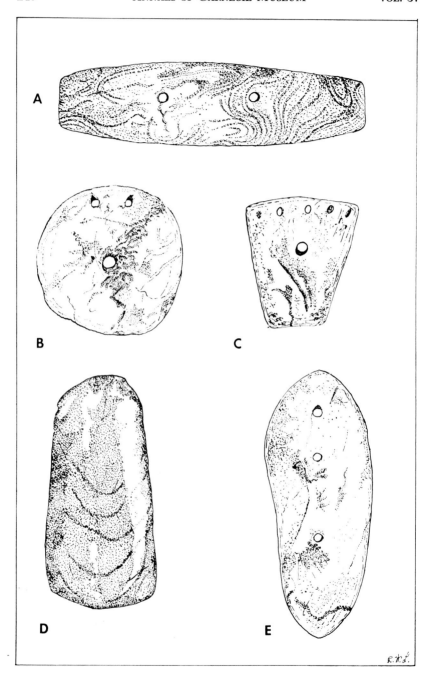

R.W.L.

Glacial Kame had specific analogies with Hopewell and that this complex could not have been earlier than Hopewell. Others looked upon Glacial Kame as contemporaneous with late Adena and believed that it carried over into Hopewell (Martin, and others 1947, p. 263). Morgan (1952, p. 85) cast serious doubts upon the association of platform pipes, the most Hopewellian-like trait with Glacial Kame sites, and suggested that the complex probably belonged to Early Woodland. In his studies of early burial cult remains in the Northeast, Ritchie (1955, p. 73) looked upon Glacial Kame as one of several widely separated cultures of the Early Woodland period possessing a formalized cult of the dead that eventually became later the orientational focus of Adena, Hopewell and cognate cultural complexes during Middle Woodland times.

On the basis of the present evidence, I believe Glacial Kame represented in its area the expression of a wide-spread burial cult upon a late Archaic base. The resemblances of Glacial Kame to Adena reflect the common adoption of the ideas pertaining to the burial of the dead but not necessarily ideas related to secular life. Like early Adena, Red Ocher, Old Copper, and the burial cult manifestations of the Northeast, Glacial Kame has its own pecularities that it does not share with the others.

Mention has already been made of the Old Copper complex in a previous section of this report as concerns the possible relationships of copper tools and ornaments in Adena with those of the earlier Old Copper complex. The priority of Old Copper in time and its nearness to the area of Adena occupation certainly points to the Old Copper complex as the donor of copper-working techniques to later manifestations in its own and adjacent areas.

The burial complex of Old Copper, especially near its end, is of particular interest because there are similarities with Glacial Kame, Red Ocher, and Adena (Wittry and Ritzenthaler, 1957, p. 310-328). Important traits were cremations, extended burials, flexed burials and

---

Fig. 24. Artifacts of the Glacial Kame complex
A. Banded slate rectangular gorget, Burch Site, Burch County, Mich. B. Circular shell gorget, Burch Site. C. Trapezoidal shell gorget, Burch Site. D. Black slate celt, Mulen Site, Randolph County, Ind. E. Sandal-sole shell gorget, Burch Site. (After Cunningham, 1948.)

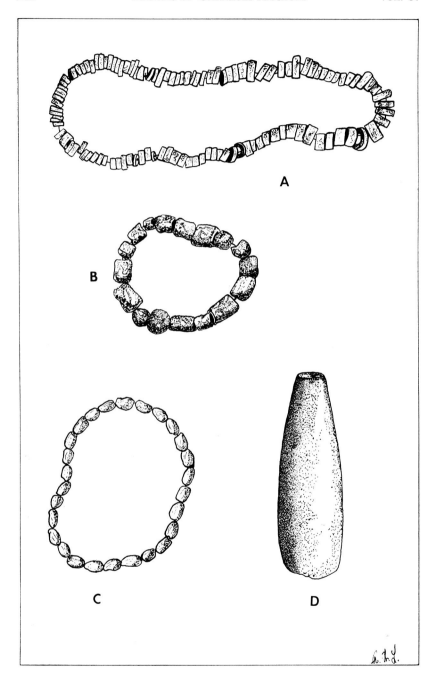

bundle burials in cemeteries often located on gravel and sand knolls. In several of these cemeteries in association with Old Copper tools were traits such as birdstones, large flint blades, red ocher, columella shell beads, and sandal-sole shell gorgets. These traits seem to indicate Glacial Kame cultural influences coming from the east and acting upon late Old Copper groups in Wisconsin (Wittry and Ritzenthaler, 1957, p. 326-327). Although the presence of Glacial Kame traits in Old Copper sites is indicative of the partial overlapping in time of these two cultures, it is of particular interest to note that most of the burial practices such as cremation, flexed and extended burials, inclusion of grave goods, and the preference for natural knolls as locations for cemeteries were present in Old Copper prior to contact with Glacial Kame. Thus, it seems quite likely that many of the traits that mark the early burial cult may have developed independently and at different times before their eventual inclusion in the burial practices of several groups living around the Great Lakes, in the Ohio Valley, and in the Northeast at the late Archaic level.

From the foregoing discussion I think it is obvious that most of the major burial practices and many of the artifact traits of early Adena were similar to those of several late Archaic manifestations surrounding, and in some cases overlapping, the area of Adena occupation. The similarities of Adena culture to Red Ocher, Glacial Kame, Old Copper, and the early burial cult manifestations of the Northeast are basic, and reflect the participation of these cultures in a cult of the dead produced by the coalescence of ideas and practices concerning the disposal of the dead that had developed in several widely scattered Archaic populations. The rise of the cult of the dead presented Archaic man with an orientational focus transcending the mundane pursuits of daily existence that had occupied his mind and deeds for several thousand years. Thus, Ritchie's (1955, p. 75) "basic core of religiosity" not only greatly changed the late Archaic populations but was also to mold many cultures in the eastern United States for the next 1500 years and to influence others up to the coming of the Europeans.

Fig. 25. Artifacts of the Glacial Kame complex
A. Disk shell beads, Burch Site, Burch County, Mich. B. Tubular copper beads, Burch Site. C. Conch columnella beads. D. Limestone tubular pipe, Mulen Site, Randolph County, Ind. (After Cunningham, 1948.)

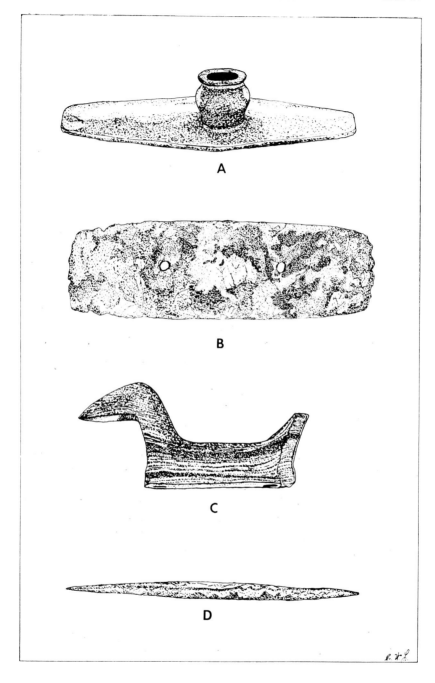

A

B

C

D

Adena as the possessor of the cult complex in the Ohio Valley had its origins and roots in the earlier Archaic just as had Red Ocher, Glacial Kame, and the cult of the dead manifestations of the Northeast, but Adena was to persist longer and to add several important innovations to the cult complex. From the practice of burying the dead in natural knolls, Red Ocher and probably Adena at about the same time began the construction of earth mounds to accomodate the inclusion of additional burials in a circumscribed and probably sacred area. At first these mounds were small and uncomplicated in structure; but by the end of Adena, mounds were large and contained elaborate tombs made of logs. Pipes, and presumably the practice of smoking, became important in the rites of the cult and pipes were buried with the dead. Stone tablets used for the preparation of paint pigments were changed from the crude forms like those found in the lower levels of the Cresap Mound into carefully executed palettes, some with engraved designs. As I have outlined in a preceding section of this report, we can trace the long development and enrichment of Adena Culture in many facets of their technology, and by inference from their works and burial practices, an increasing elaboration of social and religious customs. However, the basic cult of the dead complex persisted undiminished from the beginning to the end and was always the focus of Adena Culture.

Although I believe, as did Ritchie (1955) before me, that the origin and development of the Adena burial complex can be traced back to Archaic groups indigenous to the Ohio Valley and surrounding areas, I am sure there are those among my colleagues who will still question the validity of this position. Their objections will center mainly upon two points that I have deliberately avoided in this discussion until now—the presence of pottery in Adena and the differences of the Adena physical type when compared with earlier Archaic types.

Fig. 26. Artifacts of the Glacial Kame complex
A. Platform pipe found with burial in gravel pit in Allen County, Ind. in association with two sandal-sole gorgets and a circular disk gorget of shell. B. Copper rectangular gorget, Burch Site, Burch County, Mich. C. Banded slate birdstone, Harrison Site, Kalamazoo County, Mich. D. Copper awl, Burch Site. (After Cunningham, 1948.)

There has been a tendency for some archeologists to consider pottery as having been introduced to the Ohio Valley by physically distinctive Adena peoples along with agriculture, pipe smoking, and the mound burial complex (Webb and Snow, 1945, p. 311-313; Martin, and others, 1947, p. 263-267). I believe that the concept of the unity of these traits clouded our picture of Adena development and was responsible for leading us astray to distant Central America in search for the origins of Adena. The validity of the unit concept can best be questioned for the following reasons: 1. The presence of the cult of the dead burial complex in late Archaic groups such as Glacial Kame, Old Copper, and those of the Northeast in which pottery and pipe smoking both appear to be absent or to be very late additions. 2. The presence of pipes but not pottery with Archaic burials manifesting some cult traits found under the Adena Davis Mound in central Ohio (Baby, 1959, p. 95-96). 3. The presence of heavy, thick, cord-impressed pottery similar to Adena "Fayette Thick" associated with the Baumer and early Crab Orchard complexees of southern Archaic ancestry in the lower Ohio Valley in which the burial cult was absent (Maxwell, 1952, p. 179-184). 4. The lack of convincing evidence that agriculture was practised in the Ohio Valley during early Adena or by any of the other cultures on the late Archaic level possessing the cult of the dead. The varying combinations of these major traits among several late Archaic groups suggest to me that pottery, pipe smoking, agriculture, and the burial cult developed independently, and to trace the origin and cultural associations of one does not tell the story of the others.

The early Adena pottery represented by the "Fayette Thick" type belongs to a group of closely related, early types scattered throughout the eastern United States (Griffin, 1945, p. 225-228). As Maxwell (1952, p. 179) and others have pointed out, pottery was apparently introduced to many late Archaic groups with little or no other change in their culture. I have always been struck by the fact that pottery was not included in the grave offerings of Adena, although pottery sherds are often found in the fill of Adena mounds. The reason for the exclusion of pottery, I believe, lies in the history of the development of the Adena burial complex from the earlier Archaic cult when pottery was absent. Thus, as a later and utilitarian import into Adena culture, pottery was never considered a part of the cult paraphernalia.

PHYSICAL ANTHROPOLOGY OF ADENA

The problem of the Adena physical type is indeed a complex one. Snow (1945, p. 247-309) in his early study of Adena skeletal remains based his observations upon a Kentucky series of 78 adult skulls—46 males, and 32 females. To this series Snow (1957, p. 49) later added 19 more skulls from mounds in Ohio, West Virginia, and Kentucky. Like Hertzberg (1940, p. 83-102) before him, Snow also described the Adena physical type as that of "a large, round-headed, long-faced, medium statured group with occasional tall members." In summarizing the appearance of the Adena male Snow (1957, p. 48) stated:

"The outstanding facial profile described above is a distinctive feature of the Adena male face, found in nearly all of the male skulls in addition to the large face (both length and breadth). The forehead is typically a prominent one, bordered below by fairly sizable brow-ridges. The root of the nose is of average proportions and continues on to a prominent convex bridge that is one of the prominent features of the face. The characteristic bulge of the upper and lower jaws (alveolar prognathis) is moderate in projection and is supported by a chin that is unusually prominent for American Indian crania. Usually the cheek bones are not only of large size in themselves but they have a forward and lateral prominence that must have formed a characteristic feature of these prehistoric Indian faces. . . The lower face (mouth and lower jaw sections) is moderately full as seen from the front. One of the particular features present in at least one-half of the observed examples is the great width of the bony chin, formed by bilateral eminences rarely found among the skulls of the much earlier Shell Heap People or among the later Hopewell People."

Snow's picture of the Adena people is an accurate and carefully detailed one based on the available skeletal remains. However, the number of measurable skulls and post-cranial bones is quite limited and nearly all are from culturally late Adena mounds (Webb and Snow, 1945, p. 247-250; Snow, 1957, p. 49) belonging to the "Robbins" complex discussed in the preceding section of this report. Thus, our picture of the Adena people does not span the entire time of Adena Culture but only the upper levels of that culture after it had undergone many modifications. Knowing the end product of Adena physical development does not necessarily tell the story of what early Adena peoples were like (Plate 52).

Another complicating factor well understood by Snow (Webb and Snow, 1945, p. 247) was the fact that most of the skeletons in his series were from the elaborately prepared log tomb graves. Of the

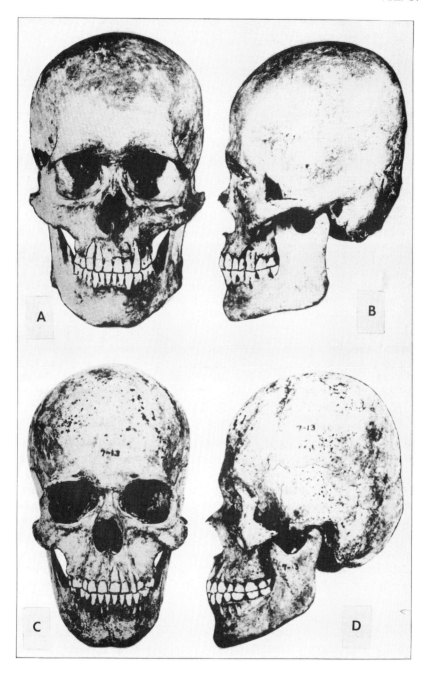

burials of determinable sex in these tombs there were nearly twice as many males as females. This fact coupled with the common practice of cremation led Snow (Webb and Snow, 1945, p. 247) to suggest that these remains were "those of a selected group, probably the important individuals of the community." The chronological outline of Adena development presented earlier in this report clearly indicates that in late Adena times greater attention was given to the elaborate burial of certain individuals than was common in early and middle Adena times where grave goods were often placed with many burials scattered throughout a mound. If, as Snow believes (and the evidence seems to support his belief at least for late Adena) the picture of Adena man is based upon the individuals of a selected group then our picture is not truly a representative cross-section of the Adena population. Snow (Webb and Snow, 1959, p. 38) has summarized the situation as follows:

"We have indicated before that the Adena people selected for the elaborate mound burial—the honored dead—cannot be regarded as representative samples of the Adena population. It seems certain that many if not most, of the ordinary people must have been cremated in the common form of burial preparation. Therefore we are dealing with a most unusual group. It is no little surprise perhaps to conclude that the Adena people stand alone and have few counterparts in the usual skeletal series of archeological origin."

Snow's "unusual group" of "honored dead" does indeed stand alone among the brachycephalic peoples of the New World. Two outstanding traits have been noted repeatedly for this group. One is the protruding and massive chin often with prominent bilateral protrusions (Webb and Snow, 1959, p. 37). The second trait is the large size of many of the males and some of the females. A male of six feet was common and some individuals approaching seven feet in height have been found, for example, Burial 40 in the Dover Mound (Webb and Snow, 1959, p. 31) and Burial 54 in the Cresap Mound. Some of the females of the Dover Mound also were more than six feet in height. Not only were these Adena people tall but also the massiveness of the bones indicates powerfully built individuals. The head was generally big with a large cranial capacity (Plate 52).

Plate 52.   The typical Adena male and female as known from late Adena tombs
A and B, male.   C and D, female.   (After Snow, 1957.)

Snow (Webb and Snow, 1959, p. 39) suggested that perhaps sexual and social selection factors may have been involved in the development of the prominent Adena chin. If, as the evidence seems to indicate, the burials in the tombs were those of a selected group such factors would have undoubtedly been of importance not only in the development of the prominent chin but also in the large stature. If only certain inbreeding individuals of the total population were members of the "selected group," genetic factors would also have played an important part in the establishment of the unique Adena physical type found in the late Adena tombs. Any changes (mutations) in the gene pool either dominant or recessive would soon be distributed among all the members of the group.

How wide-spread throughout the entire Adena population were the unique traits of the tomb burials is unknown but Snow's (Webb and Snow, 1959, p. 46) study of the cremated remains from the Dover Mound indicated that at least some individuals among these cremated remains also possessed the unique traits of the flesh burials in the tombs. Because of the common practice of cremating most of the dead, we will probably never be able to determine the full extent of these special traits in the general population.

Although the unique physical type is well known for the late Adena mounds, our information on the physical type of early and middle Adena is very scanty because of the extremely poor preservation of skeletal remains in the early mounds. For example, of the 54 burials in the Cresap Mound not one was sufficiently preserved for accurate measurements. On the basis of our observation of the badly crushed and decayed skulls in situ in the Cresap Mound, all were brachycephalic, but only two skulls were of large proportions. Although the chins were prominent on the Cresap males, none was as extreme as those noted for the late Kentucky Adena mounds. I suspect that as we gain more information on early Adena we will find a trend towards more moderate proportions and an absence of the prominent and unique traits that mark the "honored dead" of late Adena.

Snow's (1957, p. 53-54) studies of the head deformation present on the majority of the measured Adena skulls point out another difficulty in determining the normal or unaltered appearance of the Adena physical type. Nearly all skulls show some occipital flattening probably caused by strapping an infant onto a cradle board and some skulls show an additional compression brought about by some sort of head binding or bandaging that produced an almost perfectly circular skull outline. On some skulls there is a depressed groove extending from the supra-orbital depression around the posterior borders of the temporals to the adjoining parts of the occipital bone. Bindings such as a cord or thong tight enough to produce such a groove would not only greatly alter the horizontal outline and height of the cranial vault but would have also changed the facial structure. Snow (1957, p. 55) summarized the overall affects of this type of deformation as follows:

"The metric data (measurements and indices) also reflect the strong probability that this pseudo-circular type of head binding produced the characteristic Adena skull form. It will be noted that the Adena skulls, deformed as they are, are the highest known in the world. The extreme height of the skull vault would certainly be the sort of compensatory change which would result from such compressive forces. These forces would tend to limit the growth of the head in the horizontal axis (breadth) as well as that of the height. There is evidence which indicates that individuals whose remains were cremated were likewise marked by this peculiar form of head shaping [Dover Mound]."

The unusual type of head deformation practised by Adena coupled with the general brachycephalic physical type seems to have been the major reasons for Snow (1957, p. 59) suggesting that the source for Adena was "down Mexico way." Not only did he believe that there were "Adena-like" skulls from the early Zacatenco levels of the El Arbolillo, Ticoman, and Tlalilco sites, but he also suggested that we could "perhaps trace the earliest advent of the Walcolid physical type to the Tepexpan Man, found in the valley of Mexico in 1948, which has been dated as far back as 10,000 to 12,000 years."

Although there may be a superficial resemblance of Adena to the early Mexican populations, Adena's unique traits appear to be absent in the latter. I have already stated my doubts of any close cultural relationships of Adena with Mexico since the traits conjectured as being of Mexican origin were typical of late Adena and not of early Adena. The same situation occurs in our comparison of physical types. The extreme head deformation noted for Adena appears to have been typical of the late Adena "Robbins" complex but we do not know whether this type of deformation was present in the early Adena population. Although some occipital flattening was noted on some of the Cresap Mound skulls from the early levels, there were no examples of extreme deformation like that recorded for the late Kentucky remains. I am inclined to believe that extreme head deformation caused by tight skull bindings was a trait of late Adena associated with the rise of definite classes within Adena society. The skull bindings and the resulting head deformation may well have been a mark of Snow's "honored dead" that further distinguished this select group from the common people. As such, the head deformation seen in Adena had no direct relationship with similar practices in Mexico.

It is also of interest to note that bifrontal and occipital flattening, probably caused by the use of cradle boards, was present on nearly half of the Archaic Indian Knoll adult population. Thus head deformation was not unique to Adena and was present at an earlier time in the Ohio Valley.

As to the relationship of the rugged brachycephals of Adena to previous physical type classifications of the American Indian, Snow (1957, p. 57) stated:

"We believe that the roots of the Adena People are to be found in the early brachycephalic population living in the Southeast, named 'Gulf' by Hrdlicka, 'Koger's Island' by Newman and Snow, 'Centralid' by von Eickstedt, and recently, 'Walcolid' by Neumann. We take all these terms to be synonomous [sic]."

Snow (1957, p. 57) further suggested that there was a very close similarity between what might be called early representatives of the Walcolid type (Adena people) and the later Middle Mississippian type of Walcolid if the dimensions of an Adena skull little affected by deformation were utilized. He also called attention to the fact that the deformed crania of the later Tennessee Stone graves and of Copena in Alabama were similar to those of Adena in dimensions and proportions. Although Snow saw similarities of Adena with these later Walcolid peoples, he made no statements concerning the possible relationships of Adena with earlier or contemporary brachycephalic peoples living in the areas surrounding the Ohio Valley.

Neumann (1952, p. 33), as had many others before him, originally explained the differences in American Indian populations as the result of the introduction of new migrants from Asia into the New World. Since the brachycephalic Walcolid peoples differed from the earlier, typical, longheaded groups of the Archaic, the Walcolids represented a major influx of new peoples. In a more recent re-evaluation of the evidence fortified by much new data, Neumann (1960, p. 66-68) concludes that the observed differences among Indian groups resulted from gradual changes in the earlier Paleoamerind populations and not by way of new migrations. According to Neumann differentiation from a common, longheaded Paleo-Indian ancestor of a southern Archaic Iswanid and a northern Archaic Lenid variety was well on its way by at least 6000 B.C. in eastern North America and by 4000 B.C. the two varieties were clearly separable. In both of these varieties there were further gradual changes involving increase in size and brachycephalization during middle and late Archaic times. These changes mark the advent of a derived Mesoamerind population and the origin of the Walcolid and other brachycepalic varieties.

Neumann believes that the Walcolid variety, which may be associated largely with the development of Middle Mississippi Culture, had its origin among the late Archaic Iswanid peoples like those responsible for the Indian Knoll Culture of Kentucky. There is indeed good evidence for changes in the Archaic populations of Kentucky and the Tennessee Valley. Although the majority of individuals found at Indian Knoll were longheaded (dolichocephalic), there were some brachycephalic and mesocephalic individuals with high, round vaults (Snow, 1948, p. 381-452). Some of the Archaic populations in the Tennessee Valley were even more heterogeneous than those of Indian Knoll. At some sites, particularly Site Lu°25, there was a tendency towards larger size and a putative change of physical type in the upper levels towards a more brachycephalic population (Newman and Snow, 1942, p. 397-507). It was precisely in these areas of southern Archaic development that we find the later Mississippi Culture centers with a well differentiated Walcolid population by about 900 A.D.

Although Snow (1957, p. 57) suggested that Adena man was an early representative of the Walcolid variety and that there was a close similarity to the later Middle Mississippi type of Walcolid, Neumann (1960, p. 68) now believes that the Adena physical type was derived from the northern Archaic Lenid variety. Along the southern margins of the Great Lakes certain Lenid groups gave rise to the brachycephalized Adena in a fashion parallel to that of the Iswanid to Walcolid change in the South. To these brachycephalized groups of Lenid origin Neumann has applied the name Illinid.

Neumann's case for the northern origin of the Adena peoples from the Lenid population can also be supported by archeological evidence. It was precisely in those areas below the Great Lakes that we traced earlier in this report the development of the cult of the dead burial complexes. According to Neumann (personal communication) derived

Illinid populations were present in the Red Ocher Culture of Illinois and the Glacial Kame Culture of Indiana, Michigan, and Ohio. Also, the brachycephalic peoples of the late Archaic in the Northeast appear to belong to the Illinid variety. The correlation of the Illinid physical type with the various burial cult complexes indicates not only close cultural ties but also a common physical heritage.

The physical relationship of the Adena people to the Hopewellians who were contemporary with late Adena and eventually succeeded them in the Ohio Valley has been subjected to two conflicting interpretations. Snow (1945, p. 254; 1957, p. 51) believed Adena to be "strikingly" different from Hopewell since the majority of Hopewell skulls were dolichocephalic and assignable to Neumann's (1952, p. 213-253) Lenid variety. Snow (1957, p. 51) suggested that Adena and Hopewell were "clearly of different population origins." This view reflected Snow's belief in the ultimate origin of Adena in the populations of central America and their subsequent migration to the Ohio Valley. Neumann believes that the undeformed Adena skulls are very closely related to Hopewell and clearly reflect the derivation of the Illinid variety to which Adena belongs from the earlier northern Archaic Lenid population. From my own observation of Adena and Hopewell skeletal remains, I am inclined to agree with Neumann's thesis. Disregarding the brachycephalic head of Adena, which unfortunately was further distorted by deformation, the general size and many other morphological traits of Adena appear more closely related to Hopewell than to the later Walcolid peoples associated with Middle Mississippi Culture.

The socio-cultural factors that would have influenced change in the Adena population, or at least among certain groups within Adena, have already been discussed in connection with the individuals buried in the elaborate log tombs. There are also other factors of a more general nature that bear upon the problem of physical change and population differentiation that appear to be pertinent to the development of Adena from earlier Archaic man. Since neither Snow nor Neumann has detailed the operation of these factors, it seems of value to mention them here not only as an insight into the mechanism of change but also as a guide to future research.

Certainly among the most potent factors for change would have been those related to environment. During the 6000 or more years of development of Archaic Culture from near the end of the last glacial retreat until about 1000 B.C. there certainly would have been important changes in climate and the associated changes of flora and fauna. If extensive physical modification, including a tendency to round-headedness, due to environmental adaptation, can be called upon to explain the origin of Mongoloid populations in Asia over a comparable time interval (Fairservis, 1959, p. 76), are we to believe that even less extensive changes did not take place among the American Indians? Studies by Coon, and others (1950) seem to indicate that adaptation to environmental conditions either by mutation or natural selection, or by both, does play an important part in the development of racial groups. In more recent papers, Coon (1953) and Newman (1955) have pointed out that the same natural ecological factors that apply to other animal life also apply to man.

The majority of human remains known for the Archaic have come from the shell middens of the lower Ohio and the Tennessee valleys. In this situation our sample is not only slanted towards a specific climatic zone but also towards certain food preferences. What of the Archaic peoples who lived in the northern portions of the Ohio Valley, around the Great Lakes, and in the Northeast where shellfish were not a major item in the diet? What effects would different food habits have on these people? It is now a well known fact that nutrition can be an important factor in changing the human body. Boaz's (1912) early study of immigrants to America and a similar study by Shapiro (1939) of Japanese immigrants from Japan to Hawaii coupled with the U. S. Armed Forces' measurements of men who served in the First World War and the Second World War, plus recent studies on Mexican and Central American populations (Lasker, 1952; Scrimshaw, and others, 1955) clearly show that with improved nutrition there comes an increase in overall stature and a tendency towards round-headedness.

Dr. T. D. Stewart (1960, p. 259-273) in a recent paper has pointed out the remarkable homogeneity in phenotype and genotype of the American Indian and suggests "that the total time involved in the peopling of America was too limited to effect major evolutionary changes." All the New World skeletons thus for discovered show the presence of modern man over a period of only about 20,000 years. Physically these remains are similar to types known over a wide area of eastern Asia in late Pleistocene times. Stewart (1960, p. 269) stated "That these varieties represent the population from which the first Americans were derived seems highly probable, although the point in time at which the separation occurred remains to be discovered." Since, with the exception of the Eskimos and the Athapascans which on the basis of blood group and other features appear related to late Asiatic groups, the American Indian possesses none of the extreme Mongoloid characteristics, we would suspect that the separation occurred before these same features also marked the Asiatic populations.

In spite of homogeneous genotype of the American Indian, Stewart would not deny that Indians do vary particularly in stature and shape of head, but these variations can be ascribed less to changes in population heredity that have taken place in this hemisphere than to changes attributable primarily as adaptive responses to different environmental conditions in the New World. In spite of the variability seen in the American Indian, Stewart (1960, p. 262) has pointed out "that no population of comparable size has remained so uniform after expanding, in whatever time has been involved, over such a large land area."

Accepting the demonstrated physical plasticity of the Indian and other peoples to environment and nutritional standards, Stewart regarded four agencies as mainly responsible for genetic changes in a population: mixture, mutation, natural selection, and random genetic drift. Since the ancestors of the American Indians were not preceded in the New World by any different breed of men, the only mixture that took place would have been between groups with much the same genetic constitution; therefore, mixture would not have been of great importance.

The significance of gene mutation in changing a human population has not been established, but singular, non-recurrent mutations would probably have had little effect. Even the same, single mutation occurring recurrently and at numerous loci may or may not become established at any one locus. In the event a mutation did escape extinction, its utilization for population change would have depended upon the remaining two agencies of population change, selection, and genetic drift.

Natural selection is generally considered to mean that certain individuals possessing certain characteristics tend to survive in larger numbers, and leave relatively more offspring than do other individuals of the same kind possessing different characteristics (Boyd, 1950, p. 140-141). Stewart (1960, p. 265) suggests "that in man differential survival—or better, differential fertility—is brought about by all sorts of things, most, if not all of which collectively constitute the environment."

The American Indian occupied many climates, each with its own peculiar assortment of plants and animals of varying nutritive value. Each of the various habitats such as tundras, temperate forests, grassy plains, deserts, rain forests, jungles, sea-coasts, and mountains would have exerted different stresses upon the occupants, and the individuals best equipped to survive in each area would come to predominate in the population. The environment of some areas would have been less stable and more subject to climatic fluctuations than others. This would seem to have been particularly true in the northern regions of the eastern United States subjected to glaciation. From the end of the last glacial maximum until the present there is ample evidence to indicate that these regions underwent alternating cooling and warming trends that would have affected not only the flora and fauna but also man.

Coupled with natural selection would have been the agency of random genetic drift which "depends for its operation on the isolation of one small population from other populations with which it could interbreed." (Boyd, 1950, p. 154). In any given small isolated group the number of genetic combinations is always smaller than that of a larger interbreeding population to which it may have originally belonged. In such a case, some genetic combinations may no longer occur while others may become more frequent. In time, the population derived from the isolated group may deviate considerably from the original population. There is ample evidence for the isolation of Archaic groups that resulted in regional specializations of an earlier basic, wide-spread Archaic cultural tradition in the Ohio Valley and the Northeast (Dragoo, 1959, p. 139-246). The dependence upon local raw materials for the manufacture of each group's cultural items attests to limited contacts with surrounding groups. Thus, the necessary isolation for genetic drift to be an important factor in physical change was present in the Archaic and may well have been responsible for some of the changes noted in certain late Archaic populations previously mentioned.

Summary of Adena Physical Anthropology

In summary, all the above factors—differential environmental conditions, mutations, natural selection, and genetic drift—would have had time during the long development of Archaic culture in eastern North America to play their part in changing the physical attributes of man. As Neumann (1960, p. 66-68) has suggested, the origin of the

Adena people can be traced to changing peoples of the late Archaic. His contention that these changes took place in the areas below the Great Lakes correlates also with the cultural evidence for the rise of the cult of the dead burial complex in the same areas. In Adena the potent forces of socio-cultural selection can be added to the natural factors for change to account for the extreme modifications of at least certain groups in the Adena population.

The gradual disappearance of the typical Archaic physical types from among the later populations of eastern North America is to me a clear demonstration of in situ physical modification for I can see neither natural reasons for their extinction nor evidence of their annihilation by the arrival of new groups of a different physical type. That similar changes of early Archaic populations also occurred in other regions of the New World, for example, the Southwest indicates the operation on a wide scale of potent natural and cultural factors influencing physical change. Although the rate of change among different and widely separated populations varied and the form of certain modifications became peculiar to that population, there appears to have been a gradual change among nearly all groups from an earlier dolichocranial head shape towards a mesocranial or brachycranial form.

Although I have indicated my belief in the in situ origin of Adena peoples from the earlier Archaic population, I do not wish to convey the idea that there were no contacts or interactions of Adena peoples with their neighbors in surrounding areas. I have no doubt that there were physical as well as cultural interchanges between Adena and these other groups. These contacts were, perhaps, more limited and less influential during the early stages of Adena development, but in the final phase of Adena culture these contacts were to have far-reaching ramifications.

ADENA AND ITS NEIGHBORS

So far in this report we have been concerned basically with tracing both culturally and physically the origin of Adena and its subsequent development in the Ohio Valley. What, if any, new light can we shed on the relationship of Adena to contemporary and succeeding cultures in the Ohio Valley and surrounding areas?

The relationship of Adena to the Hopewell Culture of Ohio has been a problem of major interest for many years. Webb and Snow (1945) have traced the early studies of this problem and through their own observations came to the following conclusions:

1. Adena was chronologically precedent to Hopewell and culturally ancestral to it.

2. Although certain cultural elements and the physical type of Hopewell can perhaps be traced back into the Archaic, Hopewell material culture was in large part rooted in that of Adena, and many of its important burial and earthwork traits were derived from Adena prototypes.

3. The traits shared by Adena and Hopewell were those already present in late Adena and donated by Adena to the new Hopewell Culture which formed after the contact of Adena peoples with a long-headed population which had lived north of the area of Adena occupation.

4. The Adena traits seen in Hopewell would not have been available prior to the contact since these traits were brought to the Ohio Valley by Adena from distant Middle America or Mexico.

5. The result of the contact of broad-headed Adena people possessing the concept of a complex social organization with the Hopewellian long-headed people having a somewhat less highly organized society was the development of Ohio Hopewell which reached a higher level of cultural attainment than that of Adena.

6. The evidence from physical-anthropological studies indicates that some "Adena-like" individuals became, "to all intent and purpose," Hopewell people either by a mingling of blood or by actual mixing of peoples.

7. Some Adena sites continued to be occupied while early Hopewell was developed, but all Adena sites had ceased to be occupied before late Hopewell since not a single late Hopewell artifact has ever been found in any Adena site.

8. As Ohio Hopewell rose in strengeh and importance and further developed the same mound-building traits which they had adopted from Adena, some of them moved southward (and presumably in other directions) where they established the Copena Culture in northern Alabama.

Webb and Snow's speculations concerning the relationship of Adena to Hopewell were reasonably valid in 1945, but additional excavations and recent research by several workers, including Webb and associates, tend to cloud the picture as they then believed it to be. Let us examine the nature and implications of these recent findings.

As outlined earlier in this report, there is no concrete evidence to support the thesis that Adena culture, or Adena peoples, was derived from Middle America while there is ample and accumulating evidence for both the cultural and physical development of Adena in situ in the Ohio Valley from earlier Archaic manifestations. Since Adena was not the only, or even perhaps the earliest, culture possessing a distinctive burial complex in the region below the Great Lakes, many of the basic burial traits could have been available to Hopewellian peoples before their encounter with Adena. The basic themes of the burial complex were remarkably similar among several different groups scattered from Illinois to New York, only the expressions of the burial complex in terms of local artifactual variations and the degree of elaboration of burial traits seem to differ.

Point Peninsula Culture

Ritchie (1944, p. 115-186; 1955) has carefully documented the presence of the Point Peninsula culture in the Northeast which he believes to have been rooted in the earlier Archaic burial cult manifestations of the same area. If the radiocarbon dates for Point Peninsula are reasonably correct, this culture was well established in New York as early as 1000 B.C. (Griffin, 1958, p. 9-10) and thus would have been coeval with the Adena occupation in the Ohio Valley. Although the Point Peninsula culture is known best in western, central, and northern New York state and lower Ontario, similar cultures have been found in Ohio, Michigan, Minnesota, and Indiana (Martin and others, 1947, p. 251; de Paepe, 1960). As yet, our knowledge in these latter states is very incomplete due mainly to the lack of intensive archeological investigations in the areas where Point Peninsula remains have been found.

Although the Point Peninsula people show some variation in physical type, the majority were long-headed representatives of Neumann's (1960, p. 66-68) Lenid variety who preferred to situate their villages near rivers and lakes. They generally buried their dead in pits dug into level ground near the village, but occasionally natural knolls or hillsides were utilized. Bodies were usually flexed but a few extended burials have been found. Sometimes several bodies were placed in the same grave accompanied by tools and ornaments. Sometimes cremation was practised and the finding of disarticulated bundles of bones indicates that bodies were placed on platforms until they decomposed. Red ocher was often sprinkled over the bodies and associated grave offerings.

Among the artifact traits described by Ritchie (1944) for Point Peninsula are many that are like, or similar to, those found in other cultures of the eastern United States possessing traits of the burial cult. The most important of these traits are: 1. Large triangular or leaf-shaped "cache" blades. 2. Broad, thin, side-notched, and corner-notched blades. 3. Bar atlatl weights. 4. Birdstones. 5. Rectangular stone gorgets. 6. Copper awls and axes. 7. Tubular and barrel-shaped copper beads. 8. Tubular and right-angled or obtuse-angled elbow pipes of pottery or stone. 9. Curved or straight base platform pipes. 10. Pottery vessels with cordmarked or fabric impressed surfaces and vessels with decorations made by incising, punctating, dentate stamping, and rocker stamping (Fig. 27 and 28).

Many of the traits of Point Peninsula, as Ritchie (1955, p. 76-78) has suggested, have obvious similarities to those of the early Northeast burial cult manifestations, Glacial Kame, and Old Copper. Some of these traits, or variations of them, are also the same basic traits seen in the burial practices of Red Ocher and early Adena. These latter traits are of a general nature, however, and reflect the wide-spread influence and acceptance of certain burial practices and concepts by several groups living around the Great Lakes and in the Ohio Valley at the late Archaic time level. Above this early level the subsequent developments and contents of Point Peninsula and Adena seem to have been quite divergent.

Griffin (1952, p. 359) has theorized that the development of Adena culture in the central Ohio Valley produced a type of culture so attractive to the peoples to the north that there was an actual movement of some of these people from the New York area and perhaps even from

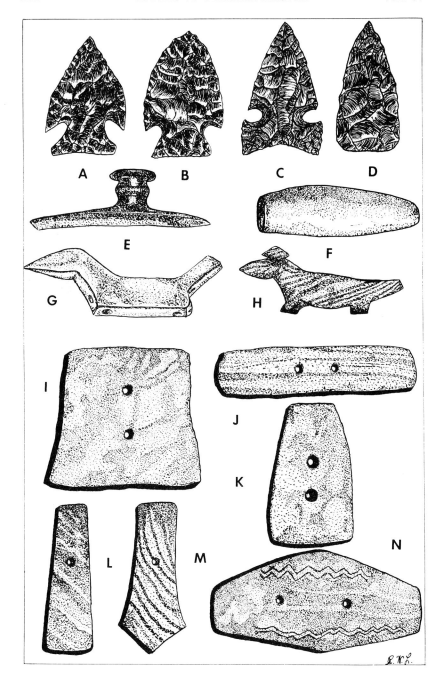

the west and north into southern Ohio where they blended with Adena to produce Ohio Hopewell. Although Griffin did not state that the New York peoples were carriers of Point Peninsula Culture, this would seem to have been the case since Point Peninsula was dominant in the New York area at that time level. His only specific reference concerning Point Peninsula and Ohio Hopewell connections was that "the ceramic material of Ohio Hopewell is certainly primarily 90 per cent, at least, northern, and has some interesting connections with the Point Peninsula pottery of the lower Great Lakes."Among the later northern Algonquians Griffin saw a number of similarities with Ohio Hopewell including hair-dress and clothing as depicted on Ohio Hopewell figurines, bilaterally symmetrical art styles, the bear as an important art motif, representations of the horned serpent and the Great Hare (an Algonquian culture hero), and antler head-dresses worn by priests. In addition to these traits Griffin suggested that the projectile points associated with Ohio Hopewell, and also those of the Illinois valley, fit much better into the northern sequence than into any other area.

I believe Griffin's thesis for the northern origin of many Hopewell traits worthy of serious consideration since it can be supported by a substantial amount of evidence. However, at what time, from what direction, and in what intensity these influences arrived in the Ohio Valley to contact Adena seem open to debate. On the basis of our present evidence, it would seem that the contact of Point Peninsula peoples of the New York area with Adena in the Ohio Valley was minimal and confined to the exchange of a few trade items with Adena groups in the Upper Ohio Valley. Also, if these Point Peninsula peoples were so active in the formation of Hopewell after their contact with Adena, I find it difficult to explain why so few Hopewell traits found their way back to the Point Peninsula peoples still living in New York while to the west in Illinois many Hopewellian traits, including the construction of large mounds, were readily adopted by the peoples in that area.

Fig. 27. **Traits of the Point Peninsula Culture. Objects from various sites in New York and Ontario**
A and B. Corner-notched blades. C. Side-notched blade. D. Leaf-shaped blade. E. Platform pipe. F. Tubular pottery pipe. G. Banded slate birdstone. H. Popeyed birdstone of slate. I. Square slate gorget. J. Rectangular slate gorget. K. Trapezoidal slate gorget. L and M. Slate pendants. N. Hexagonal slate gorget. (After Ritchie, 1944.)

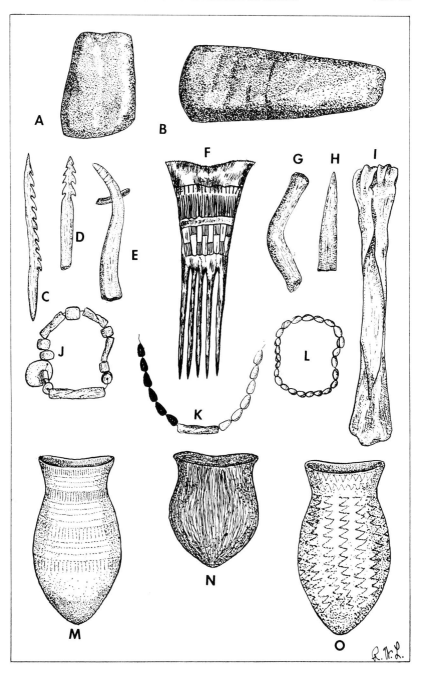

Central Basin and Illinois Hopewell

Although Point Peninsula's contacts with Adena appear to have been remote, there are interesting parallels in the content of Point Peninsula Culture with that of the Central Basin and Illinois Hopewell sequence. So strikingly similar are some of the pottery types shared by these widely separated cultures that a direct generic relationship seems to have existed (Ritchie, 1944, p. 166). It was in Illinois that long-headed Lenid peoples, similar to the Point Peninsula population, first made inroads into territory occupied by peoples physically and culturally related to Adena. Here, Lenid groups supplanted the Red Ocher culture with its close similarities to the early Adena of the Ohio Valley and established the Central Basin culture. The encounter seems to have been peaceful since Red Ocher appears to have contributed both physically and culturally to Central Basin. Probably the most conspicuous trait donated by Red Ocher to Central Basin was the practice of erecting small mounds to inclose the dead.

Opinions vary as to the origin of Hopewell in Illinois. Cole (1943, p. 300) and Bluhm (1951, p. 329) have stated their belief that the Central Basin culture in the Fulton County area was the foundation for the following Hopewell culture. McGregor (1958, p. 186) has taken a less positive position in which he has stated that "it is not inconceivable that Hopewell developed as an indigenous system from earlier woodland cultures within the Illinois River Valley" but he believes this thesis not too appealing because "as now understood Hopewell seems to appear quite suddenly, and rather full-blown, in this area." Wray (1952, p. 163) stated that "Illinois Hopewell seems to result from the expansion of a ceremonial complex, which originated in Ohio, into the Illinois and Mississippi valleys where it incorporated localized woodland traditions."

Fig. 28. Artifacts of the Point Peninsula Culture. Objects from various sites in New York and Ontario
A and B. Celts of igneous stones. C. Antler harpoon with unilateral barbs. D. Antler point with bi-lateral barbs. E. Beaver tooth chisel set in antler tine. F. Engraved bone comb. G. Antler flaking tool. H. Antler projectile point. I. Cannon bone beamer. J. Tubular and disk shell beads. L. Olivella shell beads. M. "Vinette Dentate" pottery vessel. N. "Vinette 1 Cordmarked." O. Point Peninsula rockered stamped vessel. (A-M after Ritchie, 1944; M-O after MacNeish, 1952.)

It is of particular interest to note that evidence of a cultural continuity from the earlier Central Basin culture into Hopewell appears
most strongly in the upper Illinois valley (Cole and Deuel, 1937, p.
205) while in the lower Illinois valley and in southern Illinois evidence
seems to support the encroachment and influence of a well established
Hopewell complex upon resident groups that appear to adapt many
Hopewellian burial traits without too much change in the other facets
of their lives (Maxwell, 1952, p. 186).

Prior to Hopewell times southern Illinois seems to have had a different history from that of the upper Illinois valley. While Red Ocher
and Central Basin were developing in this latter area, the Baumer
and Crab Orchard cultures dominated southern Illinois. Maxwell
(1952, p. 181-184) has suggested that the Baumer and Crab Orchard
cultures were closely related and can be derived from the Archaic of
the Tennessee Valley. These cultures were at least as early in southern
Illinois as Adena was in the Ohio Valley, but Adena influences do not
seem to have arrived in southern Illinois until after the abandonment
of the Baumer sites. Crab Orchard sites, however, manifest a greater
time depth and demonstrate an unbroken cultural continuity through
a stage of Adena influence in which many of the material traits of
Adena and Red Ocher were accepted but not the elaborate burial complex. On the late Crab Orchard sites there was a much stronger influence from the Illinois Hopewell centers in the Illinois Valley and the
burial-mound complex was accepted by at least some of the Crab
Orchard people although they retained many of their older traits in
association with the new importations.

Thus, it would seem that in spite of their closeness over a long period
of time to peoples like Red Ocher to the north and Adena to the east
who possessed a burial complex, Crab Orchard peoples were particularly resistant to accepting the concepts of the burial cult. This resistance seems indicative of the cultural solidarity and disparate origin
of the Crab Orchard Culture. As Maxwell (1952, p. 181) has suggested, the Baumer and Crab Orchard cultures of southern Illinois
were derived from the late Archaic manifestations of the Tennessee Valley that lacked a burial-mound complex. The affinities of the Red
Ocher, Central Basin, and Illinois Hopewell cultures, however, lie
with the late Archaic peoples of the Great Lakes and central Ohio
Valley where concepts of a burial cult in some form was a conspicuous
feature of all these manifestations.

The apparently conflicting ideas concerning the origin of Illinois Hopewell would seem to depend upon the viewpoint. To those workers who are most familiar with the cultural sequence of southern Illinois, Hopewell does, indeed, appear as the late arrival of a new complex that impinged upon pre-existing and unrelated cultures. The belief of those who have worked the upper Illinois valley that Illinois Hopewell was rooted in the preceding Central Basin culture seems to be equally valid and supported by the archeological evidence from that area.

Recent research on the Hopewellian manifestations of Illinois has demonstrated the presence in that area of several stages in the development of Illinois Hopewell Culture (McGregor, 1958; Griffin, 1958). It is also of particular interest to note that, although Hopewell reached its highest artistic levels in Ohio, many of the influences of Hopewell to north, south, and west of the Ohio Valley were derived from the Illinois centers rather than from those of Ohio. It seems quite significant that all major Hopewellian sites outside of central Ohio were located to the west in Illinois and adjoining areas rather than to the east. If, as Griffin has suggested, peoples from western New York participated actively in the formation of Hopewell, should we not find in that area more evidence of Hopewell influence than has been reported? Why did the peoples of the Central Basin culture in the upper Illinois valley accept so readily the influences from Ohio Hopewell? The answer to this would seem to be that they, or their very close relatives living directly above the Adena area, were the ones who participated in the development of Ohio Hopewell. Thus, there were no barriers to the movement of peoples or ideas between Ohio and Illinois.

In summary, I believe the similarities shared by Ohio Hopewell, Central Basin, Illinois Hopewell and Point Peninsula were neither accidental, nor merely the result of trade, but the result of a common physical and cultural heritage. The Lenid peoples who formed the basic populations of these cultures were decendants of the earlier populations responsible for the Old Copper, Glacial Kame, and Northeast burial cult cultures. Until Hopewell times these groups were confined to the lands surrounding the Great Lakes because Adena peoples had already staked their claim to the central and Upper Ohio Valley and, through portions of central Indiana and northcentral Illinois, Adena's Red Ocher relatives had taken up residence. For a considerable period of time the two major populations must have occupied their respective areas with only a minimum of physical and cultural exchange, but eventually Lenid peoples moved southward where they submerged the Red Ocher Culture in northcentral Illinois to form the Central Basin Culture. Both stratigraphic and typological evidence indicates that this contact with Red Ocher took place on the early Adena time level since Adena Culture in the Ohio Valley underwent another major stage in its development before Lenid peoples again penetrated the Adena area to form the basic population of Ohio Hopewell.

In western New York and adjacent areas, the Lenid peoples of the Point Peninsula Culture during the early phases of their development shared many of the basic traits of their western Central Basin relatives. At this level there seems to have been a generalized culture, similar to that of Point Peninsula and Central Basin, scattered throughout the areas around and just below the Great Lakes. In time, Point Peninsula's contacts to the west seem to have diminished and their culture expanded along somewhat different lines that eventually became the basis for later Northeastern cultural manifestations. The eastern Point Peninsula peoples were never to become active in or to share the full fruits of the Ohio Hopewell culture which their western cousins were to establish after their intrusion into the Adena area.

The many similarities of the Ohio Hopewell culture with that of Illinois Hopewell leave little doubt of the close connection between the Lenid Peoples of these two areas. So strong were these ties that at least part of the original Lenid peoples who participated in the formation of Ohio Hopewell probably came from the upper Illinois Valley.

Although the physical contribution of the Lenid peoples to Ohio Hopewell has been estimated as high as 75 per cent. (Griffin, 1952, p. 359), little credit has been given to their cultural donations to Hopewell. Basic to the view of Ohio Hopewell development expressed by Webb and Snow(1945, p. 157-217) has been the idea that Adena was chronologically precedent and culturally ancestral to Ohio Hopewell. Thus, the traits shared by Adena and Hopewell were those already present in late Adena and donated to the new Hopewell Culture which formed and prospered as the result of Adena's contact with the Lenid peoples. Webb and Snow believed that most of the important material culture traits of Hopewell, as well as the burial and earthwork traits, were rooted in the preceding Adena. Griffin (1952, p. 359), suggested that Hopewell projectile point types, some pottery types, and certain art

styles were not derived from Adena, but the ceremonial and burial practices, however, were an elaboration of those of the Adena Culture.
In the light of the sequence of Adena development presented earlier in
this report, let us examine in more detail the nature of the traits that have
been put forth as links from Adena to Hopewell (Fig. 29-30).

From late Adena sites Webb and Snow (1945, p. 157-217) found "the
beginnings of many of the customs which in Hopewell blossomed into
important and highly specialized traits." Among those Adena traits
that carry over into Hopewell were the practice of cremation, increased
use of copper and mica, artistic carving of stone and bone, the supposed
use of ear spools of perishable material in Adena that would have been
prototypes of Hopewellian stone and copper ear spools, the conventionalized figures cut into Adena tablets as encestral to later elaborate Hopewell designs, the presence of earthworks in association with Adena burial
mounds, the use of logs to construct a tomb in which important individuals were buried, and the expanded-bar gorget (atlatl weight) of Adena
which in Hopewell became ornately carved effigy forms. To these major
traits we could add many minor details pertaining to burial customs and
artifacts that were shared by Adena and Hopewell, but it is not necessary for our purpose here to list them since they have been thoroughly
discussed by Webb and Snow (1945).

Although the origin of the basic burial and artifactual traits of late
Adena, as manifested by the "Robbins" complex, can generally be traced
back into early Adena, the expression and elaboration of these traits,
plus the addition of several new traits, so clearly distinguish the "Robbins" complex from early Adena that these changes seem as profund
as the changes from Adena to Hopewell. The causes of these changes
in late Adena are crucial because the resulting new traits were precisely
those that were most important as links to Hopewell. Unlike Webb
and Snow (1945, p. 157-217) who viewed these aforementioned traits
as originating in Adena, I believe that these changes were wrought
from influences coming from outside of Adena rather than from within.
It does not seem reasonable that the majority of the artificial and burial
traits of late Adena should contrast so sharply with those of early Adena
if there was a gradual development of these traits from early forms. The
Lenid peoples who eventually predominated in the Ohio Hopewell Culture would certainly have been the main source and the efficient cause
of these changes. In order to understand the nature and limits, both in

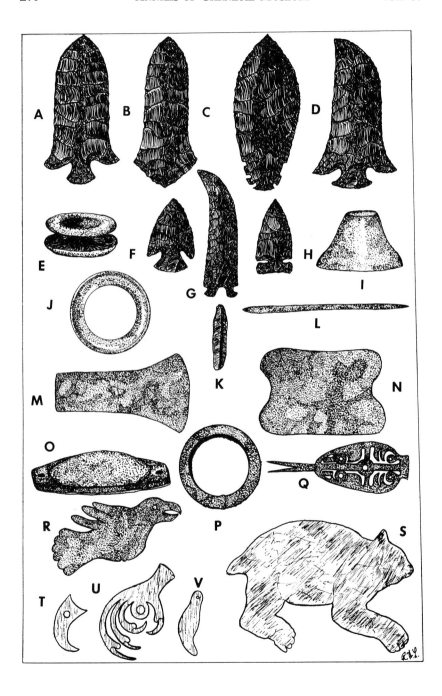

content and time, of the Lenid peoples' influence upon Adena, let us look more closely at some of these link traits.

In late Adena there was an important change in the manufacture of flint blades. The "Robbins" stemmed and "Robbins" leaf-shaped blades were much wider in proportion to length and thinner in cross-section than the earlier "Adena stemmed" and "Adena leaf-shaped" blades. Except for the retention of a stem the "Robbins" blades are more like those of Hopewell than the blades of early Adena. There also seems to have been a marked preference for Flint Ridge flint in the making of "Robbins" blades in contrast to the greater varieties of local origin used in early Adena. Although this change in blade types has received little notice before, I feel it is of as great importance as the traits pertaining more directly to burial customs.

Although the presence of zoömorphic and geometric designs on tablets, pipes, copper, and mica in late Adena has been cited (Webb and Snow, 1945, p. 163) as the source for later Hopewell motifs, I believe this assumption may be seriously challenged. The few examples of effigies on pipes and tablets made their appearance only in the late Adena "Robbins" complex. The famous human effigy pipe found in the original adena Mound by Mills (1902, p. 475) is unique in Adena. With the exception of its tubular form, the figure of the human dwarf wearing ear spools and a head dress appears as a Hopewellian style rather than Adena. The same can be said for the animal effigies portrayed on the pipes from the Welcome, Sayler Park, and Englewood mounds (Setzler, 1960, p. 451-458). Again the only thing Adena about these pipes was the tubular form.

Fig. 29. Artifacts of the Ohio Hopewell Culture
A. Corner-notched blade of obsidian. B. Pointed-base blade of obsidian. C. Leaf-shaped blade with multiple notches. D. Corner-notched blade with curved cutting edge. E. Copper ear spool. F. Corner-notched blade. G. Notched-base blade with curved cutting edge. H. Side-notched blade. I. Truncated stone cone. J. Stone ring. K. Flake knife. L. Copper awl. M. Copper celt. N. Copper plaque or gorget. O. Copper boatstone. P. Copper bracelet. Q. Copper serpent head effigy. R. Copper eagle effigy with pearl eye. S. Mica bear effigy. T. Mica claw pendant. U. Mica raptorial bird claw effigy. V. Mica bear canine pendant. A-D, F-H, J-N, Q-R, and T-V from Mound 25 of the Hopewell group, Ross County, Ohio; E from Seip Mound, Ross County, Ohio; I, O and W from the Tremper Mound, Scioto County, Ohio. (After Moorhead, 1922; Shetrone, 1926; Mills, 1907, 1916, and 1922; Shetrone and Greenman, 1931.)

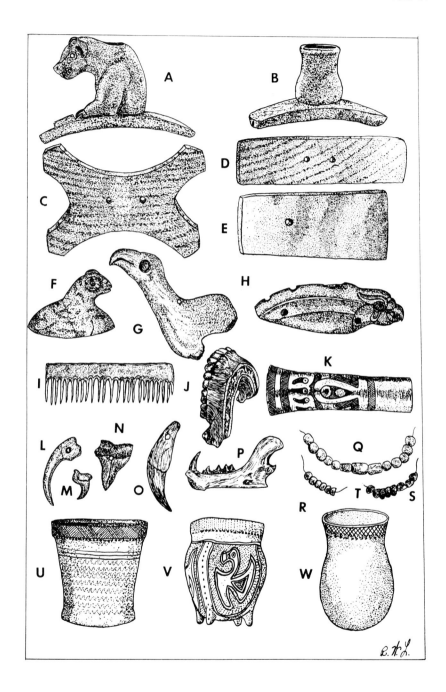

The platform pipe was a distinctive Hopewellian style that can not be derived from any Adena form. On many of these platform pipes of Hopewell was carved the effigy of an animal. In the famous Tremper Mound, Mills (1916, p. 263-398) found 145 complete and fragmentary pipes. Of the 106 pipes restored, 60 were effigies and the remainder plain. More than two-thirds of the fragmentary pipes were also effigies. Nearly every major animal and bird present in the Great Lakes and Ohio Valley regions has been depicted on hundreds of pipes from many Hopewell mounds. It is of interest, however, to note that there seems to have been a preference for aquatic animals and birds. For a people living in southcentral Ohio off the major migratory flyways, the duck seems to have been given more than its fair share of attention. Three of the four animal effigy tubular pipes known to have come from Adena mounds are also effigies of the duck while the fourth appears to be that of a wolf or bear. Can it be that the duck motif gained its importance among the Lenid peoples when they lived nearer the Great Lakes, and that it was carried into the Adena area from this source? As yet there can be no conclusive answer, but there seem to be interesting possibilities for future research along these lines. Certainly the small number of effigy pipes in Adena can hardly seem ancestral to the great profusion of effigies on a different style pipe in Hopewell.

Webb and Baby (1957, p. 99) have suggested that Adena cult designs or motifs, such as the raptorial birds depicted on a few engraved tablets, found their way into Hopewell where they became an integral part of Hopewell's fundamental religious concepts. Webb and Baby's analysis of the use of tablets in Adena for the preparation of paint pigments during burial ceremonies seems valid and supportable by the evidence from

---

Fig. 30.   Artifacts of the Ohio Hopewell Culture
A. Platform pipe with bear effigy. B. Platform pipe. C. Reel-shaped slate gorget. D. Rectangular slate gorget. E. Rectangular pendant. F. Bust-type birdstone. G. Carved bone bird head effigy. H. Bird effigy of stone. I. Turtleshell comb. J. Cut human jaw. K. Engraved section of human femur. L. Effigy bird claw of bone. M. Claw of the gray wolf. O. Perforated bear canine. P. Cut lower jaw of bob-cat. Q. Tubular shell beads. R. Pearl beads. T. Nerita shell beads. S. Olivella shell beads. U. Rocker stamped vessel. V. Tetrapodal vessel with effigy bird design. W. Incised and punctated decorated vessel. A, B and C from the Tremper Mound, Ohio. (After Mills, 1916.) E, L, M, T and U from the Harness Mound, Ohio. (After Mills, 1907.) F, G, H, J, K and U from Hopewell group, Ohio. (After Moorhead, 1922.) V from Mound City group. (After Mills, 1922.) I and Z from Seip Mound, Ohio. (After Mills, 1907.)

several mounds. Stone tablets were made and used over a long period of time in Adena, but, as in the case of the effigy pipes, the addition of the raptorial bird design, or an animal effigy like the turtle tablet from the Cresap Mound, came only in the final "Robbins" complex stage of Adena. There is no clear evidence to indicate that the raptorial bird, or any other animal motif carved in stone had any history in Adena earlier in time than the entrance of the Lenid peoples of Hopewell into the Ohio Valley.

With the exception of a bone gorget from the Florence Mound in Ohio and a shell gorget from the Crab Orchard Spring Mound in Kentucky (Webb and Baby, 1957, p. 94), both of which are very late Adena and within the Hopewell time level, all nine other representations of the raptorial bird in Adena have occurred on tablets that have no direct counterpart in Hopewell forms (Dragoo, 1959, p. 134-144). In Hopewell the raptorial bird motif was produced on stone, bone, copper, mica, shell, and pottery with the greatest of skill and in abundance. The rendition of the raptorial bird motif in Hopewell ranged from literal, naturalistic portrayals to highly conventionalized forms, but in Adena only the conventionalized motif, which seems to be a more complex concept, was employed to decorate a small number of a pre-existing and usually undecorated tablet form. If the raptorial bird design had been developed by Adena Peoples to embellish their tablets, would we not expect such an important item as the tablet as well as the design to have become important to Hopewell? Since this apparently did not happen, it would seem that the design was developed independently of the Adena tablet and probably by the Lenid Peoples of Hopewell from whom Adena borrowed it.

The expanded-center bar atlatl weight was also a new addition to the late Adena "Robbins" complex that seems to have been more closely related to Hopewell than to any trait found in early Adena. Although it is possible that the expanded-center bar may have been derived from the earlier, simple bars of Adena, it is remarkable that this item seems to have made its appearance only on the late Adena scene in association with other elements new to Adena. In Hopewell there were a number of objects, some with ornate designs, similar in shape to the expanded-center bar gorget.

Among the other major artifact traits supposedly donated by Adena to Hopewell was the increased use of copper and mica. Copper was used sparingly in early Adena for the manufacture of beads and occasionally gorgets patterned after the quadri-concave type in slate, but copper C-shaped bracelets, finger rings, and crescents seem to have made their appearance in the late Adena "Robbins" complex. Mica also came into use at the same time, but its employment in Adena was limited in quantity and confined to the making of simple designs, usually crescents that were sewn onto a garment (Webb and Snow, 1959, p. 59). In Hopewell, however, both copper and mica were abundant and used for many purposes. Copper bracelets, finger rings, axes, awls, ear spools, and "breast" plates were common, and in the case of the "breast" plates, quite different from the gorgets of Adena, were often decorated with geometric or zoömorphic designs. Many geometric and zoömorphic representations were also cut into mica and occasionally large slabs of it were used to line graves in the mounds. Again it would seem that Adena was in the position of borrower rather than donor.

At some late Adena sites, such as in the top zone of the Cresap Mound and in the Wright Mound (Webb and Haag, 1940, p. 56), rectangular gorgets have been found. This type was alien to early Adena but common in both Ohio and Illinois Hopewell and in the Point Peninsula cultures.

The "Fayette Thick" pottery of early Adena appears to have been derived from a basic pottery tradition prevalent throughout the central and northeastern United States at the late Archaic level. Although there were many local types belonging to this tradition such as "Vinette 1," "Baumer" "Fabric-Impressed," "Marion Thick," and "Fayette Thick," all shared certain basic characteristics such as great thickness, grit tempering, and cord and fabric impressions usually on both exterior and interior surfaces. The only basic internal change in Adena pottery occurred during the late Adena "Robbins" complex when the surfaces were smoothed and the vessels often were thinner. Decorations were never an important element of Adena pottery design and at those sites where decorated vessels such as "Paintsville Simple stamped" and "Montgomery incised" have been found there seem to have been influences from the Southeast on the very late Adena time level (Haag, 1942, p. 341-349).

Griffin (1958, p. 8) has stated that the basic general pottery tradition of Ohio Hopewell was certainly present in the Ohio area during the early phases of the Adena Culture. In a way this may be true, but only to the extent that both Adena and Hopewell pottery were related to a general and wide-spread early pottery tradition. There are several important characteristics in form and decoration in Hopewell pottery that can not be derived from Adena. Griffin (1958, p. 8) has suggested that Ohio Hopewell pottery was also influenced from at least three other sources. Some features of Ohio Hopewell pottery such as dentate stamping, rocker, and rocked dentate stamping were similar to the Point Peninsula Culture of New York while check stamped, complicated stamped, and simple stamped surface finishes made their way to Hopewell from cultures in the Southeast. Griffin's third influence was the introduction of zoned stamped decorated pottery from the Hopewell ceramic group in the Illinois Valley. There can be little doubt that Ohio Hopewell ceramic development was influenced from various directions and at varying times with the resulting formation of a distinctive pottery complex. What is important to our problem here, however, is the obvious relation of Ohio Hopewell ceramics to both Point Peninsula and Illinois Hopewell for it would seem that the Lenid Peoples of Ohio Hopewell already had, before their contact with Adena, a well established pottery tradition in which decorations were employed. Thus, Adena would have had nothing new to contribute from their still early level ceramic styles to the formation of the Hopewell pottery complex. On the contrary, the shift in late Adena to plain surfaced and thinner walled vessels may have been a Hopewellian influence.

Of perhaps greater significance than the changes in artifact traits in the late Adena "Robbins" complex were those changes pertaining to burial and mound-building customs. Important elaboration of certain old traits and the addition of new traits clearly indicate that strong social forces were at work in late Adena. The most conspicuous of these changes were: 1. The construction of elaborate log tombs in contrast to the simple burial pits of early Adena. 2. The concentration of fine artifacts with the individuals buried in subfloor tombs or in log inclosures on the mound floor rather than the placement of artifacts with many individuals scattered throughout the mound. 3. The placement of "trophy" skulls as burial furniture with the dead. 4. Evidence of ceremonial rites centered around the burial of several individuals not accompanied by artifacts. 5. An increase in the number of individuals cremated. 6. The establishment of major ceremonial and residential centers with an increase in the number and size of the burial mounds. 7. The construction of earthen inclosures or embankments around the mounds in these major centers.

Most of the above innovations of late Adena can best be explained as the result of the following factors: 1. The rise of a strong socio-religious ruling class constituting a selected minority of the population. 2. An elaboration and centralization of the functions of the mortuary cult by the ruling class. 3. The establishment of a more effective social organization that brought the general population under the control of the ruling class, thus making possible the group labor necessary for the construction of large burial mounds and earthworks. 4. A general population increase, or a drawing together of the Adena population.

The inadequate state of our present information concerning the development of Adena throughout its entire distribution makes it impossible to determine accurately how many of the changes in burial customs and social organization of late Adena were initiated from within the Adena culture without the benefit of external influences. Since, however, most of the traits resulting from these changes in late Adena were the same traits shared and amplified by Hopewell, I suspect that outside influences played a greater part in these changes than has been heretofore credited. If Adena peoples accepted new ideas, and I believe the evidence indicates that they did, concerning the making of artifacts and new design motifs from the Lenid peoples, would they not have also accepted new ideas concerning religious and social organization?

The extensive changes in burial practices and social organization of late Adena seem to have also coincided with the introduction of the new artifact traits. The majority of these changes made their appearance on the Adena scene relatively rapidly and without any clear-cut sequence of development from early Adena forms. At the stratified Cresap Mound there was a distinct discontinuity from early-middle Adena to the late Adena "Robbins" complex. The transition was not gradual but quite abrupt. Most Adena mounds appear to manifest either an early-middle Adena component or a late Adena "Robbins" component. Although the Cresap Mound is our best example of the sharp break in Adena Culture, a similar break seems to have taken place in a few other mounds. Unfortunately, the artifactual contents of these latter mounds were usually too meager to document the change positively. What is of importance, however, is that sufficient stratigraphic and typological evidence does exist for an alteration of Adena culture that can not be adequately explained on the basis of internal evolution alone. Since these changes in late Adena were links to Hopewell, it would seem not only possible but also probable that the Lenid peoples of Hopewell were the catalyst in this transformation either by direct physical participation or as a potent external stimulus, or both. Although the influence of the Lenid peoples on Adena is most readily apparent in the artifacts, the most potent influence of all probably was in the category of social organization.

From the distribution of the Adena and Hopewell sites in the Ohio Valley we gain some interesting insights into the probable nature of the Lenid peoples encountered with Adena.

By late Adena times, and probably at the earlier level, there were Adena sites along every major tributary stream of the Ohio River from southeastern Indiana to western Pennsylvania. Although Adena mounds have been found throughout this vast area both north and south of the Ohio River, there were in certain areas, heavy concentrations of mounds that may be termed centers. The largest of these concentrations was in the Scioto Valley in southcentral Ohio, but other major centers were located along the Kanawha River in West Virginia, in the upper Ohio Valley in northern West Virginia, near Lexington, K., and around Cincinnati, Ohio, in southwestern Ohio and eastern Indiana. Smaller clusters of Adena mounds were scattered here and there throughout the Ohio Valley.

In contrast to the great distribution of Adena sites in the Ohio Valley, the major classic Ohio Hopewell sites were located mainly in the Scioto Valley in southcentral Ohio where they overlapped the earlier Adena Scioto Valley center. Although near the east-west center of Adena culture, these main Hopewell sites tend to be in the northern portion of Adena's north-south distribution. No classic Hopewell site has ever been found south of the Ohio River nor in the long reaches of the Ohio Valley east of the mouth of the Scioto River. Across southeastern Indiana and western Ohio, however, Hopewellian materials are abundant in the surface collections and several mounds and earthworks, for example, the Anderson earthworks in Indiana (Lilly, 1937, p. 37), seem to have been of Hopewellian origin. Also, it is of particular interest to note that several of the late Adena mounds of this same area possessed many traits that could be easily assigned to Hopewell.

The distribution of early and classic Hopewellian materials and sites in the central Ohio Valley seems to indicate clearly that the Lenid peoples drove a wedge into Adena territory certainly from the northwest, and possibly from the northwest through Indiana and western Ohio and then into the Adena settlements in the Scioto Valley. It would appear that the Adena peoples in these areas were probably being influenced by the Lenid peoples before their actual physical appearance on the scene in any numbers. Thus, the way was already paved for their acceptance into, and their eventual domination of, the western and central Adena territory north of the Ohio River that was now to become the home of Ohio Hopewell.

Webb and Snow (1945, p. 330) suggested that this "mixing and blending of two different peoples brought about a hybrid vigor, genetically and culturally", that was responsible for the unique achievements that characterized Ohio Hopewell. Although many Adena peoples in Ohio and Indiana "to all intent and purpose" became Hopewell people, the majority of the Hopewell population was composed of Lenid peoples, as much as 80 per cent according to Webb and Snow (1952, p. 295). Thus, it would seem that the contributions of the Lenid people physically as well as culturally to the development of Ohio Hopewell can be shown to have been proportionally greater than that of Adena. However, the function of Adena in the formation of Ohio Hopewell can not be denied for without the blending and modification of original traits contributed by both, plus the most important factor of social contact with the resulting realinements and stresses, the conditions for rapid cultural change and social re-orientation that produced Ohio Hopewell could not have occurred.

The problem of Adena's relationships to Hopewell would have been greatly simplified if all Adena peoples in the Ohio Valley had participated actively in the formation of Ohio Hopewell and if Adena culture had ceased to exist at this point. Webb and Snow (1945, p. 335) have noted that while early Ohio Hopewell was developing in the Scioto Valley some Adena sites continued to be occupied. I believe the number of such sites was great and included nearly all the major Adena centers south of the Ohio River in Kentucky and West Virginia and the large center in the upper Ohio Valley around Moundsville, W. Va. Although this overlapping in time of the Adena and Hopewell cultures complicates our attempts to establish accurate chronologies, some of the most important questions concerning the development of the Adena and Hopewell cultures and their relationships seem to be explainable only on the basis that Adena and Hopewell in certain areas were contemporaneous for a considerable period of time. In this event, the following interpretations appear warranted:

1. Ohio Hopewell developed as the result of the intrusion of Lenid peoples from the west and north into the Ohio Valley where they first merged with and eventually dominated physically and culturally the Adena peoples in southeastern Indiana and western Ohio. The major Adena center affected by this intrusion of Lenid peoples was located north of the Ohio River in the Scioto Valley of southcentral Ohio. All the major classic Ohio Hopewell sites developed in this area are of initial Lenid intrusion and domination.

2. Although a few individuals buried in some late Adena mounds may resemble the Lenid physical type, there is generally no conclusive evidence to indicate the presence of Lenid peoples in number in any Adena mound south of the Ohio River in Kentucky and West Virginia and in the upper Ohio Valley.

3. Thus, it would seem the Lenid peoples were unable physically to extend their domination to the entire Adena territory, but many of the new concepts of the developing Hopewell culture in the Scioto Valley were diffused throughout Adena, giving rise to the late Adena "Robbins" complex. That the new traits of the "Robbins" complex were the result of diffusion seems to be attested by the fact that several of the new concepts were grafted upon, or adapted to, pre-existing Adena forms.

4. Some of the Adena peoples of the Scioto Valley may have left that area and moved in with their relatives south of the Ohio River bringing with them ideas of the developing Hopewell Culture. Although the majority of the Adena peoples living in the Scioto Valley and adjacent areas to the west may have "to all intent and purpose become Hopewell people," it is conceivable that some were not entirely content with their new situation, and would have found things more to their liking among the Adena groups outside the Lenid sphere of physical influence.

5. It is highly significant that during the development and classic Hopewell periods no major Hopewell centers were established in highly desirable areas south of the Ohio River or in the Upper Ohio Valley. The only Hopewellian penetration of these areas seems to have come after the Adena occupation had ended and at a time when the Hopewell Culture had become a loose and nebulous influence over large areas of the eastern United States. The logical explanation of Hopewell's failure to cross the Ohio River into nearby Kentucky and West Virginia would seem to be the presence of Adena peoples in sufficient numbers to hold back the tide. Such a situation implies the existence of both some physical and cultural resistance on the part of Adena peoples in these areas.

The extensive spread and development of Hopewell Culture westward through Indiana and Illinois indicates that there were no major barriers in that direction. In southern Illinois and southwestern Indiana much of Hopewell Culture was accepted by peoples who had been culturally and physically distinct prior to Hopewell. The fact that resident populations in these latter areas took on Hopewell Culture rather than being replaced by Hopewellian peoples indicates that there were limitations to the actual dispersal of Lenid peoples. In many areas the spread of Hopewell Culture depended upon other peoples who accepted the influences of Hopewell with little or no change in their populations.

6. Although in late Adena many influences were received from the developing Hopewell Culture, the general picture of Adena Culture is a conservative one. It is possible that some of the features of late Adena, such as the pulling together of Adena peoples into larger centers, came about as the result of Adena's resistance to Hopewell. If all the Adena peoples in the Ohio Valley had accepted Hopewell Culture as freely as did the peoples of southern Illinois, there would seem to have been nothing that could have prevented the establishment of important Hopewellian outposts south of the Ohio River and in the Upper Ohio Valley during early and classic Hopewell times.

Copena Culture

If all Adena peoples did not participate in, or become submerged by, the Hopewell Culture, what happened to them? Webb and Snow (1945, p. 335) made an important observation when they stated that all Adena sites had ceased to be occupied before late Hopewell since not a single late Hopewell artifact has ever been found in any Adena site. They further presumed that the reason Adena sites never show any contact with late Hopewell in Ohio was because such Adena peoples as had not been completely fused with Hopewell by middle Hopewell times had migrated down the Ohio and up the Tennessee rivers, taking with them the joint cultures of Adena and Hopewell. Webb and Snow (1945, p. 337) concluded "thus, we may speculate on the disappearance of Adena as such from the Ohio River Valley and the rise of Copena in northern Alabama along the Tennessee River Valley."

The traits of Copena (Moore, 1915, p. 171-428; Webb and De Jarnette, 1942, p. 301-305; Webb and Wilder, 1951, p. 273-277) have long been noted as similar to Hopewell and Adena. In the past Copena's similarities to Hopewell were stressed more strongly than those that would link Copena to Adena with the result that Copena was considered a southern phase of Hopewell. A recent re-evaluation of Copena's relationship to Hopewell and Adena by Webb and Baby (1957, p. 80) has led them to believe that "the cultural contribution of Adena may be evaluated correctly as greater than that of Ohio Hopewell to Copena," and they further state that "this may be possible because the contribution of Adena to Copena may have been more direct." The mixed nature of the Copena population, 68 per cent. broad-headed and 32 per cent. long-headed, seems to indicate a possible Adena population that had been both physically and culturally influenced by Hopewell before their movement into the Tennessee Valley. Once in the Tennessee Valley, however, certain distinctive elements were developed by Copena that were unlike any that had been present before in the Ohio Valley. Some of these items, such as extreme reel-shaped copper gorgets and large steatite effigy pipes, were apparently traded to Hopewell peoples back in the Ohio Valley (Webb and Snow, 1945, p. 337).

Webb and Baby (1957, p. 81) also believed that traces of Adena Culture were present in other areas of the South such as in northern Georgia at the Booger Bottom Site (Caldwell, 1952, p. 319-328). Charles H. Fairbanks in a letter to Dr. William S. Webb (Webb and Baby, 1957, p. 81) pointed out the presence of Adena-like traits at this site and suggested that certain minority types of pottery found at some late Kentucky Adena sites, such as the Wright and C. & O. Mounds may have been derived from this source. Although the evidence is suggestive of Adena, it is still too meager to draw any conclusion as to the nature and extent of Adena's part in this area.

The evidence of Adena participation in the Copena Culture is extensive. Thus, Webb and Baby's evaluation of Adena's contribution as being more direct and greater than that of Hopewell seems well founded. In Copena we certainly find our best evidence for the presence of Adena peoples who after moving from the Ohio Valley were able to establish themselves in another area and to perpetuate at least certain elements of Adena Culture in spite of strong cultural and physical influences from Hopewell and from peoples surrounding them in their new homeland in the Tennessee Valley.

East Coast Adena Sites

Although some Adena peoples appear to have moved southward to found the Copena Culture, others moved eastward out of the Ohio

Valley. The evidence of this eastward movement of Adena peoples has been traced in a study by William A. Ritchie and Don W. Dragoo (1959, p. 43-50; 1960, p. 1-80). At the time this study was made, however, the complete results of the findings at the stratified Cresap Mound were not available. Now it is possible to throw additional light on the nature of the eastern Adena materials.

Our best evidence for Adena in the East comes from the shores of Chesapeake Bay in Maryland and on the Delmarva Peninsula in Delaware where three major sites containing largè quantities of Adena objects in association with burials and pit cremations covered with red ocher have been discovered (Fig. 31).

Although various articles on the two Maryland sites have been published, a recent report, accompanied by radiocarbon dates, by T. Latimer Ford of the Maryland Archeological Society, gives the most complete résumé of the finds which number over 700 objects (Weslager, 1942; Mason, 1953; Ford, 1958). Important diagnostic Adena traits at these sites include blocked-end tubular pipes, large stemmed blades and points of Flint Ridge, Ohio, and Harrison County, Ind. flint, cones and hemispheres, gorgets and pendants of various forms, and copper beads. Other less diagnostic Adena traits found at these sites include the boat-stone and birdstone. There was also a Copena type of effigy pipe in one of the graves.

During the summer of 1960 a site nearly indentical to those in Maryland was excavated along the St. Jones River near Dover, Del. by Leon de Valinger, Director of the Delaware State Museum (Dragoo, 1961). Again burials and cremations accompanied by red ocher and artifacts were found in shallow pits in a gravel knoll. Among the important Adena items were blocked-end tubular pipes, expanded-center bar weights, reel-shaped gorgets, a copper reel-shaped gorget, slate pendant, large stemmed blades and leaf-shaped blades of Flint Ridge, Ohio, and Harrison County, Ind., flint. Although the research and final report on this site has not been completed, it appears to be in all major respects similar to the two Maryland sites both in time and contents.

At the time of our study of the Maryland Adena materials (Ritchie and Dragoo, 1959, p. 45) it was our belief that the Maryland sites were more closely related to the Upper Ohio Valley Adena sites, particularly the Beech Bottom and Natrium mounds, than to those of any other area. On the basis of available radiocarbon dates at that time we suggested that the movement of some Adena groups eastward out of the Ohio

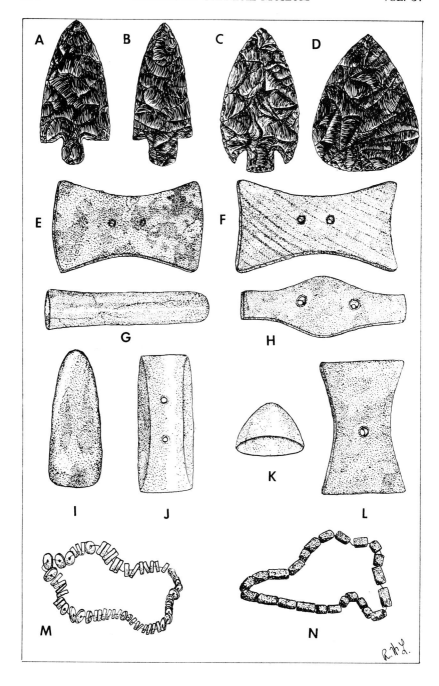

Valley took place in the late-middle Adena period rather than during the late Adena period. A re-examination of the materials from the Maryland sites and the new evidence from the Delaware site still indicates close affinities of these sites with the Adena sites in the Upper Ohio Valley, and to a lesser degree with those of Kentucky, but now typologically the remains from these sites can best be equated with the late Adena "Robbins" complex stage as found in the top zone of the Cresap Mound in the Upper Ohio Valley and typical of all late Adena sites in Kentucky. Hopewellian influences are now clearly observable in the materials from these eastern sites just as they are in the late Adena sites of the Ohio Valley. These influences are manifested particularly in the "Robbins" blade and projectile point types and in the greater diversity of gorget forms including many rectangular gorgets present usually in late Adena only and very common in Hopewell. The finding of a Copena-like pipe in one of the Maryland sites may indicate that the eastern Adena sites were on about the same time level as Copena in the South.

Although Adena objects from the Ohio Valley could have been traded to peoples along the east coast, it seems most unlikely that so many characteristic Adena traits of Ohio Valley raw materials would have been associated with nearly identical burial practices unless Adena peoples had actually been present at the Delaware and Maryland sites. The remains are so unlike any known earlier or later cultural manifestations in that area that only the movement of some Adena peoples with their burial complex and typical artifacts can logically account for their presence in that area.

Ritchie's extensive archeological studies in the Northeast indicate Adena influences also spread into that region (Ritchie and Dragoo, 1960, p. 26-62). Although some Adena traits may have filtered into New York

---

Fig. 31. Artifacts of the Adena sites in Maryland and Delaware
A-C. Variations of the "Robbins" stemmed blade. D. "Robbins" leaf-shaped blade. E. Bi-concave copper gorget. F. Quadriconcave slate gorget. G. Blocked-end straight tubular pipe. H. Expanded-center bar gorget. I. Round poll celt. J. Semi-keeled stone gorget. K. Hematite hemisphere with slate pendant. M. Disk shell beads. N. Tubular copper beads. A-H from the St. Jones River Site, Lebanon, Del., based on photographs courtesy of Leon de Valinger, Delaware State Museum. I-N from the Sandy Hill Site, Dorchester County, Md., based on photographs courtesy of T. Latimer Ford, Maryland Archaeological Society.

state from the Upper Ohio Valley earlier in Adena, the majority of traits appear similar to those of the late Maryland and Delaware Adena sites. The distribution of the Adena materials along the east coast and in the Northeast also indicates that there may have been a migration route from Chesapeake Bay to Delaware Bay, then northward via the Delaware River into New Jersey and beyond. Some Adena peoples also may have moved from the Chesapeake Bay area up the Susquehanna River into New York. Once in the Northeast these Adena peoples subsequently became responsible for the genesis of the Middlesex complex.

Middlesex complex

In the Middlesex complex of the Northeast there was generally a progressive dilution of Adena traits with increasing distance from the Adena centers in the Ohio Valley and the sites in Maryland and Delaware. However, one of the largest and most peripheral of these sites, the Long Sault Island mounds in the St. Lawrence River, produced several diagnostic Adena traits composed primarily of materials foreign to the Northeast such as Flint Ridge, Ohio, and Harrison County, Ind., flint and Portsmouth, Ohio, fireclay. Typologically some of the traits, especially the blades, of the Middlesex complex exhibit the same Hopewellian influences seen in the late Adena "Robbins" complex of the Ohio Valley and also found in the Maryland and Delaware sites.

Also present in the northeast Middlesex sites are Point Peninsula traits. Ritchie's (1937, p. 192-193; 1944, p. 113, 115, 186-187) studies have shown that Point Peninsula was primarily a western manifestation in the New York area while Middlesex was an eastern one. However, the evidence from shared traits indicates coevality and in some areas Adena peoples were probably assimilated into resident Point Peninsula populations.

At the time of our study, in 1957-1958 of the dispersal of Adena peoples we came to the following conclusion (Ritchie and Dragoo, 1960, p. 63):

"We believe that it is more than mere coincidence that the eastern, northeastern and southern extensions of Adena occurred at approximately the same time during the middle Adena period. The wide scattering of Adena traits from the homeland in the Ohio Valley cannot, we think, be explained as the wandering of traders in search of new markets or raw materials. The finding of typical Adena objects made from Ohio Valley stone materials, and in the context of the Adena ceremonial burial pattern, at these farflung outposts, can best be explained by the actual presence of Adena people. Why would groups of Adena people want or find it necessary to leave the Ohio Valley which had been their home for at least 600 years? The apparent answer to this question is that internal strife or outside force, or a combination of both these factors, drove them from the Ohio Valley. When we seek the cause of destruction in Adena, a movement of Hopewell people into the area appears to provide the logical clue."

The present study generally substantiates the above conclusions, but it is now possible to draw finer lines as to the time Adena peoples moved from the Ohio Valley and as to the probable cause and nature of these movements.

On the basis of radiocarbon dates the postulated dispersal of Adena occurred during the late-middle Adena period. With the stratigraphic evidence of the Cresap Mound plus a fuller understanding of the content and position of the late Adena "Robbins" complex over much of the Ohio Valley, it is now certain that this dispersal took place in late Adena times and after a period of considerable Hopewell influence. On the basis of stratigraphy and typology, I seriously doubt the continued, active existence of Adena Culture anywhere in the Ohio Valley much after 1 A. D. and it is quite possible that the end came even before that time.

The arrival in the central Ohio Valley of Lenid peoples and their domination of the developing Hopewell Culture certainly would have precipitated some social and cultural turmoil within Adena. In our study (Ritchie and Dragoo, 1959, p. 49) of the two Maryland sites, now bolstered by similar finding at the Adena site in Delaware, we suggested that some groups of Adena peoples, especially those in the Adena social and religious hierarchy, would probably have found the growing power of the Lenid peoples of Hopewell intolerable and would have chosen, or perhaps been forced, to leave the area. The sites in Maryland and Delaware appear to be excellent examples of the presence of ceremonial leaders who gathered their prized possessions when they moved from the Ohio Valley. It seems quite possible that these peoples and related groups who pressed on into the Northeast were no longer able to maintain the more conspicuous elements, such as mounds and earthworks, of the Adena mortuary complex because of the lack of sufficient common labor to complete such undertakings. In the East and Northeast, I seriously doubt that these groups were able to preserve their cultural identity for any great length of time. Most of their artifacts from the Ohio Valley soon were buried with the dead and the remnants of these decreasing Adena peoples were readily absorbed into local populations.

The majority of the Adena peoples who moved from the Ohio Valley probably went south where they established the Copena Culture in the Tennessee Valley. Here they were more successful in preserving some elements of Adena Culture over a greater period of time.

Thus it would seem that the disappearance of Adena Culture from the Ohio Valley can be attributed to two causes: 1. The absorption of many Adena peoples into the Hopewell Culture. 2. The gradual disruption of Adena groups surrounding Hopewell from internal strifes and frictions resulting from the social and cultural pressures of Hopewell. Undoubtedly other factors were also involved, but vastly more research must be done before all these factors can be brought clearly into focus.

Adena-Hopewell chronology and radiocarbon dates

So far in this report I have deliberately avoided extensive use of radiocarbon dates in my discussions of chronology and relationships of complexes. It seemed preferable first to establish the contents of the complexes involved and second to examine the possible relationships of the complexes on the basis of typology and actual statigraphy when present. Radiocarbon dates would have little meaning unless we knew exactly what we were attempting to date.

Radiocarbon dates have been received by many with great enthusiasm and apparent trust in their accuracy. Although carefully executed time charts based on these dates have been prepared for Adena (Webb and Baby, 1957) and Hopewell (Griffin, 1958), I must view these endeavors with considerable misgiving. In Table 3 the major radiocarbon dates for Adena, Hopewell, and related manifestations have been listed. By looking at some of these dates and the problems involved, I believe the need for caution in accepting these dates at face value can be clearly illustrated.

On the basis of radiocarbon dates from the Florence and Cowan Creek mounds in Ohio and the Drake Mound in Kentucky Webb and Baby (1957, p. 111) placed the use of these late Adena mounds between 150 and 900 A. D. based on the measured value of the carbon samples plus the range of probable error in the dating of the sample. The latest date for Adena was 1168 ± 150 (C-126) taken from the Drake Mound in Kentucky and processed at the University of Chicago laboratory. On the aforementioned charts this date was used by Webb and Baby and by Griffin as indicative of late Adena. A later dating of this same sample at the University of Michigan gave a date of 2200 ± 250 (M-19) a difference of 1032 years earlier than the first date. Obviously both these dates of the same sample can not be correct, but which one do we accept, or can we accept either one of them?

Griffin (1958, p. 5) in remarking upon the late Adena dates suggested that the dates after approximately 200-300 A. D. were too recent for Adena, but he gave no specific reasons for this belief. As I have stated previously, on the basis of typology and stratigraphy, I seriously doubt that any Adena site in the Ohio Valley would have been in existence much after 1 A. D. or perhaps even earlier. If we accept the late dates for the Drake Mound (1168 ± 150), Florence Mound (1425 ± 250), Cowan Creek Mound (1509 ± 250), and the Sayler Park Mound (1860 ± 250), then we must accept the general thesis that the Adena peoples responsible for the late Adena "Robbins" complex found in these mounds persisted relatively unchanged for several hundred years for this same late Adena "Robbins" complex was also present in mounds dated much earlier (Dover, 2605 ± 175, 2169 ± 175 and Welcome 2300 ± 200). Thus, not only does approximately 1400 years seem excessive for late Adena but we must also consider the fact that the Florence and Cowan Creek mounds were directly in the sphere of Hopewell development which according to radiocarbon dates began as early as 2285 ± 210 (C-137 Mound 25, Hopewell) in Ohio. That Adena peoples living in the midst of Hopewell could maintain the status quo unchanged for hundreds of years is not only illogical but ridiculous.

Because of the radiocarbon dates of 2605 ± 175 (C-759) and 2169 ± 175 (C-760) the Dover Mound in Kentucky was considered to be an early Adena mound by Webb and Baby (1957, p. 111. An examination of the artifactual remains and the burial traits indicate that this mound certainly falls within the late Adena "Robbins" complex and, as Webb and Snow (1959, p. 70-71) have even stated, there are certain items, such as copper bracelets and cut mica, that link the Dover Mound with Hopewell traits. In the absence of any clearly diagnostic early Adena traits like those of the lower levels of the Cresap Mound and the Toepfner Mound, the date of 2605 ± 175 (C-759) for a charcoal sample found in an upper zone of the Dover Mound seems excessively old and out of line with the typological evidence.

Until the excavation of the Cresap Mound, the radiocarbon dates from the Toepfner Mound indicated that it was the oldest Adena mound yet dated. These dates range from 2200 ± 200 (M-519) to 2780 ± 410

(C-942) or a total time span of 1190 years if the range of probable error is also included.

Three charcoal samples from the Cresap Mound were submitted to the University of Michigan for dating with the following results (Crane and Griffin, 1961, p. 116):

(M-974) 2020 ± 150 yrs. Charcoal from Feature 24, Burial 44, 13.1 to 16.1 ft. E. and 0.0 to 3.2 ft. N. at an elevation of 6.75 ft. above floor of mound; should date the middle occupation of the mound.

(M-975) 2190 ± 200 yrs. Charcoal from near edge of West Primary mound, 8.0 ft. W. and 9.2 ft. N., at an elevation of 0.8 ft. above floor of mound and should date an early period in the construction of the mound.

(M-976) 2240 ± 150 yrs. Charcoal found in fill in sub-floor tomb (Feature 28, Burial 54). A fire had been built over the tomb, and with collapse of the logs the charcoal fell directly into the tomb. Sample was found 7.5 ft. E. and 2.1 ft. S. at depth of 0.0-0.8 ft. below floor of mound and should date Feature 28 and an early phase in the construction of the mound.

Although the Michigan dates for the Cresap Mound are consistent within themselves, they seem to be somewhat late on the basis of their stratigraphic position within the mound and the typological resemblance of the associated features and artifacts to those of the Toepfner Mound in Ohio dated much earlier. As a check on these dates additional samples were submitted to Gulf Research Laboratories and the results were received while this report was in press (personal communication to author from Dr. M. T. J. Weismann, Gulf Research Laboratories, Dec. 11, 1963).

(Gulf) 2506 ± 175 yrs. Charcoal found in the bottom of sub-floor tomb (Feature 28) in direct association with the cremated skull fragments of Burial 54. This sample should be contemporaneous with sample M-976 dated at 2240 ± 150 yrs.

(Gulf) 3685 ± 123 yrs. Charcoal from a mass of burned material found in the fill of the West Primary mound at an elevation of 1.2 ft. above the floor of the mound. This sample was near sample M-975 which was dated at 2190 ± 200 yrs.

Thus, the dates for the lower levels of the Cresap Mound range from 2020 ± 150 (M-974) to 3685 ± 123 (Gulf) or including probable error a span of 1938 years. The internal structure of the lower zones of the Cresap Mound indicates that it was built over a considerable period of time, but not of the magnitude of possibly 1938 years as indicated by the radiocarbon dates. However, the average of the five dates of 2528 years seems a fairly reasonable approximation for the general time level during which the lower zones of the Cresap Mound were constructed.

At the Cresap Mound the late Adena "Robbins" complex was stratigraphically distinct from the lower zones containing the early Adena materials and the dated charcoal samples. Thus, if our radiocarbon dates are correct, the late "Robbins" complex at the Cresap Mound came after 2020 ± 150 (M-974), the latest date for the early Adena zones. Only a few miles down the Ohio River, however, the Welcome Mound had been in the "Robbins" complex stage at 2300 ± 200 (M-903) and even farther downstream in Kentucky at the Dover Mound the "Robbins" complex had come into vogue at 2605 ± 175 (C-759). Are we to believe that it took the changes seen in the late Adena "Robbins" complex nearly 600 years to move up the Ohio Valley?

The dates for the Adena materials at the West River Site in Maryland range from 1630 ± 400 (M-418) to 2310 ± 200 (M-416) or a span of 680 years for an assemblage of traits extremely homogeneous in nature and representative of the Late Adena "Robbins" complex strongly influenced by Hopewell. All evidence strongly points to the transfer of this material from the Ohio Valley at a rather specific time and it is most unlikely that it took nearly 700 years for these items after they arrived in Maryland to end up in graves. To complicate and cloud the matter even further a rerun of sample M-418 first dated at 1630 ± 400 gave another date of 2030 ± 250, a difference of 400 years. How many other samples if tested again would produce results different from those now available?

I believe the above examples illustrate the problems in attempting at this time to rely on the accuracy of radiocarbon dates. It would seem that we are a long way from having the kind of dates that can be used to establish finely drawn chronological distinctions among sites. To attempt to use them for this purpose now is only misleading and confusing. Typology and stratigraphy still remain our best tools in the ordering of sites and complexes.

Theoretically the radiocarbon dating method is scientifically sound under ideal conditions. Unfortunately the samples that have usually been available for dating have been far from ideal. We seldom find the type of sample in a mound that fits all the necessary requirements of kind, size, location, and definite association with distinct and diagnostic cultural materials. In addition, there is the problem of contamination of the sample by modern carbon due to the presence of plant life and micro-organisms that could result in the sample being dated much later than its true age. Other factors may affect the sample that would result in an earlier date. After the samples have been taken to the laboratory, it is obvious from the wide differences in dates given for the same sample that there are factors in the preparation and counting of the sample that can and do affect the validity of the date. Dates from many sites are urgently needed if we are to solve the problems of radiocarbon dating and make it a standard tool of the archaeologist. Only after samples with sufficient cultural associations from many sites have been dated will we, perhaps, be able to determine the causes of the troubles that presently cast shadows on the radiocarbon method.

Unlike some of my colleagues who have considered radiocarbon dating as totally inadequate and hopeless to the point of believing it would do no good to submit samples from sites, often very important sites, I feel that we have derived some benefits and that we should keep trying to perfect our methods both in the field and the laboratory. Until we are more sure of all the problems involved in achieving accurate dates and their application to cultural manifestations, it will be necessary to exercise extreme caution in the use of radiocarbon dates. To accept the present dates without careful analysis of their relationship to the typological and stratigraphic evidence can lead only, (and I am afraid already has led) to confusion and misinterpretation of the archeological record.

In spite of obvious inconsistencies and inaccuracies of the present dates, it is possible to make some general deductions that appear reasonably valid. With the exception of four dates, all the other dates for Adena in the Ohio Valley are at least 2000 years old. In the case of date 1168 ± 150 (C-126) the rerun gave a new reading of 2200 ± 200 (M-19) which indicates that the three other dates earlier than 2000 years may also be questionable. Thus, it would seem that Adena was near its end about 2000 years ago. This is a date that seems to be basically substantiated by the typological and stratigraphic evidence as close to a terminal date for Adena.

Webb and Baby (1957, p. 112) are certainly correct in suggesting that the earliest dates for Adena have not been measured, for certainly all our present dates have come from large and well established Adena sites. Considering the evidence from all sources, I suspect the earliest dates for a recognizable Adena manifestation will come close to 3000 years ago and overlap the dates for the late Archaic.

If we use an average of the dates for the West River Site in Maryland as representative of the eastern movement of Adena peoples from the Ohio Valley, we again arrive at a date of about 1900 years ago when if we include the date 1630 ± 400 (M-418) later rerun and dated at 2030 ± 250 (M-418). Typologically the eastern Adena sites are very late Adena with strong Hopewell influences. Thus from this eastern site comes additional evidence for the end of Adena culture soon after 2000 years ago. It is also of interest to note that a sample from a site in Georgia having cross-ties with late Adena in Kentucky also has been dated at 2104 ± 140 (C-933) (Libby, 1955, p.111; Webb and Baby, 1957, p. 81).

The radiocarbon dates for Hopewell sites in Ohio and Illinois indicate that Hopewell overlapped the late stage of Adena by perhaps 200 years but continued for several hundred years after the end of Adena. The dates from some of the Illinois sites of 2336 ± 250 (C-152), 2300 ± 250 (M-256), 2500 ± 300 (M-15), and 2200 ± 250 (M-20) may indicate, as has been suggested in this report, that the roots of Ohio Hopewell lay among the Lenid peoples of the Illinois Valley.

The four dates for Ohio Hopewell ranging from 2285 ± 210 (C-137) to 1890 ± 200 (M-650) are so limited in number and from only two sites that any statements made concerning Hopewell dates in Ohio can be only tentative. If they are reasonably correct they certainly overlap the late Adena occupation culturally represented by the "Robbins" complex with its evident Hopewell influences. How long the great Hopewell sites in the Ohio were occupied remains unknown, but it seems that by 500 A. D. the classic Hopewell period had come and gone. In the meantime influences from Hopewell in Ohio and Illinois had spread to many surrounding areas where peoples not originally part of the Hopewell Culture accepted many Hopewell practices and traits that were to survive into late prehistoric times.

In Table 3 are included the dates for Point Peninsula and Old Copper because these dates overlap or continued back into Archaic time many of the traits that later find their way into Adena and Hopewell. The Point Peninsula dates certainly suggest considerable antiquity for that culture beginning in late Archaic and overlapping both the Adena and Hopewell occupations in the Ohio Valley. The latest of the Old Copper dates would also overlap both the early Point Peninsula and Adena dates. Radiocarbon dates from many late Archaic and early burial cult manifestations in the Great Lakes region and the Ohio Valley are urgently needed. At present, the few available dates are entirely inadequate to be of value for comparative purposes.

TABLE 3. RADIOCARBON DATES

Sample	Site	Substance	Date B.P.	Reference
Ohio Valley Adena:				
M-974	Cresap Mound, W. Va.	Charcoal	2020±150	G
M-975	Cresap Mound, W. Va.	Charcoal	2190±200	G
M-976	Cresap Mound, W. Va.	Charcoal	2240±150	G
Gulf	Cresap Mound, W. Va.	Charcoal	2506±175	L
Gulf	Cresap Mound, W. Va.	Charcoal	3685±123	L
M-903	Welcome Mound, W. Va.	Charcoal	2300±200	F
C-923	Toepfner Mound, Ohio	Charcoal	2377±150	A
C-942	Toepfner Mound, Ohio	Charcoal	2780±410	A
M-517	Toepfner Mound, Ohio	Charcoal	2300±200	D
M-518	Toepfner Mound, Ohio	Charcoal	2280±200	D
M-519	Toepfner Mound, Ohio	Charcoal	2200±200	D
M-520	Toepfner Mound, Ohio	Charcoal	2350±200	D
M-521	Toepfner Mound, Ohio	Charcoal	2410±200	D
M-929	Clough Mound, Ohio	Charcoal	2120±200	G
M-570	Sayler Park, Ohio	Charcoal	1860±200	D
C-214	Cowan Creek Mound, Ohio	Charcoal	1509±250	A
C-874	Florence Mound, Ohio	Charcoal	1425±250	A
C-759	Dover Mound, Ky.	Charcoal	2650±170	A
C-760	Dover Mound, Ky.	Charcoal	2169±175	A
C-126	Drake Mound, Ky.	Wood	1168±150	A
M-19	Drake Mound, Ky.	Wood	2200±250	B
M-908	Gaines Mound, Ky.	Charcoal	1975±200	F
M-909	Gaines Mound, Ky.	Charcoal	2070±200	G
M-31	Newt Kash Hollow, Ky.	Vegetal	2650±300	B
Eastern Adena:				
M-416A	Site 18 An 18, Md.	Charcoal	2310±200	F
M-417A	Site 18 An 18, Md.	Charcoal	1850±200	F
M-418	Site 18 An 18, Md.	Charcoal	1630±400	C

M-418	Site 18 An 18, Md.	Charcoal	2030±250	C
M-419B	Site 18 An 18, Md.	Charcoal	1960±200	G
M-419C	Site 18 An 18, Md.	Charcoal	1700±250	B
M-420B	Site 18 An 18, Md.	Charcoal	2110±200	G
M-927	Site 18 An 18, Md.	Charcoal	2300±200	G
Y-933	St. Jones River Site, Del.	Charcoal	2225±80	K

Hopewell:

C-136	Mound 25, Hopewell, Ohio	Charcoal	1951±200	A
C-137	Mound 25, Hopewell, Ohio	Shell	2285±210	A
C-139	Mound 25, Hopewell, Ohio	Wood	2044±250	A
M-650	Rocky Fort Mound, Ohio	Charcoal	1890±200	D
M-928	West Mound, Ohio	Charcoal	1830±200	G
C-152	Havana Group, Md. 9, Ill.	Wood	2336±250	A
M-256	Weaver Site, Ill.	Shell	2300±250	D
M-15	Pool Site, Ill.	Shell	2500±300	B
M-183	Pool Site, Ill.	Charcoal	1740±250	B
M-20	Havana, Ill.	Wood	2200±250	B
M-558	Wilson Mound, Ill.	Charcoal	1950±200	D
M-559	Wilson Mound, Ill.	Charcoal	2000±200	D
M-443	Bedford Mound group, Ill.	Charcoal	1930±250	D
M-444	Bedford Mound group, Ill.	Charcoal	1940±250	D
M-445	Bedford Mound group, Ill.	Charcoal	1720±250	E
M-446	Bedford Mound group, Ill.	Wood	1550±250	E
M-164	Knight Site, Md. 8, Ill.	Shell	1700±300	M
M-378	Steuben Site, Ill.	Charcoal	1660±250	C
M-380	Steuben Site, Ill.	Bone	1650±250	C
M-439	Steuben Site, Ill.	Shell	2110±200	G
M-440	Steuben Site, Ill.	Charcoal	1325±200	G
M-441	Steuben Site, Ill.	Charcoal	1275±200	G
M-545	Steuben Site, Ill.	Charcoal	1900±200	G
M-548	Steuben Site, Ill.	Charcoal	2010±200	G
M-560	Rutherford Mound, Ill.	Charcoal	1525±200	D
M-489	Irving Site, Ill.	Charcoal	1180±250	C
M-578	Kuhne Site, Ill.	Charcoal	1670±200	E
M-579	Kuhne Site, Ill.	Charcoal	2210±250	E
M-580	Kuhne Site, Ill.	Charcoal	1790±300	E
M-453	Liverpool Mounds, Ill.	Wood	1470±200	E
A-80	Dickson Mound group, Ill	Wood	1990±250	H

M-760	Caterpillar Mound, Ill.	Wood	2010±150	G
M-758	McDougal-Hartman Mound, Ill.	Wood	2270±200	G
M-759	Renchville Mound, Ill.	Wood	1990±200	G
L-00	Twenhafel Site, Ill.	Charcoal	2900±650	I
L-431c	Twenhafel Site, Ill.	Bone	1440±100	I

Point Peninsula:

C-192	Oberlander 2, N.Y.	Charcoal	2817±170	A
C-192	Oberlander 2, N.Y.	Charcoal	3080±200	A
M-640	Morrow Site, N.Y.	Charcoal	2527±250	E
M-51	Williams Mound, Pa.	Charcoal	2800±300	B
M-194	Killarney Bay, Ont.	Charcoal	2180±300	B
M-428	Killarney Bay, Ont.	Skin	2040±200	E
C-608	Burley Site, Ont.	Charcoal	2619±220	A
M-850	Serpent Mounds, Ont.	Charcoal	1830±200	

Old Copper:

C-836	Oconto, Wis.	Charcoal	5600±600	A
C-837	Oconto, Wis.	Charcoal	7510±600	A
M-643	Osceola, Wis.	Bone	3450±250	E
M-644	Reigh Site, Wis.	Bone	3660±250	E
M-658	Riverside Cemetery, Mich.	Bone	3040±300	D

Northeast Burial Cult:

C-794	Hunter Site, Red Lake, N.Y.	Charcoal	4881±400	A
C-794	Hunter Site, Red Lake, N.Y.	Charcoal	3920±300	A
M-494	Orient No.2 Site, N.Y.	Charcoal	2900±250	C
M-586	Sugar Loaf Hill, N.Y.	Charcoal	3000±300	C
W-543	Jamesport, N.Y.	Charcoal	2720±220	F
M-659	Andrews Site, Mich.	Bone	3170±300	F

REFERENCES FOR TABLE 3

A. Libby, W. F. 1955. Radiocarbon dating. Ed. 2, p. 91-100. University of Chicago Press.

B. Crane, H. R. 1956. University of Michigan radiocarbon dates, 1: Science, v. 124, p. 666-668.

C. Crane, H. R., and James B. Griffin. 1958. University of Michigan radiocarbon dates, 2: Science, v. 127, p. 1099-1101.

D. Crane, H. R., and James B. Griffin. 1958. University of Michigan radiocarbon dates, 3: Science, v. 128, p. 1119-1120.

E. Crane, H. R., and James B. Griffin. 1959. University of Michigan radiocarbon dates, 4: American Journal of Science Radiocarbon Supplement, 1, p. 176-177.

F. Crane, H. R., and James B. Griffin. 1960. University of Michigan radiocarbon dates, 5: American Journal of Science Radiocarbon, 2, p. 33-180.

G. Crane, H. R., and James B. Griffin. 1961. University of Michigan radiocarbon dates, 6: American Journal of Science Radiocarbon Supplement, 3, p. 111-116.

H. Shutler, Dick, Jr., and Paul E. Damon. 1959. University of Arizona radiocarbon dates, 2: American Journal of Science Radiocarbon Supplement, 1, p. 60.

I. Olson, Edwin A., and Wallace S. Broecker. 1959. Lamont natural radiocarbon measurements, 5: American Journal of Science Radiocarbon Supplement, 1, p. 21.

J. Olson, Edwin A., and Wallace S. Broecker. 1961. Lamont natural radiocarbon measurements, 7: American Journal of Science Radiocarbon Supplement, 3, p. 169.

K. Rouse, Irving to Don W. Dragoo. Personal letter of August 14, 1962. Yale University radiocarbon dates.

L. Weismann, M. T. J. to Don W. Dragoo. Personal communication of Dec. 11, 1963. Gulf Research Laboratories radiocarbon dates.

M. Griffin, James B. 1958. The chronological position of the Hopewellian culture in the eastern United States. Anthropological papers no. 12, Museum of Anthropology, University of Michigan, p. 9, 13.

REFERENCES

Baby, Raymond S.
1949. Cowan Creek Mound explorations. Ohio Historical Society, Museum echoes, v. 22, p. 54-55. Columbus.

Baby, Raymond S. and Asa Mays, Jr.
1949. Exploration of the William H. Davis Mound. Ohio Historical Society, Museum echoes, v. 32, No. 12, p. 95-96. Columbus.

Bache, Charles and Linton Satterthwaite, Jr.
1930. The excavation of an Indian mound at Beech Bottom, West Virginia. University of Pennsylvania, Museum journal, v. 21, p. 132-187. Philadelphia.

Baker, Frank C. and others
1941. Contributions to the archaeology of the Illinois River Valley. Transactions of the American Philosophical Society, v. 32, pt. 1, p. 1-209. Philadelphia.

Bell, Robert
1958. Guide to the identification of certain American Indian projectile points. Oklahoma Anthropological Society. Special bulletin no. 1. 104 p. Oklahoma City.

Black, Glenn A.
1934. Archaeological survey of Dearborn and Ohio counties. Indiana history bulletin, v. 11, p. 173-260. Indianapolis.
1936. Excavation of the Nowlin mound. Indiana history bulletin, v. 13, no. 7, p. 201-342. Indianapolis.
1946. The Cato Site, Pike County, Indiana. Indiana Academy of Science. Proceedings, v. 40, p. 18-22. Indianapolis.

Bluhm, Elaine A.
1951. Ceramic sequence in Central Basin and Hopewell sites in central Illinois. American antiquity, v. 16, no. 4, p. 324-329. Menasha.

Boaz, Franz
1912. Changes in bodily form of descendants of immigrants. 573 p. Columbia University Press, New York

Boyd, William C.
   1950.   Genetics and the races of man. 435 p. Little, Brown and
           Co., Boston.

Cadzow, Donald
   1933.   Mr. George Fisher's discoveries in western Pennsylvania,
           Pennsylvania archaeologist, v. 3, no. 3, p. 3-5, Milton.

Caldwell, Joseph, and others
   1952.   The Booger Bottom mound, a Forsythe period site in Hall
           County, Georgia. American antiquity, v. 18, no. 4, p. 319-
           328. Menasha.

Caldwell, Joseph R.
   1958.   Trend and tradition in the prehistory of the eastern
           United States. American Anthropological Association.
           Memoir 88, v. 60, no. 6, pt. 2, 88 p. Menasha.

Carpenter, Edmond S.
   1951.   Tumuli in southwestern Pennsylvania. American anti-
           quity, v. 16, no. 4, p. 329-346. Salt Lake City.

Catlin, George
   1860.   Letters and notes on the manners, customs, and condition
           of the North American Indian. J. W. Bradley, Phila-
           delphia.

Chard, Chester S.
   1961.   Invention versus diffusion: the burial mound complex of
           the eastern United States. Southwestern journal of an-
           thropology, v. 17, no. 1, p. 21-25. Albuquerque

Cole, Fay-Cooper and Thorne Deuel
   1937.   Rediscovering Illinois. 295 p. University of Chicago
           Press, Chicago.

Cole, Fay-Cooper
   1943.   Chronology of the Middle West. American Philosophical
           Society. Proceedings, v. 86, no. 2, Philadelphia.
   1951.   The Baumer focus. In "Kincaid, a prehistoric Illinois
           metropolis." p. 184-210. University of Chicago Press.
           Chicago.

Coon, Carlton, and others
1950. Races . . . a study of the problems of race formation in man. 153 p. Charles C. Thomas, Springfield, Ill.

Coon, Carlton S.
1953. Climate and race. Smithsonian Institution, annual report 1953. p. 277-298. Washington.

Crane, H. R.
1956. University of Michigan, radiocarbon dates, 1. Science, v. 124, p. 666-668.

Crane, H. R. and James B. Griffin
1958. University of Michigan radiocarbon dates, 2. Science, v. 127, p. 1099.

Cranc, H. R. and James B. Griffin
1958. University of Michigan radiocarbon dates, 3. Science v. 128, p. 1119-1120.

Cunningham, Wilbur M.
1948. A study of Glacial Kame in Michigan, Ohio and Indiana. Occasional contributions from the Museum of Anthropology of the University of Michigan, no. 12, p. 1-45. Ann Arbor.

DeHaas, Wills
N.D. The mound builders, their monumental and art remains. MS. Catalog No. 2430. Bureau of American Ethnology. Washington.

de Paepe, Duane
1959. An archaeological survey of Starke County, Indiana. Indiana Historical Bureau. 44 p. Indianapolis.

Dragoo, Don W.
1949. Origins of the Adena Culture.
Manuscript on file at the Graduate School of Indiana University. Bloomington.
1951 Archaeological survey of Shelby County, Indiana. Indiana Historical Bureau. 37 p. Indianapolis.
1955. The Linn Mound, an Upper Ohio Valley Adena stone mound. Pennsylvania archaeologist, v. 25, no. 1, p. 58-69. Milton.

Dragoo, Don W. (Continued)

1956.   Excavations at the Watson Site, 46HK34, Hancock County, West Virginia. Pennsylvania archaeologist, v. 26, no. 2, p. 59-88. Milton.

1959.   Archaic hunters of the Upper Ohio Valley. Annals of Carnegie Museum, v. 35, p. 139-245. Pittsburgh.

1959.   An unusual cache of Adena tablets. Pennsylvania archaeologist, v. 29, no. 3-4, p. 134-144. York, Pa.

1961.   An Adena burial site in Delaware. Eastern States Archeological Federation. Bulletin 20, p. 12. Trenton.

Engberg, Robert M.

1930.   Archeological work in Westmoreland-Fayette counties. Western Pennsylvania historical magazine, v. 13, no. 2, p. 67-103. Pittsburgh.

Fairservis, Walter A., Jr.

1959.   The origin of oriental civilization. 192 p. Mentor Books, New York.

Faulkner, Charles H.

1960.   A Point Peninsula-like focus in Indiana. Indiana history bulletin, v. 37, no. 10, p. 124-136. Indianapolis.

1960.   The Red Ochre Culture: an early burial complex in northern Indiana. Wisconsin archeologist, v. 41, no. 2, p. 35-49. Lake Mills, Wis.

Fetzer, E. W. and William J. Mayer-Oakes

1951.   Excavation of an Adena burial mound at the Half-Moon Site. West Virginia archeologist, no. 4, p. 1-25. Moundsville.

Ford, T. Latimer

1958.   Adena traits in Maryland. Eastern States Archeological Federation. Bulletin 17, p. 10-11. Trenton.

Funkhouser, W. D. and William S. Webb

1929.   The so-called "Ash Caves" in Lee County, Kentucky. University of Kentucky reports in anthropology and archaeology, v. 1, no. 2, p. 37-112. Lexington.

Goslin, Robert

1957.   Food of the Adena people. In "The Adena people No. 2" by Webb and Baby. p. 41-46. The Ohio Historical Society. Columbus.

Greenman, Emerson F.
  1932.   Excavation of the Coon Mound and an analysis of the
           Adena Culture. Ohio State archaeological and historical
           quarterly, v. 41, p. 366-523. Columbus.
Griffin, James B.
  1942.   Adena pottery. American antiquity, v. 7, no. 4, p. 344-358.
           Menasha.
  1943.   Adena village site pottery from Fayette County, Ken-
           tucky. University of Kentucky. Reports in anthropology
           and archaeology, v. 5, no. 7, p. 667-672. Lexington.
  1954.   The ceramic affiliation of the Ohio Valley Adena culture.
           In "The Adena People" by Webb and Snow. University of
           Kentucky. Reports in anthropology and archaeology, v. 6,
           p. 220-246. Lexington.
  1948.   An interpretation of the Glacial Kame culture. Occasional
           contributions from the Museum of Anthropology of the
           University of Michigan, no. 12, p. 46-51. Ann Arbor.
  1952.   Editor. Archeology of eastern United States. 392 p. Uni-
           versity of Chicago Press. Chicago.
  1960.   Climatic change: a contributory cause of the growth and
           decline of northern Hopewellian Culture. Wisconsin
           archeologist, v. 41, no. 2, p. 21-33. Lake Mills, Wis.
Haag, William G.
  1942.   The pottery from the C. and O. mounds at Paintsville.
           University of Kentucky. Reports in anthropology and
           archaeology, v. 5, no. 4, p. 341-349. Lexington.
Hayden, Harry
  1941.   Tumuli burials along Cheat River. Pennsylvania archae-
           ologist, v. 11, no. 1, p. 5-7. Milton, Pa.
Hennen, R V.
  1909.   West Virginia Geological Survey, County reports and
           maps. Marshall, Wetzel, and Tyler counties. Morgan-
           town.
Hertzberg, H. T. E.
  1940.   Skeletal material from the Wright Site, Montgomery
           County. In "The Wright mounds" by Webb and Haag,
           University of Kentucky. Reports in anthropology and
           archaeology, v. 5, no. 2, p. 83-102. Lexington.

Homsher, G. W.
    1884.   The Glidwell Mound, Franklin County, Indiana. Smithsonia Institution. Annual report for 1882, p. 721-728. Washington.

Jordan, Douglas F.
    1959.   Adena and blocked-end tubes in the Northeast. Bulletin of the Massachusetts Archaeological Society, v. 20, no. 4, p. 49-61. Attleboro.

Kellar, James H.
    1960.   The C. L. Lewis stone mound and the stone mound problem. Indiana Historical Society. Prehistory research series, v. 3, no. 4, p. 357-481. Indianapolis.

Lasker, Gabriel Ward
    1952.   An anthropometric study of returned Mexican emigrants. Proceedings 29th International Congress Americanists, v. 3, p. 242-246.

Libby, Willard F.
    1955.   Radiocarbon dating, ed. 2. University of Chicago Press. Chicago.

Lilly, Eli
    1937.   Prehistoric antiquities of Indiana. 293 p. Indiana Historical Society. Indianapolis.

Magrath, Willis H.
    1945.   The North Benton Mound: a Hopewell site in Ohio. American antiquity, v. 11, no. 1, p. 40-46. Menasha.

Martin, Paul and others
    1947.   Indians before Columbus. 582 p. University of Chicago Press. Chicago.

Mason, J. Alden
    1953.   New discoveries in the Choptank River, Delmarva Peninsula and their implications. Eastern States Archaeological Federation, Bulletin 12, p. 6. Trenton.

Mayer-Oakes, William J.
    1955.   Prehistory of the Upper Ohio Valley. Annals of Carnegie Museum, v. 34. 296 p. Pittsburgh.

Mayer-Oakes, William J. (Continued)
1958. Radiocarbon dates from the Upper Ohio Valley. Eastern States Archeological Federation. Bulletin 17, p. 13. Trenton.

Maxwell, Moreau S.
1951. Woodland cultures of southern Illinois. Logan Museum publications in anthropology. Bulletin 7, Beloit College, Beloit, Wis.
1952. Archeology of the lower Ohio Valley. In "Archeology of eastern United States" (ed. by Griffin). p. 176-189. University of Chicago Press. Chicago.

McGregor, John C.
1958. The Pool and Irving villages: a study of Hopewell occupation in the Illinois River Valley. 232 p. University of Illinois Press. Urbana.

McMichael, Edward V.
1956. An analysis of McKees Rocks Mound, Allegheny County, Pennsylvania. Pennsylvania archaeologist, v. 26, no. 3-4, p. 129-151. Milton.

McNeish, Richard
1958. Preliminary archaeological investigations in the Sierra de Tamaulipas, Mexico. Transactions of the American Philosophical Society, v. 48, pt. 6, p. 1-210. Philadelphia.

Miller, F.
1878. Mound in Trumbull County, Ohio. Smithsonian Institution, Annual Report of the Board of Regents for the year 1877, p. 268. Washington.

Mills, William C.
1902. Excavation of the Adena Mound. Ohio State archaeological and historical quarterly, v. 10, p. 452-479. Columbus.
1907. Exploration of the Edwin Harness Mound. Ohio archaeological and historical quarterly, v. 16, p. 113-193. Columbus.
1909. Explorations of the Seip Mound. Ohio archaeological and historical quarterly, v. 18. no. 3, p. 269-321. Columbus.
1916. Exploration of the Tremper Mound. Ohio archaeological and historical quarterly, v. 25, p. 263-398. Columbus.

Mills, William C. (Continued)

1917.   Exploration of the Westenhaven Mound. Ohio archaeological and historical quarterly, v. 26, p. 227-266. Columbus.

1922.   Exploration of the Mound City group. Ohio archaeological and historical quarterly, v. 31, p. 423-584. Columbus.

Moore, Clarence B.

1915.   Aboriginal sites on Tennessee River. Journal of the Academy of Natural Sciences of Philadelphia, ser. 2, v. 16, pt. 2, p. 170-428. Philadelphia.

Moorehead, Warren K.

1917.   Stone ornaments of the American Indian. 448 p. Andover Press. Andover.

Morgan, Richard G.

1952.   Outline of cultures in the Ohio Region. In "Archeology of eastern United States" edited by Griffin, p. 83-98. University of Chicago Press. Chicago.

Morse, Dan F.

1959.   Preliminary report on a Red Ochre Mound at the Morse Site, Fulton County, Illinois. Papers of the Michigan Academy of Science, Arts, and Letters, v. 44, p. 193-206. Ann Arbor.

Narona, Delf

1957.   Moundsville's mammoth mound. West Virginia archaeologist, no. 9, 55 p. Moundsville, W. Va.

Neuman, Georg K.

1937.   Preliminary notes on the crania from Fulton County, Illinois. In "rediscovering Illinois" by Cole and Deuel. p. 227-264. Chicago.

Neuman, Georg K.

1952.   Archeology and race in the American Indian. In "Archeology of eastern United States" edited by Griffin. p. 13-34. University of Chicago Press. Chicago.

1960.   Origins of the Indians of the middle Mississippi area. Proceedings of the Indiana Academy of Science, v. 69, p. 66-68. Indianapolis.

Newman, Marshall T. and Charles E. Snow
1942. Preliminary report on the skeletal material from Pickwick Basin, Alabama. In "An archeological survey of Pickwick Basin in the adjacent portions of the states of Alabama, Mississippi, and Tennessee" by Webb and De Jarnette, Bureau of American Ethnology, Bulletin 129, p. 393-507. Washington.

Newman, Marshall T.
1953. The application of ecological rules to the racial anthropology of the aboriginal New World. American anthropologist, v, 55, 311-327.

Ritchie, William A.
1944. The Pre-Iroquoian occupation of New York state. Rochester Museum of Arts and Sciences, Memoir 1, 416 p. Rochester.

Ritchie, William A. and Don W. Dragoo
1959. The eastern dispersal of Adena. American antiquity, v. 25, p. 43-50. Salt Lake City.
1960. The eastern dispersal of Adena. New York State Museum and Science Service. Bulletin 379, p. 1-80. Albany.

Ritzenthaler, Robert, ed.
1957. The Old Copper Culture in Wisconsin. Wisconsin archaeologist, v. 38, no. 4, p. 185-329. Lake Mills, Wis.

Ritzenthaler, Robert and Arthur Niehoff
1958. A Red Ochre burial in Ozaukee County. Wisconsin archaeologist, v. 39, no. 2, p. 115-120. Lake Mills, Wis.

Schmitt, Karl
1952. Archeological chronology of the Middle Atlantic states. In "Archeology of eastern United States" edited by Griffin, p. 59-70. University of Chicago Press, Chicago.

Schooley, Matthew
1902. The Peters Creek Indian mound, Monongahela Valley, Pennsylvania. 15 p. Homestead, Pa.

Scrimshaw, Nevin S. and others
1955. Nutritional problems of children in Central America and Panama. Pediatrics, v. 16, p. 378-397.

Setzler, Frank M.
  1930. The archaeology of the White Water Valley. Indiana history bulletin, v. 7. no. 12, p. 373-418. Indianapolis.
  1931. The archaeology of Randolph County and the Fudge mound. Indiana history bulletin, v. 9, no. 1, 51 p. Indianapolis.

Setzler, Frank M.
  1960. Welcome Mound and the effigy pipes of the Adena people. Proceedings of the United States National Museum, no. 3441, v. 112, p. 451-458. Washington.
  1960. Welcome mound and the effigy pipes of the Adena people. West Virginia archeologist, no. 12, p. 4-14. Moundsville, W. Va.

Shapiro, Harry L.
  1939. Migration and environment. New York.

Shetrone, Henry C.
  1920. Culture problem in Ohio archaeology. American anthropologist, v. 22, no. 2, p. 144-172.
  1926. Exploration of the Hopewell group of prehistoric earthworks. Ohio archaeological and historical quarterly, v. 35, p. 1-227. Columbus.
  1930. The mound builders. 508 p. Appleton, New York.

Shetrone, Henry C. and Emerson F. Greenman
  1931. Explorations of the Seip group of prehistoric earthworks. Ohio archaeological and historical quarterly, v. 40, p. 343-509. Columbus.

Snow, Charles
  1948. Indian knoll skeletons of Site No. 2, Ohio County, Kentucky. University of Kentucky reports in anthropology and archaeology, v. 4, no. 3, pt. 2, p. 367-532. Lexington.
  1957. Adena portraiture. In "Adena People No. 2" by Webb and Baby. p. 47-60. Ohio Historical Society. Columbus.

Solecki, Ralph
  1952. Exploration of an Adena mound at Natrium, West Virginia. Bureau of American Ethnology. Bulletin 151, p. 313-395. Washington.

Spaulding, Albert C.

1952. The origin of the Adena Culture of the Ohio Valley. Southwestern journal of anthropology, v. 8, p. 260-268. Albuquerque.

1955. Prehistoric cultural development in the eastern United States. In "New interpretations of aboriginal American culture history," 75th anniversary volume of the anthropological Society of Washington, p. 12-27. Washington.

Squier, E. G. and E. H. Davis

1848. Ancient monuments of the Mississippi Valley. Bartlett and Welford, 306 p. New York
From Smithsonian contributions to knowledge.

Starr, S. F.

1960. The archacology of Hamilton County Ohio. Journal of the Cincinnati Museum of Natural History, v. 23, no. 1, 130 p. Cincinnati.

Stewart, T. Dale

1960. A physical anthropologist's view of the peopling of the New World. Southwestern journal of anthropology, v. 16, no. 3, p. 259-273. Albuquerque.

Swauger, James L.

1940. A review of F. H. Gerodette's notes on the excavation of the McKees Rocks Mound. Pennsylvania archaeologist v. 20, no. 1, p. 8-10. Milton.

Thomas, Cyrus

1894. Report on the mound explorations of the Bureau of Ethnology. Twelfth annual report of the Bureau of American Ethnology. Washington.

Townsend, Earl

1959. Birdstones of the North American Indian. 719 p. Indianapolis.

Vaillant, George

1930. Excavations at Zacatenco. Anthropological papers of the American Museum of Natural History, v. 32, pt. 1, p. 1-197. New York.

1931. Excavations at Ticoman. Anthropological papers of the American Museum of Natural History, v. 32, pt. 2, p. 199-439. New York.

Vaillant, George (Continued)
    1935.   Excavations at El Arbolillo. Anthropological papers of the American Museum of Natural History, v. 35, pt. 2, p. 139-279. New York.

Webb, William S.
    1939.   An archaeological survey of Wheeler Basin on the Tennessee River in northern Alabama. Bureau of American Ethnology. Bulletin 122, 214 p. Washington.

    1940.   The Wright mounds, sites 6 and 7, Montgomery County, Kentucky. University of Kentucky reports in anthropology and archaeology, v. 5, no. 1, p. 1-134. Lexington.

    1941.   Mt. Horeb earthworks, Site 1, and the Drake Mound, Site 2, Fayette County, Kentucky. University of Kentucky reports in anthropology and archaeology, v. 5, p. 135-218. Lexington.

    1942.   The C. and O. mounds at Paintsville. University of Kentucky reports in anthropology and archaeology, v. 5, no. 4, p. 297-372. Lexington.

    1943.   The Riley Mound, Site Be15, and the Landing Mound, Site Be17, Boone County, Kentucky with additional notes on the Mt. Horeb Site, Fa1, and Sites Fa14 and Fa15, Fayette County. University of Kentucky reports in anthropology and archaeology, v. 5, no. 7, p. 580-672. Lexington.

    1950.   The Carlson Annis Mound. University of Kentucky reports in anthropology and archaeology, v. 7, no. 4, 267-354. Lexington.

Webb, William S. and Raymond Baby
    1957.   The Adena people No. 2. Ohio Historical Society. 123 p. Columbus.

Webb, William S. and David De Jarnette
    1942.   An archaeological survey of Pickwick Basin in the adjacent portions of the states of Alabama, Mississippi, and Tennessee. Bureau of American Ethnology. Bulletin 129, 536 p. Washington.

Webb, William S. and John B. Elliott
    1942.   The Robbins mounds, sites Be3 and Be14, Boone County, Kentucky. University of Kentucky reports in anthropology and archaeology, v. 5, no. 5, p. 373-499. Lexington.

Webb, William S. and W. D. Funkhouser
  1940. Ricketts site revisited. University of Kentucky reports in anthropology and archaeology, v. 3, no. 6, p. 205-269. Lexington.

Webb, William S. and William G. Haag
  1947. The Fisher Site, Fayette County, Kentucky. University of Kentucky reports in anthropology and archaeology, v. 7, no. 2, p. 47-104. Lexington.

Webb, William S. and Charles E. Snow
  1945. The Adena people. University of Kentucky reports in anthropology and archaeology, v. 6, p. 1-369. Lexington.
  1959. The Dover Mound. 72 p. University of Kentucky Press. Lexington.

Webb, William S. and Charles G. Wilder
  1951. An archaeological survey of Guntersville Basin on the Tennessee River in northern Alabama. 278 p. University of Kentucky Press. Lexington.

Webb, William S. and others
  1952. Prehistoric Indians of the Ohio Valley. 23 p. Ohio State archaeological and historical Society. Columbus.

Weslager, C. A.
  1942. Ossuaries on the Delmarva Peninsula and exotic influences in the coastal aspect of the Woodland pattern. American antiquity, v. 8, no. 2, p. 142-151. Menasha

Willey, Gordon and Philip Phillips
  1958. Method and theory in American archaeology. 278 p. University of Chicago Press. Chicago.

Wittry, Warren and Robert Ritzenthaler
  1957. The Old Copper complex: an Archaic manifestation in Wisconsin. Wisconsin archeologist, v. 38, no. 4, p. 311-329. Lake Mills, Wis.

Wray, Donald E.
  1952. Archeology of the Illinois Valley: 1950. In "Archeology of eastern United States" edited by Griffin, p. 152-164. University of Chicago Press. Chicago.

INDEX